ASIAN VEGETABLES

GARDENING • COOKING • STORYTELLING

The Wang Sisters 黃
Stéphanie, Caroline, and Patricia

Translated by J. C. Sutcliffe

AMBROSIA

To our mother,
Who has always been with us

The house we grew up in was, thanks to our mother, a wonderful, peaceful haven surrounded by flowerbeds that she tended in the same way she looked after the people around her: with patience and kindness.

From May to October, the perennials took turns brightening up the garden. Orange day lilies dominated the back entranceway, and climbing the stairs became a sweet, colourful battle. Dazzling purple morning glories languorously wound their way up a wooden trellis behind the house, big white peonies held court over the ants near the side door, and delicately scented lily of the valley carpeted the beds at the front.

Every winter, our mother leafed through seed catalogues looking for annual flowers that would add even more colour to the garden. In spring, she sprinkled cherry tomato seeds in flats by the kitchen window. Then, once the hot weather arrived and until the advent of autumn, she would put on her light blue jogging pants, a Florida T-shirt, and a straw hat, and go outside to tend the garden.

We learned early on how to help in the garden: watering, weeding, gathering leaves. These tasks may have seemed like chores to us then, but we always took great pleasure in harvesting the sweet cherry tomatoes.

As with her garden, our mother took a lot of care with meal planning. She was always on the lookout for new recipes to try, making sure that our meals were balanced and flavourful.

Our mother was also interested in family history. She loved chatting with one of her older brothers, who was working on their family tree, and also wanted to complete our father's family tree, having taken a particular interest in our paternal grandfather. She took charge of meticulously arranging and dating all the family photos, from her childhood in Madagascar, to which her family had immigrated from China, up to her life in Quebec.

We have all inherited our mother's interest in gardening, cooking, and our family's stories, and in our own way, we each seek the path she mapped out.

In 2007, our mother died of cancer. Wild nature somewhat regained the upper hand in her garden, along with the perennials that stubbornly kept on flowering, year after year, in the same place our mother had carefully planted them.

Ten years later, following her involvement with peasants and farmers' organizations, attracted to a way of life closer to nature, and wanting to launch her own project, Stéphanie started growing Asian vegetables at Le Rizen, a farm she founded in Frelighsburg, Quebec. In 2017, as she was writing a newsletter for customers who had signed up for her vegetable baskets, she felt an urge to introduce these little-known vegetables. Caroline, with her nutrition training and interest in food, began collaborating on the newsletters by writing note cards explaining how to use and cook the vegetables.

Interest in these Asian vegetables is growing, yet there are very few resources on the subject. The idea to write a book about them through the lens of our family history was born. Patricia, who had already begun collecting our family tales, would tell our family's cooking and gardening stories, and weave in all the memories.

We have built this book together, as sisters — a book in which gardening, cooking, and family history converge to pay homage to our love of food and to our family, with the aim of helping people discover and appreciate these locally grown Asian vegetables.

CONTENTS

Preface by Jean-Martin Fortier 6

Preface by Elisabeth Cardin 7

OUR FAMILY

From China to Quebec via Madagascar 11

A culinary heritage 16

The Wang sisters 19

A few words on Le Rizen farm 20

An invitation to travel ... 21

ASIAN VEGETABLES

What are Asian vegetables? 26

A difficult breakthrough 27

From Asia to Quebec, for increased food sovereignty 28

Vegetables: Good for the body, great on the plate 33

Chinese medicine and us 34

Our choice of Asian vegetables 36

Understanding Cantonese: Our family language 40

THE BASICS OF CHINESE AND ASIAN COOKING

A playground 45

Crucial ingredients 47

Useful tools 53

Basic techniques 54

A YEAR LIVING ACCORDING TO THE SEASONS

Benefiting from market-garden knowledge 67

WINTER

Using the time while the garden sleeps to plan for next year 72

Starting off: Answering some questions 73

Planning the garden 74

Planning what to grow 76

Ordering seeds 77

The first indoor sowings 80

SPRING

Stéphanie's burnout story 92

Set to work! The first round of planting out and plunging your hands into the soil 94

Specifics of cold-loving vegetables 97

Battling insects 98

BOK CHOY 108

Roasted bok choy 117

Gaspé turbot, lobster, and tatsoi with XO sauce 119

The fish and seafood of Madagascar 121

Rustic sticky rice with bok choy 123

CHOY SUM 124
Speedy steamed choy sum 131
Cantonese fried rice with choy sum 133
Marinated tofu 133
From Marie-Thé to Marie Wang 134

GAI LAN 136
Grilled gai lan 143
Lightly braised gai lan with miso and pancetta 145
Gai lan with sizzling oil (*Biang biang gai lan*) 147

MUSTARD GREENS 148
Japanese sesame salad (*Goma-ae*) 157
Nabe with miso and butter 159

EDIBLE CHRYSANTHEMUM 160
Chrysanthemum-stuffed crêpes (*Bings*) 167
Maple-sautéed chrysanthemum 169
Chrysanthemum pesto noodles with edamame 171
It's never too late (to learn to cook) 173

CELTUCE 174
Dungeness crab with celtuce, mint, goat yogurt, oxalis 179
Quick-pickled celtuce 183
Celtuce leaf and dried cranberry salad 183

SUMMER
Harvest time 192
Harvesting techniques 194
The particularities of heat-loving vegetables 200

AMARANTH 206
Soups and fruits 211
Amaranth soup 213
Lentil and amaranth dhal (*Thotakura pappu*) 215
Amaranth romazava-style 217
Tomato rougail 217

MALABAR SPINACH 218
Malabar spinach stir-fry with ginger and Sichuan pepper oil 225
Malabar spinach and black-eyed peas curry
(*Valchebaji ani gule*) 227

SHISO 228
Laotian meat salad (*Laap*) 235
Spring rolls with shiso and duck 237
Shiso and lychee sorbet 239
A chef's vision 241

OKRA 242
Crispy roasted okra (*Kurkuri bhindi*) 249
Lacto-fermented okra 251
Okra with mushrooms 253

ASIAN EGGPLANT 254
Asian eggplant achar 259
Garlicky roasted Asian eggplant 261
Arctic char, miso eggplant, saké kasu 263
Steamed pork-stuffed Asian eggplant 267
Danielle Laou, unstoppable cook 268

ASIAN CUCUMBER 270
Cold noodles (*Liǎng miàn*) 277
Asian cucumber and shiso cocktail 279

LUFFA 280
Luffa spread 287
Luffa and chicken stir-fry 289
Culinary shocks 291

LEMONGRASS 292
Tom kha gai soup 297
Grilled chicken with lemongrass and Siling labuyo chili
(*Gà nướng sả ớt*) 299
Lemongrass panna cotta 301

FALL
The final sprint 310
Closing up the garden 311
Extending the life of vegetables: Freezing,
fermenting, and some Chinese methods 314
Reconnecting with these preserved foods 319

CHINESE CABBAGE 320
Kimchi 325
Glazed baluchoux with teriyaki sauce 327
Chinese cabbage sauté with bacon and chili 331
January 1st in Nosy Be 333

FINAL WORDS 335

ACKNOWLEDGEMENTS 336

GARDEN GLOSSARY 339

INDEX 340

SOURCES 342

APPENDICES 344

PREFACE BY JEAN-MARTIN FORTIER

The book you hold in your hands is a treasure. Not only because it celebrates vegetable seasonality and the job of the market gardener that often goes with it, but also because this is the first time that readers have been offered an in-depth look into the fabulous universe of Asian vegetables — the so-called new crops that have existed in Asia for millennia.

When I took my first steps in market gardening, encountering Asian vegetables like bok choy, tatsoi, and Chinese cabbage, to name just a few, was an eye-opening discovery. Today, they are well-known classics that are easy to grow and also pique customers' curiosity at the farmers' market on Saturday mornings.

One of the most wonderful revelations from this "branch" of vegetables is that several of them withstand summer heat very well, while others are very resistant to the cold temperatures of spring, fall, and even winter.

Asian summer vegetables, such as different varieties of eggplants, cucumbers, and Chinese okra, make way for cold-loving Asian vegetables in the fall and winter, such as edible chrysanthemum and stem lettuce. While these vegetables bring diversity to our plates, they also help us reach a bigger goal: achieving out-of-season food autonomy.

In fact, cold-climate Asian vegetables are very well suited to the northern gardening we see spreading in Quebec. Thanks to these plants' biology, making them frost-resistant and able grow in cold and low light conditions, combined with low-tech solutions (basic shelters, cold frames, unheated or minimally heated greenhouses), we see more and more market gardeners growing fresh vegetables year-round in Quebec. Asian vegetables are a part of this revolution, which is why I have long been interested in growing them.

Despite my experiments, I was blown away to see all these other Asian vegetables in uncommon shapes, textures, and flavours that grow so abundantly at Le Rizen. I had never seen, heard of, or eaten — never mind thought of selling — several of these vegetables. And this is why this book is so interesting.

By providing detailed instructions for growing fifteen Asian vegetables, this book saves gardeners several years of trial and error, allowing us to grow them success-fully on the first attempt. This makes this book a real gold mine, whether for home gardens, commercial market gardens, or ornamental gardens.

But this book is much more than just a horticultural manual; through the recipes and the family stories accompanying the vegetables, we discover the extent to which the vegetables are rooted in a way of life. As we read how to grow, cook, and eat them, we also absorb a harmony inspired by traditional Chinese wisdom, which works with the seasons' natural rhythms.

Thank you, Stéphanie, Caroline, and Patricia, for taking the time to share your secrets and your enthusiasm. I encourage every one of us to collectively pursue the discovery of all this richness, which in Canada is still largely unexplored.

PREFACE BY ELISABETH CARDIN

We are at the dawn of a farming revolution that is both gentle and necessary. A revolution full of benevolence, culture, growth, diversity, and age-old knowledge. This book is part of a rational and sensitive movement that reminds us of the importance of welcoming harmony back into the heart of our food-related activities and ecosystems — both natural and human.

Despite the initial good intentions behind it, industrial food — and consequently its megafarms and supermarkets — upended the natural equilibrium that existed previously, when humans lived according to the rhythms of nature and the seasons, and were connected to one another. Luckily, we soon realized the seriousness of the damage it caused to the health of soil, water, animals, and human communities (not to mention the disappearance of so many animal species and vegetable varieties). We now know how imperative it is that we return to local methods of production, on a human scale, diversified, ecologically sound, and with local food sovereignty.

Food is the ultimate connection that links us to the earth and to other people. It can also be the quickest way to heal everything that got broken while we weren't paying attention.

Cooking is the meeting point between nature and culture, between resources and knowledge. Anyone with even a passing interest in Canada's culinary history quickly understands that it isn't all beans and bacon or potatoes or maple syrup. Canadian cuisine is a multi-layered melting pot. It reflects the incredible diversity of the cultures that have come together on this vast fertile territory. Don't all families tell stories with their recipes? The settlement of the first Cantonese people in Canada in 1788, with a more significant wave in the second half of the nineteenth century, along with other Asian families who followed later, have made an enormous contribution to enriching our own cultures with flavour and knowledge. And their history becomes, in some small way, *our* history.

Organic Asian vegetables that are suited to our climate? What an excellent idea. Vegetables are true witnesses to history, bearers of memories, and masters of adaptation. They are to cooking what words are to poetry. They carry a particular ancestral memory. They whisper stories of labour and poverty, and above all, of love and hope. They narrate the way in which we have chosen to use the resources at our disposal: the diversity in gardening reflects culinary and cultural diversity.

By choosing to invite vegetables eaten in different parts of the world and yet grown locally to us into our own cooking, we are choosing to write our shared history and to define a future cuisine for us all. A cuisine rich in flavour and colour. A cuisine adapted to our northernness and concerned for the well-being of human and natural communities.

At its heart, the Wang sisters' work is just that: a meeting between nature and culture, and between the past and the future.

And all this in the most moving and flavourful balance.

OUR FAMILY

我們一家

The migratory route of our family over three generations

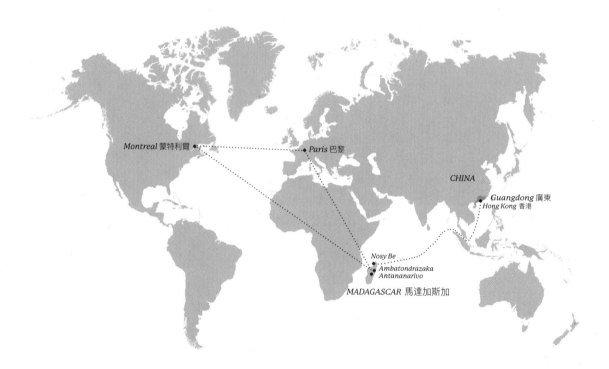

Montreal 蒙特利爾

Paris 巴黎

CHINA

Guangdong 廣東
Hong Kong 香港

Nosy Be

Ambatondrazaka
Antananarivo

MADAGASCAR 馬達加斯加

FROM CHINA
TO QUEBEC
VIA MADAGASCAR

Our family comes from far away. Like so many generations before them, our grandparents were born in the Chinese countryside in Guangdong province. This province in the south of China is the cradle of Cantonese culture. Living conditions were tough there in the early twentieth century, and many people left the country, some of them for the isle of Madagascar, in the south of Africa, to find work. Our mother's father was only twelve years old when he made the long journey by boat across the Indian Ocean. He later returned briefly to China to get married before making the reverse journey, and his wife joined him later. Our paternal grandfather had a different journey: he was a general in the Chinese national army and was exiled, first to Taiwan and then to Hong Kong, before settling to retire in Madagascar with our grandmother. She is the only grandparent who was not born in Guangdong; she was born in Hong Kong, like our father.

So Madagascar is where our parents, aunts, and uncles grew up, alongside a mixed population off the coast of Africa. This island, whose indigenous population is African-Asian in origin, was a French colony at the time. Our mother grew up on Nosy Be, a paradisiacal island on the country's northwest coast, while our father grew up in Ambatondrazaka, a city 186 mi (300 km) north of the capital. Our parents grew up speaking Cantonese but quickly adopted French at the schools they were sent to, mainly in Antananarivo, the capital. As young adults, they left the island to continue their studies: our mother studied Chinese in Paris, and our father studied business administration in Sherbrooke, Quebec, where his mother and sister Marie later joined him. Eventually, all our aunts and uncles ended up leaving Madagascar to settle in France or Canada.

After having a long-distance relationship by letter and getting married in Paris, our parents settled in Montreal, Quebec, where we grew up with all the cultural baggage that precedes us. Although we speak only a little Cantonese, we are still deeply connected to our family via a very Chinese trait: the love of food.

Our Laou grandparents and their children,
including our mother, Nicole, in her mother's arms.

Our Wang grandparents and their children:
our aunt Marie on the left and our father, Henri, on the right.

Our mother under the Nosy Be palm trees in Madagascar.

Our mother's Chinese passport.

Our father and his parents in Madagascar.

Our parents' wedding in Paris, France.

Our father in Antsirabe, Madagascar.

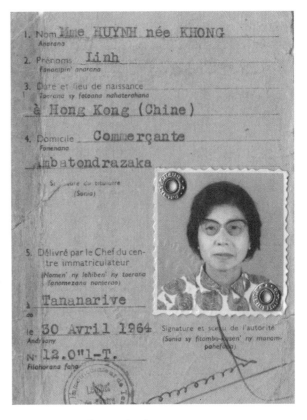

Our grandmother Monique's Malagasy driver's licence.

A CULINARY HERITAGE

Food holds a central position in Chinese culture. Meals are shared with family and friends, and celebrations are accompanied by feasts. Cantonese people in particular love to eat and are known even within China for their ability to cook "almost everything that flies in the sky, swims in the water, or walks on four legs," according to a popular expression. In many Asian cultures, when you bump into someone you know or receive visitors, the first thing you do is ask the person if they have already eaten. In Cantonese, this is: *Sik tso faan mei aa?*

At home, our mother cooked some Cantonese recipes and a lot of recipes from the magazine *Coup de Pouce*, which meant a lot of French- and Québécois-inspired dishes. We learned to cook with her, particularly baked goods like muffins or crêpes. In winter, we loved helping her make wontons — this was a big production that took an entire Sunday afternoon. We chatted as we wrapped the ground meat mixture in the square pastry sheets. When evening came, we devoured these mouthfuls of flavour with a homemade chicken stock and a sauce unique to our family, made from soy sauce and ketchup.

Our interest in and appreciation for vegetables is not new. As we grew up, there was always a vegetable on the plate, whether in our school lunches, in meals at home, or at family gatherings. Vegetables are at the heart of Chinese cooking. "Eat" in Chinese literally means "eat rice," and the Chinese character for "vegetable" is also used to mean "dish." Meat is generally less present on the plate: consumption of animal protein is around ten times lower in China than it is in Western countries.

Our mother cooked some Asian vegetables: bok choy, gai lan, and Asian eggplant, which she would bring back from her occasional trips to Montreal's Chinatown, and watercress, which she grew in her garden and added to the rice porridge (congee) that we ate every Sunday lunch. We can remember seeing her at the kitchen table, separating the leaves from a huge bunch of watercress sitting on newspaper.

We were also lucky enough to grow up with two very generous aunts, Dany and Marie, who still today prepare proper feasts for us every time we visit them. Whenever we are with our aunt Marie and our cousins, either for a visit or at the cottage, we can spend entire days cooking and eating ... all the while talking about food as well. We share anecdotes about dishes we have tasted, we hold spontaneous tasting sessions, and we plan our future meals. At our aunt Dany's house, the table is always overflowing with tasty homemade dishes, including the Cantonese classics we adore: roast pork belly, barbecue pork (char siu), sweet red bean (adzuki) soup ... And every time, we leave our aunts' houses with meals or baked goods like baos (small stuffed steamed buns) or moon cakes.

Caroline, Stéphanie, and Patricia.

THE WANG SISTERS

These faraway places where our family once lived, unknown to us as children, have entered our hearts and minds in the form of flavours and fragments of memory handed down to us over the years. In turn, our respective interests have led us to launch projects in different parts of Quebec, in quite separate fields. This book brings together the colours, expertise, and lived experiences of each one of us as a way of tracing our family, cultural, and culinary heritage.

CAROLINE is the oldest of the three sisters. She has always been interested in food and cooking, especially baking and local food specialities.

When she was studying nutrition, Caroline travelled to Madagascar on a research internship with plans to volunteer and to discover the land where her parents grew up. While completing her master's in health sciences (community health), she carried out a research project on the social and psychosocial determinants of health.

After Caroline finished studying, she set up a private practice in nutrition, with a particular interest in food-related habits and behaviours. Working in Gatineau, and serving Quebec remotely as a dietitian, she shares information and tools for better eating and well-being with her clients.

Caroline loves nature as well as travelling and relaxing.

From a very early age, **STÉPHANIE** has been inspired by farm life as a way of putting into practice the concept of living in harmony with nature.

At the age of twenty, a year after her mother died, Stéphanie headed off with only her backpack on a solo trip across China for nine months, during which she reconnected with the riches of her family and cultural heritage. When she was twenty-three, a ten-month internship with Indian farming organizations changed her life and opened her eyes to the crucial role of farmers in food sovereignty of communities across the world.

Once back in Canada, Stéphanie continued to be involved in the international peasant movement La Via Campesina while working with the Union Paysanne and the National Farmers Union. At the same time, she completed a master's degree in agricultural sociology, focusing on the legal and administrative aspects of Quebec farming. She worked and did various internships on organic market farms, including at Les Jardins de la Grelinette, where she explored the magnificent Brome-Missiquoi region.

Since opening Le Rizen in 2016, Stéphanie has realized her dream of having a positive influence on the world through an essential job that feeds her body, her mind, her heart, and her community in a healthy way.

PATRICIA, the youngest of the sisters, works in the music and culture industries. Although food is not at the centre of her life, she loves eating and cooking in her own time.

After studying the violin, and later cultural action studies, she worked for several years as a project manager at Regroupement du conte in Quebec, where she fell in love with the power of speech. She regretted how little she knew about her parents' and grandparents' lives, as the stories had not been handed down through the generations. In 2019, she set off to meet her family with a little tape recorder. This journey took her to France and inspired her to learn more Cantonese, her family's mother tongue.

Now settled in Rimouski, she is a violinist and podorhythmist in traditional music bands (Salicorne, Germaine) and in the GGRIL collective. She also leads a few projects of her own: LIEUES, which blends traditional Chinese and Québécois music; and HOYI, in which she explores music linked to her family heritage and the ways in which it resonates with her family's life stories. She is also engaged in various cultural projects linked to living heritage.

Patricia's work aims to gather people, to reflect musically on the mixing of cultures, and to tell beautiful stories.

A FEW WORDS ON LE RIZEN FARM

Le Rizen began producing organic Asian vegetables in the charming village of Frelighsburg, located in southern Quebec, very close to the United States border. The village is part of the Brome-Missisquoi region, which is itself situated in the tourist area of the Eastern Townships.

During the farm's early years, all the labour was done by hand. Le Rizen then migrated to a farming system in which the ground is worked by a tractor, or a two-wheeled minitractor,* and in which transplanting* and harvesting are carried out by hand. With the help of a few employees as well as ad hoc volunteers, this system allows almost an acre (in other words, the equivalent of the surface area of two Olympic swimming pools) to be used for growing Asian vegetables every season.

As well as growing over forty varieties of Asian vegetables and plants, all organic, every year, Le Rizen also makes a range of artisanal products, such as sauces, kimchi, and other lacto-fermented foods to make use of the farm and neighbouring farms' surplus of vegetables. The majority of these items are sold locally, at public markets, grocery stores, and restaurants within 62 mi (100 km) of the farm.

Climate and hardiness zone at Le Rizen

Stretching south along the plains of the St. Lawrence River, Brome-Missisquoi enjoys a long, hot summer, which has earned it the nickname Quebec's Florida. More widely, this region is in the climate hardiness zone called North temperate. In this zone, the low temperatures during the long winters can plunge to −22°F (−30°C), but luckily they then give way to a fairly hot summer, which can be shorter or longer depending on the exact geographic location, which allows a beautifully diverse range of vegetables to be grown, particularly those that grow quickly and like cooler temperatures.

In Frelighsburg, the growing site of Le Rizen is in hardiness zone 5a. The growing season out in the field can go from early May to mid-November, including a frost-free period from early June to mid-September. A great many vegetables can be grown in zone 5a, including some that we usually associate with tropical climates. Interestingly, Frelighsburg is on the forty-fifth parallel, the same latitude as northeast China, so we can expect to grow the same vegetables here.

---

* The words followed by an asterisk are defined in the Glossary on page 339.

AN INVITATION TO TRAVEL ...

Although two oceans separate us from the land of our ancestors, our family's food memories allow us to travel the many kilometres of their migration back to them. Throughout these pages we revisit the flavours, stories, and traditions that define us — our family and ourselves.

We have drawn from our own experiences, scoured the literature, and interrogated our nearest and dearest to introduce you, in numerous ways, to fifteen Asian vegetables that are suited to our climate and that grow just as well in the field as they do in a backyard or on a balcony.

We have brought together both talented chefs who have made the conscious choice to source organic and local Asian vegetables, and friends and family who are also passionate about cooking to create original and varied dishes. The recipes will launch you into their worlds, where you will discover new cooking techniques and different flavour combinations.

We have considered the challenges of getting started in vegetable growing and shared some pathways for achieving balance in feeding one's community without exhausting oneself in order to collectively reach food sovereignty.

Together, we will experience the four seasons that make up the gardener's year in a North temperate climate. From winter planning to spring seeding, summer harvesting, and autumn preserving, a cycle of meaningful tasks unfolds for anyone wanting to live, with humility and respect, in harmony with nature. In its essence, farming follows the rhythms of the natural world, in all its whims and abundance.

So we now invite you on a voyage to the heart of our familial, culinary, and cultural universe, which crosses four continents, three generations, fifteen vegetables, four seasons, and forty recipes.

We hope that you will enjoy leafing through this book as the seasons pass or dipping in according to your needs and interests, and that you will have as much pleasure discovering, celebrating, and sharing the Asian vegetables grown here as we have had writing this book.

ASIAN VEGETABLES

亞洲蔬菜

WHAT ARE ASIAN VEGETABLES?

Asian vegetables are plants that are grown and eaten as vegetables in Asia. In this book, we will pay particular attention to vegetables from East Asia (China, Japan, Korea), South Asia (India), and Southeast Asia (Thailand, Vietnam, Laos).

The plant's origin is not as important as its significance in the Asian culinary tradition — some of these vegetables were originally from Europe or Africa.

Loved and sought after, particularly by the Asian diaspora, these vegetables can be found in Asian grocery stores in big cities around the world.

A DIFFICULT BREAKTHROUGH

Each year we see new Asian vegetables appearing in seed catalogues, on grocery shelves, on the tables at farmers' markets, on television programs, on the menu at locavore restaurants, and in backyard vegetable gardens. But we must confess that this breakthrough has been on the slow side, and that their introduction has been a bit of a drip feed.

Why did these vegetables, which are so delicious and nutritious, and which have enormous potential in the North temperate climate of countries like our own, take so long to make an appearance in our grocery stores and backyards and on our plates? Obviously because they are little known, look different, and sometimes have an unusual texture or flavour. But these are not the only reasons.

According to the English market gardener Joy Larkcom, a pioneer who in 1991 published a reference work dedicated to growing Asian vegetables in a Western context, the mystery behind the West's late discovery of the potential of Asian vegetables is due, among other things, to the challenges surrounding their names. First, there is the difficulty of pronouncing the names, which in many cases are romanizations or transcriptions of their Asian names. Then there is the confusion arising from the fact that it isn't unusual for an Asian vegetable to have more than one name. This is the case with bok choy, which is also known as pak choi simply due to a different way of romanizing the name. Another challenge is that several different vegetables share the same name; for example, the Chinese characters used for bok choy in Cantonese are the same characters used in Mandarin for napa cabbage. We have experienced this confusion ourselves during discussions with our family as we wrote this book!

With this book, we are honoured to contribute our cultural heritage, our experiences in the field, and our research in order to advance the spadework begun by all those who believed, and still believe, in the potential of Asian vegetables from seed to fork — or from seed to chopsticks!

FROM ASIA TO QUEBEC, FOR INCREASED FOOD SOVEREIGNTY

Without agroecology, food sovereignty is just a slogan.
Without food sovereignty, agroecology is just a technology.

— La Via Campesina

Access to food is a fundamental right recognized by every country in the world. Food security means having access to sufficient quantity, and to food that meets the cultural and nutritional needs of every person. But it was for the purpose of "feeding the world" that we saw monocultures of genetically modified plants being imposed on the global farming landscape, the privatization of natural resources, and the inclusion of food in the world trade agreements undermining local food systems.

The concept of food sovereignty was developed by the international farming movement La Via Campesina. Food sovereignty offers a planetary objective that considers the power relations at the heart of the food system and tries to transform them in order to give back ownership and resource control to the people who actually produce the food. In concrete terms, this is translated as the right of communities to farm their land and to decide what is grown and how much of it, the way in which the food is produced and with what resources, and what they put on their plates.

To attain food sovereignty, we need more than ever an agroecological farming system as described in these pages: a way of farming based on community; a way of farming aligned with a lifestyle and a means of production that are in harmony with nature; a way of farming that is incorporated into profoundly transformed political and cultural systems from the perspectives of social justice and economic viability.

We firmly believe that increasing the presence of agroecologically grown Asian vegetables in our gardens, on our plates, and in the collective imagination contributes to our food sovereignty for several reasons.

Eating seasonally

In recent years, we have seen a surge of enthusiasm and a collective awareness of the advantages of eating food that is organic, in season, and local. This is a good thing, because it allows us to ensure a high level of quality, freshness, and traceability.

The most effective way to sustain local agriculture is, in our opinion, to buy directly from a farm or a trusted farming collective or cooperative by going to your area's public markets, shopping at farm stands, or ordering from a farmer online. By doing this, you will naturally eat seasonally, which is, according to traditional Chinese medicine, better for your body.

Facilitating access to high-quality vegetables

In specialized grocery stores and in supermarkets, Asian vegetables are generally imported and conventionally grown. Their freshness also varies from one place to another.

Some market gardeners, however, act as pioneers by specializing in the production of Asian vegetables. They fill the crying need in diverse communities for access to local vegetables that are good quality and grown agroecologically.

Celebrating cultural, farming, and food diversity

The cultivation and consumption of Asian vegetables support diversity on three different levels.

First, an interest in the culinary traditions of others is usually accompanied by curiosity and a feeling of proximity, which help break down many existing cultural barriers. Second, visiting alternative food sources, such as farm stands and farmers' markets, brings us closer to farms — places with a story and a face — feeding our need for connection with the land while supporting the local economy. Finally, the agroecologically grown foods found at these alternative sources are different and are produced differently: with respect for humans and the environment. They are, therefore, far from what is found in conventional distribution networks: industrialized food that is standardized and dehumanized.

In our opinion, the present and future of food sovereignty depends on diversity at all levels.

Growing and eating more sustainably all year

Asian vegetables offer farmers greater diversity in what they can grow and, consequently, what we eat in a North temperate climate. Beyond kale, Swiss chard, spinach, and lettuce, a bounty of Asian greens exist. They are delicious, nutritious, versatile in cooking, and cold-loving, which allows us to grow them in the field from May to November. We only need to use floating row covers* early and late in the season — an accessible, inexpensive method with a small environmental footprint.

Among these Asian leafy greens, those of the botanical family* Brassicaceae (formerly known as cruciferous), such as bok choy and tatsoi, are among the vegetables with the best yield when grown in minimally heated or even unheated greenhouses. As more and more market gardeners use greenhouses to prolong the growing season, it's a safe bet that Asian leafy greens will have a prime spot on our plates in the middle of winter.

In addition, since the majority of more commonly known leafy greens quickly go to flower in the hotter months, their availability is often limited in full summer. It is therefore worth exploring the idea of growing Asian leafy greens, which are from traditionally hot countries, in order to enhance options in the summer season.

Growing our food autonomy through agroecology

Food autonomy is essentially the proportion of food produced and then consumed in a single community. In Quebec, we produce the equivalent of 90% of the fresh and preserved vegetables that are consumed annually in the province. However, this production is seasonal: a significant amount is produced and exported in the summer, and we need to import the majority of vegetables eaten in winter.

There are several ways to increase our food autonomy, and growing Asian vegetables is one to consider. By applying organic or agroecological growing techniques, choosing varieties* and cultivars* suited to the climate, and deepening our knowledge of the particularities of Asian vegetables, it becomes possible to grow a great number of them, summer and winter.

We would like to see many more of these vegetables being grown in the years to come, although not at any price. We believe that many farms at a human scale, dotted across the farming landscape and using agroecological practices to grow produce destined for local markets, will be more resilient and nourishing than a handful of big farms focused on exporting food.

Here and elsewhere, the emergence of small farms is on an upward trend. After spending time in the cities and at school desks, a growing number of people eventually decide to live on the land, in the countryside. This, in our opinion, is where agricultural production should happen.

VEGETABLES: GOOD FOR THE BODY, GREAT ON THE PLATE

Often neglected by the young and the not-so-young, vegetables are delicious, adding freshness to a menu (thanks to their water content) and bringing colour, texture, and flavour to a plate. In addition, they contain multiple nutrients and compounds that are beneficial for the body, providing high doses of fibre, vitamins, and minerals. This is even more true for Asian vegetables, which include numerous dark leafy greens, a sign of nutrient richness.

Growing your own vegetables, cooking with good recipes, and continuing or sharing family or popular traditions are all activities that can contribute to the pleasure of eating vegetables.

Moreover, Asian vegetables offer a range of exciting possibilities: new flavours, textures, smells, and recipes. They allow us to dive into different culinary universes and explore. Eating vegetables is even more inviting when you know Asian vegetables!

Chinese medicine and us

Since childhood, we have strolled the streets of Montreal's Chinatown. We went to Chinese school there, as well as restaurants, patisseries, and import stores — but rarely to the stores selling Chinese herbs.

Sometimes our mother, in kind with other family members, would consult a Chinese herbalist, who would prescribe a range of herbs. When she returned home, new and unusual odours would tickle our nostrils.

When we had digestive troubles, our mother would make us a porridge (congee) that contained nothing but rice and water. When we started feeling better, she would sprinkle small chunks of ham on top. What a relief to finally be able to eat food that tasted of something!

We didn't know that these were practices anchored in the knowledge of traditional Chinese medicine, and even today we still have much to learn.

As we put this book together, we had the chance to talk with acupuncturist Claude Émile Racette to better understand Chinese medicine as it pertains to Asian vegetables. The author of *Manger le dragon: Compendium sur la diétothérapie en médecine chinoise* gives us the following brief introduction to traditional Chinese medicine, which also offers a window for understanding Chinese culture in general.

Traditional Chinese medicine and Asian vegetables

CLAUDE ÉMILE RACETTE, ACUPUNCTURIST AND DIET THERAPY PRACTITIONER IN TRADITIONAL CHINESE MEDICINE

The definition of health in traditional Chinese medicine is based on seeking equilibrium among the body, emotions, and nature, with the aim of preserving one's vitality and avoiding illness. All of this knowledge, which aims to balance one's life with one's environment and the seasons, has been built over the course of centuries to form a medical system that is the foundation of traditional Chinese medicine.

This medicine is based on the notion of vital energy, called Qi, which corresponds to the energy or strength of the body. Good health results from the combination of energy produced via the body's physiological functions, such as digestion and breath, and the innate energy that already exists in the body, like parental heritage or genetic capital.

Traditional Chinese medicine aims to maintain, revitalize, or rebalance this vital energy from an understanding of the movements or the energy between the different parts of the body. In the frame of this medicine, we evaluate the energy imbalances and use the most appropriate tools according to the context, including energetic movement to cultivate vitality within the body, mind, and spirit (such as Qi Gong), dietetics (using food), pharmacopoeia (using herbs), massages, and acupuncture.

Seeking equilibrium implies two "qualities" or "movements" of the body's vital expression and nature: yin and yang. These two vital forces, opposing and complementary, must be in equilibrium within a body and the body must be in equilibrium with its environment in order to maximize vitality and maintain good health. The yin designates what cools, slows, and moistens the body; the yang is what warms, activates, and dries it.

Foods for preventing illness, healing, helping you adapt to your environment

Diet therapy is an approach in which foods are used, alone or in combination with herbs from the Chinese pharmacopoeia, to prevent or treat health problems. It is an important aspect of traditional Chinese medicine.

This approach attributes properties to different foods, along with an action that can be identified as yin or yang within the body. Depending on whether their nature is cooling or warming, the foods can contribute to activating or slowing down certain physiological functions. Foods will therefore be chosen according to these actions in order to bring the body into equilibrium, treat health problems, or allow the person to better adapt to the climate and the seasons.

For example, in the context of traditional Chinese medicine, digestive problems caused by a cold condition will be improved by a diet made up of yang-type foods, such as ginger, onion, and leek, which warm and give energy.

In traditional Chinese medicine, local and seasonal foods are best, allowing us to adapt to our environment and maintain good health. Foods are chosen according to whether they are yin or yang, and also for their specific actions within the body according to their flavour. For example, spring is the traditional season for cleansing the body. According to traditional Chinese medicine, bitter and acidic foods will activate the liver and help eliminate waste from the body.

Asian vegetables according to traditional Chinese medicine

According to traditional Chinese medicine, green and fibrous Asian vegetables, like most presented in this book, are rich in nutrients and fluids, and trigger specific actions in the body by their sweet, bitter, or spicy flavour.

With the exception of mustard greens and shiso, which are more yang, and luffa, which is neutral, all the Asian vegetables in this book are yin. Several of the yin vegetables taste bitter, which is considered a good stimulant for the digestive and hepatic functions. Bitter vegetables increase saliva and stomach acid, which help to moisten and lubricate the intestines, thus facilitating movements within the intestinal tract. Bitter foods also facilitate the elimination of liquids by stimulating the kidneys, which has a diuretic action. Moreover, bitter foods satisfy the appetite and prevent constipation and edema.

Asian vegetables are your best allies to maintain the vitality of the body and prevent a great many health problems.

Ultimately, traditional Chinese medicine is a holistic medical system that balances out Qi based on a collection of practices and life behaviours, including training the body and mind, taking herbs and other products from the Chinese pharmacopoeia, and making food choices according to our vital energy, the seasons, and the places we live.

OUR CHOICE OF ASIAN VEGETABLES

From the vast range of Asian vegetables, we have chosen fifteen to introduce in this book. Why these rather than the others, and how did we discover them?

Some of the vegetables we chose, particularly bok choy and Asian eggplant, are connected to the recipes that our mother sometimes used to cook at home, and that our aunt Dany makes when we have family gatherings at her house.

Others are served in the Cantonese restaurants of Montreal's Chinatown, where we go as a family to celebrate birthdays. This is the case for gai lan, which you can taste in dim sum restaurants, as well as Chinese cabbage.

And others are inspired by big celebrations — weddings or Chinese New Year — in the heart of Montreal's Madagascan Chinese community, where a dozen traditional Cantonese dishes are served to hundreds of guests, between dances ranging from the cha-cha-cha to the macarena via the traditional Malagasy afindrafindrao.

Stéphanie tasted several other of these vegetables (edible chrysanthemum, Chinese lettuce or celtuce, and okra) on her pilgrimages to China and India. She got to know others by growing them from seeds from suppliers in Canada and the United States.

Our selection includes some more familiar vegetables that have been available for years in both grocery stores and conventional and organic farms (bok choy, Chinese cabbage, Asian eggplant, Asian cucumber). We also want to introduce you to the less common vegetables (amaranth, Malabar spinach, shiso) that are mainly found in Asian markets.

We have also chosen to include vegetables that work in the garden as well as on the plate: some suited to our chilly springs and falls, and others that prefer the summer heat; vegetables from different botanical families and with diverse flavours, textures, colours, and shapes. While some of them are easy to grow, others present more of a challenge in the garden.

Finally, having been grown at Le Rizen for several years now, these Asian vegetables have all proved their agronomic potential in the North temperate zone, not to mention the interest they add to dishes and the fact that they are generally appreciated by the public.

The fifteen vegetables in our selection include ten greens, four fruit vegetables, and one herb. We principally eat the leaves of the greens, or leafy greens. We include Chinese lettuce in this category because, as well as being a lettuce variety, it grows like a green even though we mainly eat the stem. The fruit vegetable is a food that we cook as a vegetable but that is, botanically speaking, the fruit of its plant.

Buying Asian vegetables

Specialized Asian grocery stores generally sell most of these fifteen vegetables year-round, but they are imported and cultivated using unknown production methods. Supermarkets stock the best known of these vegetables, either year-round or in season, but usually not organic varieties. You can also buy the most common of these vegetables from natural or health food stores and farm stands or market gardeners with a diverse range of offerings, whether organic or not, and usually in season. And while we wait for new market gardeners to specialize in Asian vegetables, whether organic or not, you will also find some of the less common vegetables (amaranth, okra, lemongrass) sold by gardeners who specialize in African vegetables.

Note: At the time of writing this book, Le Rizen was the only farm in Quebec growing all of these vegetables organically. There is thus a lot of room for Asian organic farms, particularly far from the big cities in which most of the offerings are currently found.

Growing Asian vegetables

Growing Asian vegetables is no different from current market-garden production. The difficulty rating we have given each of our fifteen vegetables is linked to the effort, time, and equipment needed to obtain commercial-quality harvests.

Beginners will appreciate the vegetables that grow easily: they are generally not attacked by insects, need no physical protection, and are less demanding in terms of soil fertility.

The intermediate level includes brassicas that have to be covered by nets at all times to protect them from plant pests, and other crops that need physical protection at the beginning and end of the season for warmth. Some crops need a moderately fertile soil but must be watered regularly. That said, you can try growing these vegetables without protection, especially if appearance and yield are not priorities for you.

If you are looking for a challenge or have several years of gardening or farming experience, the advanced category is for you. Here you will find vegetables that absolutely need physical protection to deter insects organically or to keep warm early and late in the season. These crops stay in the field for a long time and have greater needs in terms of soil fertility, and they require regular watering. The right choice of cultivars is important for obtaining high yields.

The following chart shows the fifteen vegetables in the order they appear in the book, with the exception of Chinese cabbage, which we write about last. This classification broadly follows the order in which they will be ready for harvest when grown outdoors. They are sorted by botanical family, type of vegetable, and preference for heat or cool weather. You will also see the difficulty level of growing them and where to find them for sale. This is not an exhaustive classification; rather, the aim is to give you pointers to certain types of sellers if you want to get your hands on one of them.

		Asian grocery stores	Supermarkets	Natural or health food stores	Specialized farms or market gardeners (Le Rizen and others)
Brassicaceae					
BOK CHOY	Leafy green · Cold-loving · Intermediate	✓	✓	✓	✓
CHOY SUM	Leafy green · Cold-loving · Intermediate	✓			✓
GAI LAN	Leafy green · Cold-loving · Intermediate	✓			✓
MUSTARD GREENS	Leafy green · Cold-loving · Intermediate	✓		✓	✓
CHINESE CABBAGE	Leafy green · Cold-loving · Easy	✓	✓	✓	✓
Asteraceae					
EDIBLE CHRYSANTHEMUM	Leafy green · Cold-loving · Easy	✓			✓
CELTUCE	Leafy green · Cold-loving · Easy	✓			✓
Amaranthaceae					
AMARANTH	Leafy green · Heat-loving · Easy	✓			✓
Basellaceae					
MALABAR SPINACH	Leafy green · Heat-loving · Easy	✓			✓
Lamiaceae					
SHISO	Leafy green · Heat-loving · Easy	✓			✓
Malvaceae					
OKRA	Fruit vegetable · Heat-loving · Easy	✓			✓
Solanaceae					
ASIAN EGGPLANT	Fruit vegetable · Heat-loving · Easy	✓	✓	✓	✓
Cucurbitaceae					
ASIAN CUCUMBER	Fruit vegetable · Heat-loving · Intermediate	✓		✓	✓
LUFFA	Fruit vegetable · Heat-loving · Easy	✓			✓
Poaceae					
LEMONGRASS	Herb · Heat-loving · Intermediate	✓	✓		✓

 Leafy green

Fruit vegetable

Herb

Cold-loving

Heat-loving

● Easy to cultivate: Does not require physical protection.

○ Intermediate: Requires physical protection.

● Advanced: Requires physical protection, heat, or special attention.

UNDERSTANDING CANTONESE: OUR FAMILY LANGUAGE

Coming from Guangdong, our family speaks Cantonese, one of seven major Chinese languages, which also include Mandarin (or standard Chinese), spoken by the greatest number of people in China and the second-most spoken language in the world. Cantonese is commonly spoken in the provinces of Guangdong and Guangxi, as well as in Hong Kong and Macau. The first waves of Chinese immigrants were predominantly from Guangdong. It is this diaspora that founded the first Chinatowns all over the world, especially in Canada, and that made the Cantonese language known outside of China.

Although each Chinese language is spoken differently, they all use the same writing system based on Chinese characters, also called sinogram. This means that despite the variety of spoken languages, the written characters are similar. Certain regional differences in spoken language, however, do lead to variations in writing.

Note also that two different writing systems exist alongside each other: traditional Chinese characters and simplified Chinese characters. The second, as the name suggests, is intended to reduce the complexity of some of the traditional characters by decreasing the number of elements. Simplified Chinese characters were gradually introduced in continental China by the Communist Party in the context of the Cultural Revolution, with the aim of increasing literacy rates. Traditional writing is still used in Hong Kong, Macau, and Taiwan, and in some Chinese diasporas around the world.

The romanized jyutping system

All Chinese characters are monosyllabic; in other words, each character is expressed orally by one syllable that has one or more meanings. They are also tonal: each character has a pitch relative to the others; an error in pronunciation or tone of one syllable can thus completely change the meaning of what's being said. Luckily, romanizing systems have been developed in order to transcribe the pronunciations of Chinese languages into the Latin alphabet and to indicate the tones in various ways. In Cantonese, one of these transcription systems is jyutping (pronounced *yütping*), while in Mandarin pinyin (pronounced *pin-yin*) is the official romanization system. Here are a few tips to help you decode jyutping and help you correctly pronounce the Cantonese names that you will find at the beginning of the section about each vegetable.

In jyutping, the nine Cantonese tones are simplified into six. They are indicated by the numbers 1 to 6 after each syllable to denote both the relative pitch of each sound and its movement.

DESCRIPTION OF THE TONES ACCORDING TO THE ASSIMIL METHOD

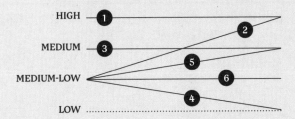

<u>TONE 1:</u> flat and high
<u>TONE 2:</u> rising from medium-low to high
<u>TONE 3</u>: flat and medium
<u>TONE 4:</u> descending from medium-low to low
<u>TONE 5:</u> rising from medium-low to medium
<u>TONE 6:</u> flat and medium-low

Note that tone 5 can also be described as initially descending and then rising.

The pitch of the sounds is relative, which means that tone 4 for one person will not have the same pitch as it will for another person. The key point is that their tone 4 will be lower than their tone 3, and that it will descend.

Jyutping is counterintuitive at times:

J is pronounced Y
C is pronounced like a soft CH
Z is pronounced like a soft TS
G is pronounced ike a soft K
OE or EO are pronounced like the French "E"

Here are some examples of jyutping pronunciation with our vegetables, indicated in brackets and followed by a description of the appropriate relative pitches. We will use the same jyutping for the names of the vegetables and at other places in the book.

Baak6 coi3 (bok choy)
[baak], flat medium-low tone
[choy], flat medium tone

Zi2 sou1 (shiso)
[tsi], tone rising from medium-low to high
[sow], flat high tone

hoeng1 maau4 (lemongrass)
[heung], flat high tone
[mao], tone descending from medium-low to low

Chinese names of the vegetables

NOT ONE BUT SEVERAL GREENS!
Chinese communities throughout the world are numerous, so in essence each has its own dialect and a multitude of names for the same vegetable. In addition, some names are spoken more than written, and vice versa. For each vegetable, we have aimed to present the name (or names) by which it is most commonly known in Canada, whether that is in day-to-day conversation or on the shelves of Asian grocery stores. This gathers together the information found in the scarce existing literature and matches what our Chinese-origin family has observed in the Quebec and Canadian contexts.

One character, many meanings

A single Chinese character usually has many meanings. Its use within a word made up of two or three characters refers to just one of these meanings, but it is not always easy to know which one, even for a Chinese speaker.

When two meanings of a character seem appropriate, we have indicated this with a slash: possible meaning of character/other possible meaning of character.

Some characters are also used for pronunciation and not for their definition. If this is the case, or if there is too much uncertainty surrounding the meaning, we have indicated this with a question mark.

THE CHINESE NAMES OF OUR VEGETABLES WILL BE PRESENTED AS FOLLOWS:

1. traditional Chinese characters/simplified Chinese characters, if these exist

2. jyutping/pinyin, if available

3. (meaning of the first character | meaning of the second character | meaning of the third character, if there is one)

In cases where certain Chinese characters are used only in Cantonese or only in Mandarin, we have separated out the names and presented them in each language.

<u>TIP:</u> To indicate tone, pinyin usually uses accents instead of the Arabic numerals used by jyutping.

For example, lemongrass is hoeng1 maau4 (jyutping) and xiāngmáo (pinyin).

THE BASICS

Of Chinese and Asian Cooking

一些基本

A playground

Whenever we talk about food, our uncle Jean loves to repeat these words: "Everything has changed. It's not the same anymore!" According to him, because the Asian vegetables grown here today are produced in conditions different from those of his childhood, because they are harvested differently (manually in Madagascar and often mechanically in North America), and because Chinese condiments are no longer prepared the same way and are now produced in industrial quantities, it is impossible to reproduce the exact flavour of the Chinese dishes of days gone by — at least those that his parents and he himself used to cook and enjoy in Madagascar.

Our uncle is not being nostalgic but rather calling for us to adapt the cooking method depending on the precise taste of each food, each ingredient. In light of this, we invite you to pay particular attention to the flavour of each vegetable or ingredient that you use. It might vary according to cultivar, the place it was grown, the way it was produced, or the time between harvest and eating. Can you tell the difference?

For us, the love of cooking resides in the pleasure of experimenting while keeping an open and curious attitude. Although recipes are obviously useful, they offer one unique version of a dish, while taste varies with each person. The ability to improvise and adapt is priceless when it comes to cooking; you also need to have the necessary ingredients on hand and a little knowledge of basic techniques.

Of course, a variety of techniques can be used for each task. The way to measure the amount of water necessary for cooking rice is a good example. The method widely shared and passed down in our extended family is to use the phalanx or palm of the hand: pour rice into the rice cooker, then fill it with water up to half of the second phalanx of the middle finger when put vertically on the surface of the rice; or fill with water up to about three quarters of the height of the palm laid flat on the rice. However, some members of our family have switched to a more quantifiable measure, such as two parts water to one part rice, or simply trust their experienced eye.

We encourage you to familiarize yourself with the ingredients and basic techniques of Chinese and Asian cooking, enjoy discovering the new flavours of the forty recipes in this book, and be inspired to improvise and create your own gastronomic delights.

CRUCIAL INGREDIENTS

Although naturally tasty, Asian vegetables are elevated when accompanied by various aromatics, spices, oils, or sauces, among other things.

The ingredients mentioned in this section figure in the recipes in this book and are typically used in Chinese cooking and other Asian cuisines, such as Japanese, Korean, Vietnamese, Thai, or Indian. Generally speaking, it is easy to obtain these items from supermarkets, Asian grocers, or online, or from specialty stores or local businesses.

AROMATICS AND SPICES

GARLIC
Added at the start of the cooking process in a stir-fry. Often chopped, it elevates all dishes with its pronounced flavour.

GINGER
Added at the start of the cooking process in a stir-fry or a stock, giving an aromatic and lightly spicy flavour. The skin is edible when young and fresh. If not, peel with a knife or scrape the skin off with a spoon.

Storage tip: Rinse the whole piece of ginger, let the outside dry at room temperature for a few minutes, then seal in a bag and freeze. Use without defrosting or peeling: grate or thinly slice before chopping. This is particularly good for preserving fresh, local, organic ginger, with its thin pink skin, which usually keeps for only two weeks in the fridge.

GREEN ONION
The white part can be stir-fried with garlic and ginger, while the green part is often chopped into rounds and sprinkled as a garnish before serving.

CILANTRO LEAVES
Sprinkle as a garnish before serving to give an aromatic flavour. Goes well with lentils, chicken, and pork.

LIME
Squeeze lime on immediately before serving to give a hint of freshness and acidity.

COCONUT MILK
Made from the pulp of crushed coconut. Gives a nice scent and brings thickness/creaminess to soups, sauces, curries, marinades, and rice.

THAI (OR BIRD'S-EYE) CHILI
A long thin chili, red or green. Very spicy.

KOREAN CHILI (GOCHUGARU)
Fruity and not very spicy, it turns food red. Essential in kimchi.

SICHUAN PEPPER
A floral, citrusy berry that looks like a peppercorn and produces a tingling sensation in the mouth. A staple of Sichuan cooking. Sometimes labelled as prickly ash or wild pepper. Red Sichuan pepper is more common than the green variety, which has a more herby flavour.

ALLSPICE (ALSO KNOWN AS JAMAICAN PEPPER)
The fruit of a tree that grows in Mexico and the Antilles, whose flavour is reminiscent of cinnamon, cloves, pepper, and nutmeg. Used in sauces, marinades, rice, roast meat, and desserts.

SESAME SEEDS (WHITE AND BLACK)
Added when serving for their nutty flavour and crunchiness. The toasted seeds have a more pronounced flavour. You can either buy them toasted or toast them yourself in a dry frying pan over medium heat for three to five minutes.

FENUGREEK SEEDS
Slightly bitter flavour. Add aroma to soups, stews, vegetables, chicken, and rice. Often used in Indian cooking.

CORIANDER SEEDS
Light, musky, citrusy flavour. Add to season stocks, marinades, fish, seafood, and baked goods. Go well with parsley, lemon, and ginger.

CUMIN SEEDS
Warm, aromatic, slightly bitter flavour. Popular in North African, Middle Eastern, Indian, and Mexican cooking to flavour soups, curries, tajines, stews, marinades, pulses, sausages, vegetables, couscous, and rice.

MUSTARD SEEDS
Spicy, mildly bitter flavour. Season sauces, curries, marinades, and pulses.

STAR ANISE
Fruit of the Indian almond tree, which grows in South China, with aromatic flavours of liquorice and pepper. Flavours soups, sauces, stewed dishes, pork, chicken, duck, and desserts.

TURMERIC
A rhizome in the same family as ginger, coloured from yellow to dark orange with a pronounced earthy, warm flavour. Often dried and ground, it seasons and colours soups, sauces, lentils, eggs, chicken, fish, shellfish, rice, and even yellow mustard.

FIVE SPICE POWDER
A blend of ground spices of Chinese origin comprising Sichuan pepper, star anise, cinnamon, cloves, and fennel. Used in marinades and for seasoning meat.

CURRY POWDER
A blend of ground spices of Indian origin, usually containing chili, pepper, turmeric, cumin, cinnamon, coriander, cardamom, ginger, nutmeg, and cloves. Used in curries and Singapore noodles.

SALT AND PEPPER
As in every type of cooking, used to balance the flavour of a dish.

SUGAR
To soften the bitterness of a food, we sometimes add a little sugar — granulated sugar, cane sugar, brown sugar, liquid honey, or pure maple syrup.

NOTE
The aroma and flavour of spices increase during cooking. Add them whole in slow-cooked dishes, and ground in dishes that are cooked quickly. You can also fry them in a dry pan or brown them in oil before adding other ingredients or incorporating them into dishes. We cook whole spices over medium heat and ground spices over low heat, taking care not to burn them. Ground spices are heat-sensitive, so our tip is to mix them with wet ingredients such as garlic, onion, or ginger, or with a little water, before frying them in oil.

CORNSTARCH

A starch extracted from maize.

Frequently used in Chinese cooking to thicken sauces and soups and to marinate meat before frying. It gives dishes a shiny appearance as well as a velvety texture.

Compared with flour, cornstarch cooks more quickly and thickens more effectively, and is also flavourless.

It is also used to coat foods before frying, giving them a thin, crispy crust.

SAUCES

SOY SAUCE

Essential in Chinese, Japanese, and Southeast Asian cooking, soy sauce adds colour and a salty umami flavour to sauces, stir-fries, stewed dishes, noodles, rice, and so on.

Originally from China, it is obtained by fermenting soybeans and wheat, and then aged in a brine and filtered.

Each Asian cuisine has its own soy sauce. The Chinese version contains more soybeans than wheat, while the Japanese version (shoyu) has equal proportions of both. The Chinese version also ferments for longer than the Japanese version, giving it a darker colour and a sweeter taste.

Black soy sauce can be light or dark. It is darker, sweeter, or thicker if it has fermented for longer, or if caramel or molasses have been added. In Chinese cooking, light soy sauce is commonly used, while dark sauce is more common in Japanese cooking.

White soy sauce is rarer, and is produced with more wheat and fewer soybeans than regular soy sauce, which gives it a light, translucent colour and a milder taste.

Whenever possible, choose the soy sauce appropriate for the type of cuisine.

Wheat-free and low-sodium versions of soy sauce are also available.

TAMARI

Of Japanese origin, this can easily be substituted for soy sauce.

Produced in a similar way to soy sauce, it is darker and thicker, and contains little to no wheat. Check the ingredients list to be sure.

Like Japanese soy sauce, tamari has a shorter fermentation period than Chinese soy sauce.

Being grain-free, it is naturally alcohol-free, but alcohol can be added for shelf stability.

OYSTER SAUCE

This sauce is made from oyster extract and offers a flavour of molluscs and a salty, sweet umami taste.

Commonly used in Chinese cooking, it adds aroma to vegetables, noodles, rice, stir-fries, and marinades.

There is also a mushroom-based vegetarian version as well as a gluten-free version.

HOISIN SAUCE

Made from fermented soybeans and seasoned with sesame seeds, garlic, and spices, among other things (sometimes including sweet potato), hoisin sauce has a sweet and salty flavour and a thick texture.

Often used in Cantonese cooking, stir-fries, and marinades. This is the perfect sauce for Peking duck, a roasted duck served with small crêpes and green onions — we love this dish!

FISH SAUCE

Essential in Southeast Asian cooking, this sauce is also used in the south of China. Made from fish or shellfish (often salted, fermented anchovies), which gives it a salty, aromatic umami, flavour, as well as a pronounced smell that softens with cooking.

The most common kind is *nước mắm*. *Mắm nêm* is also interesting: it smells very strong and contains pineapple, sugar, and spices.

Fish sauce goes well with garlic, lime, and red pepper flakes.

It is used in sauces, salad dressings, soups, stir-fries, noodle dishes, and marinades for grilled meat.

There is also a seaweed-based vegetarian version. Mushroom-flavoured soy sauce is also a good substitute.

PASTES AND FERMENTED BEANS

SWEET SAUCE (TIÁNMIÀN JIÀNG, 甜麵醬)

Also known as sweet soybean sauce or paste, this is actually a sauce or paste made from sweetened flour.

Thick and dark brown, it is made from fermented wheat flour, sugar, salt, and sometimes fermented soybeans. It has a sweet, salty umami taste. It is used in cooking in northern China, in stir-fry sauces, and as a condiment.

SWEET/SPICY SOYBEAN PASTE

This paste is made from fermented soybeans and can be either sweet (dòubàn jiàng, 豆瓣醬) or spicy (là dòubàn jiàng, 辣豆瓣醬).

Used in stir-fries, as a condiment, or to replace sweet sauce.

MISO

A paste made from fermented soybeans, often combined with a cereal (rice, barley, or another grain), salt, and other ingredients.

Miso comes in different colours, from white to dark brown. As with soy sauce, the longer the fermentation, the darker the colour and the more pronounced the flavour. It has a salty umami and sometimes sweet taste.

Added at the end of cooking, particularly to soups and sauces.

FERMENTED BLACK BEANS

Neither a paste nor a sauce, this is made from black soybeans fermented with salt, also called salted black beans.

Slightly sweet, fairly dry, with a salty umami flavour.

Used in stir-fry sauces or to add flavour to steamed dishes, it is common in Cantonese and Sichuan cooking.

Goes well with garlic, ginger, and chili.

OILS

SESAME OIL

A beautiful amber colour, highly aromatic.

Add a little at the end of cooking to lend a rich flavour of grilled sesame to vegetables, noodles, and sauces.

CHILI OIL

Comprising oil, red pepper flakes (from Sichuan province for an authentic flavour), and spices or aromatics such as garlic, star anise, or Sichuan pepper.

A condiment that adds a delicious kick to vegetables, noodles, and sauces.

We prefer to make our own version or buy it at some local Asian restaurants.

WINES AND VINEGARS

RICE COOKING WINE

A secret ingredient that balances flavours and makes dishes more flavourful, just like at a Chinese restaurant. It adds a depth to dishes.

It is produced by fermenting rice, contains alcohol, and is slightly salty and sweet.

Used for deglazing stir-fries as well as in marinades, sauces, and dumpling and wonton stuffings.

It comes in light and dark varieties. The best known is Shaoxing rice cooking wine, from the city of Shaoxing, a dark cooking wine with a more complex flavour than the lighter version. Light rice cooking wine is ideal for delicate steam-cooked dishes. There is also a cooking liquor, similar to light rice cooking wine, but with a less sweet, more pronounced taste.

Like traditional wine, rice wines of superior quality are suitable for drinking. But rice cooking wine is salty and not intended to be drunk.

You can replace rice cooking wine with cooking sherry. Other possibilities include saké, which gives a softer flavour; mirin, for a sweeter flavour; or vegetable, mushroom, or chicken stock.

Saké is a Japanese alcoholic drink made from fermented rice that can also be used like wine in cooking.

Mirin is a Japanese cooking wine. Similar to saké, it is sweeter and less alcoholic. It is a classic ingredient in teriyaki sauce.

RICE VINEGAR

Very common in Asian cooking, particularly Chinese and Japanese.

Produced by fermenting rice or rice wine, it is less acidic than white vinegar, apple cider vinegar, or wine vinegar.

Different types of rice vinegar include white (colourless or pale yellow), red, and black. Black Chinkiang rice vinegar, originally from the city of Zhenjiang, has a malted flavour and is perfect for dipping dumplings.

Rice vinegar goes well with soy sauce and sesame oil. It adds flavour to salads, dips, soups, marinades, stir-fries, stewed dishes, noodles, and sushi rice.

Alternatives: White or red rice vinegar can be replaced with apple cider vinegar or white or red wine vinegar. Black rice vinegar can be replaced with balsamic vinegar.

NOTE

There is a multitude of Asian condiments available in a variety of brands, varieties, and flavours. We suggest that you read the ingredients carefully when buying something. For a more authentic, better-tasting product, opt for the condiments with the fewest number of additives whose ingredients are as natural as possible.

In addition, sauces (such as soy sauce or tamari) and fermented pastes (such as miso) can be very salty. The amount of sodium varies between products, and some come in a low-sodium version. In recipes, do not hesitate to adjust the suggested quantities of condiments depending on the product you have and, of course, your own preferences.

USEFUL TOOLS

Here we list some tools that are useful in Chinese and Asian cooking. You can find them in shops in Chinese neighbourhoods, Asian grocery stores, or online.

WOK

Woks cook differently than frying pans. They have the advantage of rapidly cooking at a high temperature, which allows you to sear food in oil, giving the dish a charred flavour called *wok hei* — literally, "the breath of the wok." We use woks not only for stir-fries but also for any dish that would be cooked in a frying pan. In the latter case, we lower the temperature.

Choosing a good wok: Make sure it is big enough, with a thin base, not non-stick (so you can heat it to a high temperature without damaging the coating), made of pretreated cast iron or steel that you treat before using. If you don't have a wok on hand, you can still use a large frying pan, ideally not non-stick, made of cast iron or stainless steel.

A metal spatula, long and wide, is needed to adequately stir the food in the wok.

BAMBOO STEAMER

The bamboo steamer is a traditional tool for steaming food. It is placed above a wok or a saucepan containing boiling or simmering water. In the steamer, you can cook or heat one or more layers of food at the same time while transferring the steamer's characteristic plant flavour.

You can also buy steamers made of stainless steel, which are easier to maintain than bamboo baskets. Over time, the latter can become misshapen, broken, or even mouldy as a result of residue stuck between the bamboo slats.

RICE COOKER

This is a no-brainer for fuss-free rice: No need to monitor the cooking process so that the rice doesn't stick to the bottom of the saucepan. It is also useful for steaming vegetables or other food. Be aware that pressure cookers can also be used as rice cookers. Once cooked, the rice can dry out if left too long in the cooker and kept warm.

CHOPSTICKS

Chopsticks replace forks, and allow you to enjoy food a small mouthful at a time. We also use chopsticks in cooking; for example, stirring noodles or moving fried food around in oil. We prefer wooden chopsticks since they are natural, more pleasant in the mouth, and heat resistant. There are also chopsticks for children that are easier to use, which is a good way to start off.

BASIC TECHNIQUES

There are a thousand and one ways to cook Asian vegetables. Here we show you a few basics for preparing the vegetables in this book. Afterward you will be able to develop your own recipes to make them shine.

PREPARATION

Asian vegetables are prepared like other vegetables. Their preparation changes depending on the vegetable and the desired use. We're including a few general tips that can be applied to all the vegetables in this book. For specific information, see the respective section for the vegetable in question.

   · Rinse well in a large bowl of water or under running water, then drain in a sieve or by shaking.

   · Depending on the vegetable and the desired use, either keep the vegetable whole or chop it. For more uniform cooking, chop into equally sized pieces. You can also separate leaves from stems (see below for more details).

EATING

The fifteen vegetables introduced in this book can all be eaten raw, cooked, lacto-fermented, or dried. Some of them — for example, shiso and Asian cucumber — are most often enjoyed raw, while several others are usually cooked. Shiso and lemongrass can also be used to infuse dishes and drinks. To learn more about preserving methods, such as canning, lacto-fermentating, or dehydrating, see "Extending the life of vegetables" on page 314.

COOKING

Here you will find our favourite methods for cooking the vegetables in this book. Generally speaking, they should be cooked for as short a time as possible, to limit loss of flavour, texture, and nutrients. To get an idea of the cooking time for each vegetable, you can use the table giving blanching times (see "Preserving" on page 345) and then add a few extra minutes to make sure the vegetable is cooked through.

BLANCHING

Cooked for a few minutes in boiling water and then immediately plunged into ice water to stop the cooking process. This method gives vegetables a vibrant colour and preserves the flavour, texture, and colour of vegetables once frozen.

To blanch, bring a large volume of water to boil; for example, 16 cups (4 L) water for 1 lb (500 g) of vegetable. You can add salt to the water, particularly for green vegetables, to increase the temperature and speed up cooking. Start counting the cook time from when you add the vegetables to the boiling water. For ice water, simply fill a bowl or sink with cold water and ice cubes, or hold the vegetables under very cold running water.

STEWING

Cooked slowly in a simmering liquid over low heat; for example, in a soup, sauce, or stewed dish. Vegetables — in particular Asian eggplant and luffa, which act like sponges — take on the flavours of the dish in which they are stewed.

STEAMING

Cooked, covered, over boiling or simmering water. This method limits flavour and nutrient loss, since the vegetables are in limited contact with the water.

To do this, use a pot, a steamer, or a rice cooker. The technique is the same for all: Fill the container with ½ to 1 inch (1 to 2.5 cm) of water, then place an elevated support at the bottom of the pan — either a grill, a metal steamer, or a bamboo steamer basket — ensuring that the bottom of the support is not touching the water. Then lay the vegetables directly on this support, or in a stainless steel tray placed on top of the support. We usually bring the water to a boil before adding the food, although it is possible to boil the water afterward. In both cases, cover to cook.

Steam-cooking is a very common Chinese cooking method, much more so than using the oven. You can cook anything with this method: vegetables, protein foods, stuffed rolls (baos), dumplings, desserts, and more. You can also reheat cooked food by steaming instead of microwaving.

BRAISING

The vegetables are covered and cooked slowly, either in their own juice or with a small amount of liquid at the start of cooking. This is a very practical method because it needs neither a support nor much water. For greens, you can use this method instead of blanching or steam-cooking. After rinsing, place the vegetables in a pot, cover, and cook for a few minutes until they are wilted.

SAUTÉING

Cooked in oil in a wok or frying pan, over high or medium-high heat. This method allows you to brown the vegetables and briefly cook them so that they remain slightly crunchy.

Method:

   · Sort the vegetables according to the length of cooking time. If desired, first blanch or brown those that need more cooking; for example, gai lan or Asian eggplant.

   · Prepare all the ingredients first, including the sauce, so as not to interrupt the rapid cooking.

• Heat the wok so that the vegetables don't stick to it. Add the oil and distribute evenly over the wok's surface as you hold the handle to turn it in all directions. When the oil is hot, add aromatics: ginger, garlic, or the white part of green onion. Stir, then add the vegetables, starting with the ones that need the longest cooking time. Stir with a spatula or jiggle the wok as if flipping a pancake so that the vegetables jump (in French, *sauter* literally means "to jump"). If desired, add liquid — water, stock, or sauce — to facilitate cooking and enhance the flavour. Stir until you have finished cooking, or even cover for a few minutes, until the vegetables are as tender as you want them.

ROASTING OR GRILLING
Cooked in the dry heat of the oven or barbecue, with or without oil. This method makes fruit vegetables tender and juicy and greens crunchy, and gives a delicious grilled flavour.

DEEP-FRYING
Cooked in oil at a high temperature. Coat the vegetables first so that they are soft on the inside and crunchy on the outside. You can dunk them in batter, flour them, or coat them in cornstarch. Choose an oil that can withstand high temperatures, such as canola or peanut oil, and cook between 300° and 350°F (150° and 180°C). The vegetables are cooked when they rise to the surface. Drain them on paper towels before serving.

Since this method adds a significant amount of fat to the vegetable, another possibility is to cook the battered vegetables in the oven between 400° and 450°F (200° and 230°C).

GREENS
Cooking stems and leaves Chinese-style
When it comes to greens, particularly those that are mature or large, it is usual to cook the stems for longer than the leaves for uniform doneness. Whether blanching, stewing, or sautéing, separate the leaves and stems, cook the stems first, and then add the leaves toward the end of cooking, when the stems are nearly tender. Cook greens until the colour is vibrant and texture is tender-crisp.

SAUTÉING ABCS

You will have heard the term "stir-frying" used to describe Asian sautéing. This is sautéing with a wok that, unlike a frying pan, adds a charred flavour to the dish. A stir-fry can consist of vegetables only or multiple foods (vegetables, protein foods, starches).

For the basic technique, see the vegetable sautéing method on page 54. You can add the protein food after adding the sauce, and then bring to a boil once more to finish cooking.

Our aunt Dany makes a beef and rice noodle stir-fry by browning the ingredients separately in oil and salt: garlic and ginger, bell peppers, bean sprouts and green onions, marinated beef, scrambled eggs, rice noodles. Then she mixes them together and sautés them with a sauce.

Cooking tips
• Use a high or medium-high heat and avoid overloading the wok so that you can maintain a high temperature.

• Use a cooking oil such as vegetable oil or canola oil.

• Wait for the protein food to be nicely browned before stirring or flipping so that it doesn't stick to the wok and has an optimal flavour.

Creating your sauce
You can combine any of the following ingredients to make a sauté sauce. For a well-balanced sauce, choose a fat as well as ingredients that bring salt, sweet, acid, and perhaps umami or spice. Note that some of these condiments offer several of these characteristics; for example, hoisin sauce is both salty and sweet.

• Chicken, vegetable, or mushroom stock

• Light or dark soy sauce

• Oyster sauce

• Hoisin sauce

• Sweet sauce (*tiánmiàn jiàng*)

• Sweet or spicy soybean paste

• Fermented black beans

• Sesame oil

• Chili oil

• Rice cooking wine (Shaoxing or other variety)

• Rice vinegar

• Sugar

• Pepper

• Salt

Sauce ideas

Although you can use only water or stock to moisten a sauté, here are some possible combinations for a stir-fry sauce:

· <u>For a classic stir-fry</u>: soy sauce, oyster sauce, Shaoxing rice cooking wine

· <u>For a subtle flavour</u>: chicken stock, soy sauce, sesame oil

· <u>For a complex sauce</u>: chicken stock, Shaoxing rice cooking wine, light and dark soy sauce, oyster sauce, sesame oil, sugar, pepper, salt

The secret of cornstarch

To thicken a sauce while avoiding lumps, whisk cornstarch into a cold liquid before stirring it into hot foods. The heat activates its thickening properties when the mixture is brought to a boil.

<u>Continue by using one of the following methods</u>:

· Add the cornstarch to the sauce mixture before adding the sauce to the sauté at the end of cooking. Bring the sauce to a boil while stirring, and cook until the sauce has thickened, still stirring continuously.

· Dilute the cornstarch in cold water in equal parts; for example, 1 tbsp (15 mL) of cornstarch in the same quantity of water. Gradually add this mixture to the sauté at the end of the cooking process, stirring constantly. Let it simmer until the sauce has thickened. This method is also used to thicken Asian soups, such as sweet and sour soup.

In both cases, avoid overcooking the cornstarch, otherwise it may separate and lose its thickening effect.

Invent your own sauté

The only limit to the number of stir-fry combinations is your imagination! We suggest aiming for three to five ingredients, which can include vegetables, protein foods, and noodles or rice. The key is to find a balance between textures and flavours by combining, for example, a soft ingredient (noodles, tofu) with a naturally sweet ingredient (bok choy, carrots, green onions) and an ingredient with an umami flavour (mushrooms, meat).

· In addition to the vegetables discussed in this book, you could add snow peas, sugar snap peas, bean sprouts, broccoli, carrots, leeks, celery, onions, mushrooms, zucchini ...

· Protein foods could include tofu, tempeh, pulses (edamame, chickpeas, beans), eggs, shrimp, scallops, pork, chicken, beef ...

COOKING VEGETABLES BY THEMSELVES

Whether Asian vegetables are the star of the dish or served as a side, it doesn't take a lot to lift them up so they burst with flavour.

You can simply blanch or steam them, roast or barbecue them, and then drizzle with a mixture of soy sauce, the oil of your choice, and a sweet ingredient. A quick swirl of oyster sauce also works well. For more flavour, sprinkle with chopped green onions, finely julienned ginger, fresh cilantro, or fried garlic. To fry garlic, simply sauté minced garlic in oil until it turns golden—this is absolutely wonderful on cooked vegetables.

Cooked or raw, vegetables also go well with a dressing.

CREAMY SESAME DRESSING

Caroline's creamy sesame dressing can be used with any combination of greens or other vegetables, and even with rice or noodles.

To make about ⅓ cup (75 mL) of dressing, combine the following in a small bowl or sealable jar:

· 2 tbsp (30 mL) sesame butter

· 2 tbsp (30 mL) water

· 1 tsp (5 mL) liquid honey

· 1 tsp (5 mL) rice vinegar

· 1 tsp (5 mL) sesame oil

· 1 tbsp (15 mL) minced fresh ginger
(a piece about ½ inch/1 cm thick)

· ¼ tsp (1 mL) soy sauce or tamari

COOKING SIDE DISHES

OTHER ASIAN VEGETABLES

Bean sprouts

- The sprouts of soy or mung beans

- Can be eaten raw or cooked, in salads, wraps, soups, and stir-fries

- Add at the end of cooking to preserve crispness

Daikon

- Asian radish shaped like a big white carrot with a slightly sweet and spicy flavour that softens when cooked

- Serve grated with sashimi and tempura, or pickled in *bánh mì* (Vietnamese sandwiches)

SEAWEED AND MUSHROOMS

Seaweed and mushrooms bring an umami flavour to dishes. They can be used fresh or dried; if the latter, soak in water to rehydrate.

There are many kinds of seaweed, harvested anywhere from Asia to America to Europe: arame, dulse, hijiki, sea lettuce, nori, wakame, kombu, to name a few.

Shiitake and enoki mushrooms are among the most commonly used Asian mushrooms.

- Shiitake: large, fleshy cap; slightly acidic flavour, more pronounced once dried; brings out the flavour of soups, stir-fries, and stews

- Enoki: white, long, and thin; slightly crunchy flesh, delicate flavour; often added to soups and stir-fries

Other kinds of mushrooms are also used in Chinese cooking, including the ear-shaped species* that grow on certain tree trunks. They are often found dried, to be soaked in water (15 to 60 minutes in warm water) before cooking. Added to soups, salads, stir-fries, and stews.

- Wood ear (Judas's ear) (黑木耳 hak1 muk6 ji5): particularly appreciated in Asia; beige or dark brown in colour, gelatinous in texture

- Cloud ear (雲耳 wan4 ji5): close relative of the wood ear but smaller, thinner, and more delicate

NOODLES

There is a great variety of Asian noodles, available either fresh (from the refrigerated section of Asian grocery stores) or dried:

- Wheat noodles, either with or without egg

- Rice noodles and vermicelli

- Mung bean vermicelli (also called cellophane noodles or glass noodles): they look like rice noodles but are made from mung beans; they become translucent and slightly rubbery once cooked

- Soba noodles: made from buckwheat, often mixed with wheat; a classic of Japanese cuisine

RICE

Rice is the perfect accompaniment to many Asian dishes. It comes in several colours: white, brown, red, even black. There are three lengths of grains: short, medium, and long. Some examples:

- Sticky rice: short-grain rice, becomes sticky during cooking; well-liked in Chinese cooking, for instance when steamed in a lotus leaf with, for example, chicken and shiitake mushrooms

- Sticky rice flour: flour used in desserts, such as the sesame balls found in dim sum restaurants and Chinese New Year cakes called *nin4 gou1* in Cantonese

- Calrose rice: medium-grain rice, slightly sticky; ideal for sushi

- Jasmine rice: long-grain rice originally from Thailand and Cambodia; very perfumed and slightly sticky, this is our favourite everyday rice

- Basmati rice: long-grain rice from India and Pakistan (in Hindi, *basmati* literally means "perfumed"); it is a highly aromatic, non-sticky rice

Long-grain rices tend to harden as they cool; they can be reheated or used in fried rice.

Cooking rice properly

To cook rice, you can use a rice cooker or a pot.

- For red and black rice: Soaking in water for 8 to 24 hours (or in hot water for 2 to 3 hours) facilitates the cooking process. Drain the rice afterward.

- For most kinds of rice: Rinse the rice to clean it, so that it doesn't stick, and simply for a better result. To rinse, pour the rice into the cooking vessel, fill with water, then slosh the water and rice around with your hand. Drain and repeat at least two more times or until the water remains clear.

- Then add water. Depending on the type of rice and the cooking method, you will need between 1¼ and 2¼ cups (300 to 560 mL) of water for every 1 cup (250 mL) of rice.

FOR 1 CUP (250 ML) OF RICE:
White rice: 1¼ cups/300 mL (in rice cooker) to 1½ cups/375 mL water (in saucepan)

Brown rice, long-grain: 1¼ cups/300 mL water; short-grain: 1½ cups/375 mL water

Red rice: 1½ cups/375 mL (soaked rice) to 2 cups/500 mL (unsoaked rice) water

Black rice: 1¾ cups/425 mL (soaked rice) to 2¼ cups/560 mL (unsoaked rice) water

- Adjust the volume of water depending on the desired texture; for firmer rice, use less water. Over time you will learn to do it by eye without measuring the volume of water.

- In the rice cooker: Cover and start the cooker. When it stops, leave covered for 10 to 15 minutes.

- In a saucepan: Bring to a boil, cover, and simmer over low heat for about 15 minutes (up to 45 minutes for darker rices) or until all the liquid is absorbed and holes are starting to appear on the surface of the rice. Remove the pan from the heat and let rest, covered, for 10 minutes.

TOFU

A plant source of protein, tofu is made from coagulated soy milk, drained and pressed. It can be eaten raw or cooked, and takes on the flavour of the foods it is cooked with.

Firm or extra-firm tofu can be fried, stir-fried, grilled, stewed, or added to soup. To season, either marinate (see the Marinated Tofu recipe on page 133) or use Luffa Spread (see recipe on page 287).

Soft or silky tofu is a good substitute for yogurt and can be added diced to stocks/broths or delicate dishes. It can be used in desserts, or serve it with ginger-flavoured syrup.

MEATS

In stir-fries, meats like beef, pork, or chicken are usually ground or finely sliced, and marinated before cooking. Here are a few tips for achieving tender, juicy, flavourful slices of meat just like at a Chinese restaurant.

Choosing the right cut

The best cuts of meat for slicing are:

- Beef: flank is best, also chuck
- Pork: particularly shoulder, butt; also loin, tenderloin
- Chicken: breast or dark meat

Cutting technique

To slice meat, especially tougher beef or chicken, always cut against the grain, that is, perpendicular to the muscle fibres. To make cutting easier, you can partially freeze the meat to be chopped—for 30 to 60 minutes, or until the flesh is firm. Below is the best way to prepare beef flank:

- Remove the tendons (the white parts)
- Cut the meat along the grain (in the direction of the muscle fibres) into pieces 2 to 2½ inches (5 to 6 cm) long; partially freeze
- Cut each strip against the grain into thin slices (¼ inch/ 0.5 cm)

Tenderize and marinade

To tenderize chunks of beef or pork, we first massage the meat by hand with a little water and baking soda before adding it along with the other ingredients to the marinade. If you have added too much baking soda, rinse the meat well and drain before adding to the marinade.

Other meats can be massaged with a little water and soy sauce or oyster sauce before adding them along with the other ingredients to the marinade.

Then use your hands to mix everything well, cover, and refrigerate for 15 to 30 minutes to marinate.

Basic marinade ingredients

- For flavour: oyster sauce or soy sauce
- For texture: cornstarch and vegetable oil

Optional ingredients

- For flavour: Shaoxing rice cooking wine and/or sesame oil

For a sample marinade, see the recipe for Luffa and Chicken Stir-Fry on page 289.

Cooking

Once the meat is marinated, sear it in a preheated wok or frying pan with oil, or blanch it before finishing off the cooking in the wok or frying pan. This marinated meat can also be added to a soup.

With all of these culinary basics in hand, our year of Asian vegetables can begin!

A YEAR LIVING ACCORDING TO THE SEASONS

跟隨四季節奏的一年

Now that you are familiar with our selection of Asian vegetables and the basics of Chinese and Asian cooking, we are going to take you on a journey through a gardening year divided into four seasons: winter, spring, summer, and fall. In each season, you will discover the steps of vegetable growing as well as some recipes for you to enjoy.

The year starts in winter. It is a time marked by rest but also by the planning and preparation for the gardening season to come.

In spring we plunge our hands back into the soil. This is the time to adopt the good habits that will accompany us throughout the season, like stretching, staying hydrated, and establishing realistic objectives. We grow vegetables that like the cool weather: fast-growing brassicas such as bok choy, choy sum, gai lan, and mustard leaves, as well as chrysanthemum and celtuce, which all deserve to be known.

Summer is a time of abundant harvests. Heat-loving vegetables star here. We will discover amaranth, Malabar spinach, shiso, okra, Asian eggplant, Asian cucumber, luffa, and lemongrass.

Fall and the return of cool nights spell the end of summer vegetables. This is when the cool-loving vegetables return in force: Chinese cabbage shines now. We also talk about how to preserve food and, of course, about kimchi.

For each of the fifteen vegetables, you will find key information about its name; its historical and geographical context; and how to recognize, grow, store, and cook it. We will also introduce you to a wide variety of recipes — something for every taste. Traditional Chinese or Asian recipes, of course, but also modern creations. Vegan, vegetarian, omnivore, and gluten-free recipes. Simple, fast meals as well as more elaborate fare. Salads, soups, appetizers; condiments and side dishes; dishes with pulses, tofu, seafood, chicken, and meat; desserts; and even a cocktail.

The Appendices contain a table on preserving vegetables by refrigerating, freezing, or dehydrating; as well as dates for the vegetables' milestones for indoor sowing and planting out. We hope you will find these tools useful in both the garden and the kitchen to optimize and enjoy the full potential of the Asian vegetables we have chosen.

BENEFITING FROM MARKET-GARDEN KNOWLEDGE

Over the years, Le Rizen farm has applied knowledge developed and used in organic market gardening to new crops, and this, combined with trial and error, is how Stéphanie has gradually deepened her knowledge of Asian vegetables in Quebec. We can now confirm with certainty that it is possible to obtain excellent results and abundant harvests if you follow a few simple and affordable tips and techniques.

As we share our best tips about growing Asian vegetables, we hope to inspire you to use some in your own garden, whether you have a little vegetable bed just for fun or are part of a more seasoned entreprise that is already growing several vegetables. We hope that however much space you have for growing vegetables and whatever your level of knowledge, you will be able to benefit from the expertise developed by commercial growing operations to improve the yield of your harvest.

In this book, we won't go into too much detail about all the technical, scientific, and agronomic aspects of market gardening; for example, weeding, composting, or watering. There are already excellent reference works on these subjects, and we advise you to consult them if you want to do further reading.

Regardless of whether you tend toward the same agricultural model as Le Rizen, the aim is to help you obtain a greater quantity of vegetables from each of your plants all season long, while also respecting your own goals, resources, values, and needs.

WINTER

USING THE TIME WHILE THE GARDEN SLEEPS TO PLAN FOR NEXT YEAR

In winter, the snow blanket, cold, and limited light are natural obstacles to outdoor gardening. This is the perfect season to take the time to plan the garden you want to see bloom in the coming year, as well as the Asian vegetables you would like to grow.

Gardening is creating. We often unconsciously create a garden in our own image. Whether this is a commercial, community, or personal garden, planning — setting out in detail the steps that will allow us to reach our intended goals — is always the key to success. It is during planning, which generally happens between December and March, that all the decisions are made about the coming growing season. Normally, once the plan has been established, all we have to do is execute it, which leaves more room for serenity and an unharried mind during the season.

STARTING OFF: ANSWERING SOME QUESTIONS

What is my vision for this project?

First of all, allow yourself to dream. You can draw, write, and reflect on everything that comes to mind when you think about your project: what you want to do, with whom, for what reasons (values, motivations, intentions), and where. What is your vision for the short, medium, and long term?

What are my resources?

Now make a list of all the resources available for your project.

HUMAN: How many hours per week will you be able to devote to your project? What are your strengths and weaknesses? Will you have any help? Do you want to take on help?

LAND: Do you have access to a garden or piece of land? If yes, what are its dimensions and characteristics (type, fertility, orientation, drainage, soil compaction, access to water and electricity, and so on)? If you rent a plot, be sure to spell out the terms of the lease or agreement with your landlord.

MATERIALS: Do you have access to tools (shovel, hoe,* broadfork,* etc.), equipment (insect netting, floating row covers, occultation tarps,* etc.), and infrastructure (greenhouse, seed room, washing station, etc.)?

KNOWLEDGE AND EXPERTISE: What do you know already? What do you want to learn more about through books and other resources? Would you like to do any training or work at an experienced market farm?

FINANCIAL: How much money do you want to invest in the project? Even setting up a medium-size garden bed can be fairly expensive if you are starting from zero (buying books, equipment, seeds, soil, fertilizer, etc.). If your ambition is to start a small business, it is possible to begin with minimal investment (it's how Le Rizen was started), but it might take more of your time. Be careful not to go too far into debt before you are sure you want to carry on.

What is my goal for this season?

Now that you have a clear picture of your resources, you are in a position to create a realistic goal for the coming season. It will be easier and more enjoyable to attain it because you will have lower levels of daily stress.

For example, if you want to enjoy abundance by producing a whole range of pestos from different greens to see you through the winter, there's no point burdening yourself with a bunch of luffa and okra plants. On the other hand, if you don't have much time to devote to your garden, you will appreciate restricting your growing upfront to low-maintenance vegetables like chrysanthemum, celtuce, and amaranth.

For commercial producers, a goal of a particular revenue figure that covers costs, meets needs, and leaves some left over to save is often suggested. But you can have goals of a different kind, such as increasing your self-sufficiency or practising self-care throughout the season so that you don't end up burned out, or perhaps not working weekends so you can spend more time with your family.

What are the specific objectives that will allow me to reach my goal?

Once you have figured out your end goal, it's important to specify objectives that will allow you to reach it. These might target several different areas, such as finance, productivity, work and family balance, commercial development, or something else.

For example, if your goal is to increase your food autonomy, your objectives might be:

• Set aside space in your vegetable garden for foods that you can preserve and store for the winter (Chinese cabbage to make kimchi, root vegetables, etc.)

• Build a greenhouse on your property to extend the growing season

If your goal is to practise daily self-care, your objectives might be:

• Drink 8 cups (2 L) of water a day

• Take more breaks during the day

• Do some warm-ups, stretching, or other physical exercise for a few minutes a day

If your goal is to not work weekends, your objectives might be:

• Find and train an employee to replace you at the Saturday market

• Let your customers know that you won't be answering calls or emails on weekends

PLANNING THE GARDEN

Now it's time to sharpen your pencils and design your dream garden! A walkway here, a border there, a vegetable bed beside the patio, a row* of Chinese eggplants in a south-facing spot ... The important thing is not to lose track of your objectives and to really consider the space you have at your disposal to turn your project into a reality.

DRAW THE GROWING AREAS

This is where you choose the size and shape of your growing areas. Your choice is influenced by, among other things, the characteristics of your land (available growing area, relief, orientation) and your preferred agricultural methods.

Here are some growing layouts to consider:

LINEAR: In market gardening, the standard growing surface is rectangular in shape and is called a bed. The width and length are not significant, but the rectangle shape has the advantage of making many things easier, including planning, moving around, standardizing of equipment, facilitating work that needs to be done with a tractor or a two-wheeled minitractor, and maintenance.

CIRCULAR (mandala): Spiral or concentric rings are attractive and energizing. They work well with growing areas that will be worked by hand, such as vegetable beds and perennial herb gardens.

OTHER: The shape of growing area is restricted only by your imagination.

RAISE BEDS AND MAKE THEM PERMANENT

Whatever design you choose, you can create a mound so that the growing surface is raised in relation to the ground. This gives the roots extra deep aerated, rich soil.

Your growing areas can be permanent. This consists of clearing marked walkways so that you do not walk on the growing beds. By maintaining the beds in the same spot each year and working only the top level of soil, you do not have to remake the mounds each year. The benefits are many: the soil is less compacted and, therefore, has better structure, which allows better circulation of water and air — conditions that facilitate microbial life and thus soil vitality.

STANDARDIZE THE GROWING AREAS

There are several advantages to standardizing the growing areas — in other words, dividing the garden into blocks or parcels containing an equal number of beds of the same size.

First, it simplifies successive seed planting, which is needed for a continuous harvest of any vegetable with a short growing season, such as Asian greens. For example, if you calculate that you need a 6.5 ft (2 m) row of bok choy every month, you simply need to sow a new row every month.

Furthermore, standardizing the beds lets you optimize your equipment, especially floating row covers and insect netting, which you can buy and then cut down to a length that works for all your growing beds.

CONSIDER CROP ROTATION

Crop rotation is an ancient farming practice that is effective for maintaining soil health and reducing the risk of disease and harmful insects. Agronomic science recommends waiting an average of three to four years, or more depending on the specific disease, before trying to grow the affected crops in the same spot. Whatever the size of your garden, you can develop a crop-rotation plan to suit the available space.

For example, if you have six beds in your vegetable garden, you can plant each one with a different botanical family, and the following year move each crop a bed over, and so on, so that the same family is grown in the same bed only once every six years.

The table on the following page is an example of a six-year crop-rotation plan that allows more and less demanding Asian vegetables to be alternated. In year 1, beds 1, 3, and 5 receive compost to prepare the soil for spring, with the idea of planting vegetables that need high soil fertility. At the end of the summer, you can plant green manure that will allow you to add organic matter and nutrients back into the soil before planting less demanding vegetables the following season. The kinds of green manure mentioned in the table are a guide only, and can be adapted (for more on green manure, see "Nourishing the soil" on page 94).

Because the available space in the garden imposes physical limits on your project, you will be consulting back and forth between your garden plan and the next stage of planning what you will be growing. The challenge is to plant the right quantity and a diverse range of vegetables in the space available, plan on successive sowings of different seeds over the season — so you don't have too many or too few vegetables — and always keep your goals in mind.

SIX-YEAR CROP-ROTATION PLAN

	BED 1	BED 2	BED 3	BED 4	BED 5	BED 6
	Heavy feeders	Light feeders	Heavy feeders	Light feeders	Heavy feeders	Light feeders
Spring	Compost		Compost		Compost	
Crops	Solanaceae · *Asian eggplant*	Brassicaceae · *bok choy* · *choy sum* · *gai lan* · *Chinese cabbage* · *mustard greens*	Cucurbitaceae · *luffa* · *Asian cucumber*	Amaranthaceae · *amaranth* Asteraceae · *celtuce* · *chrysanthemum*	Poaceae · *lemongrass* Malvaceae · *okra*	Basellaceae · *Malabar spinach* Lamiaceae · *shiso*
Fall: **green manure**	Oat and pea, or fescue		Buckwheat		Rye	

PLANNING WHAT TO GROW

Plan what to grow according to your established objectives and the garden plan. You can use software like Excel to do this, specialized software for planning market gardens, or indeed good old pen and paper. At Le Rizen, we use Excel to generate multiple tables and planning tools: information tables, work plans, master plan, and project plans.

INFORMATION TABLES

Information tables gather all the basic information you need to plan how you will grow the vegetables in this book. The tables contain a mine of information for each of our fifteen vegetables, such as the number of plants necessary to feed one person, our advice for increasing germination rates of certain more capricious vegetables, growing time, and space between plants.

ADDITIONAL TOOLS

If you're aiming at a grander growing scale, you can create a work plan or project plan for each vegetable.

WORK PLANS

These are tables for each individual vegetable, detailing precise information about that season's growing work plan; for example, the different cultivars to be planted, the number of seeds you want to sow, and the specific dates on which you plan to plant the seeds, plant out, and harvest. The information in these sheets also helps you with garden planning. For example, you might set aside a certain portion of the garden if you want to produce a specific quantity of one vegetable.

MASTER PLAN

By compiling all the information from the individual vegetable sheets into a single table or master plan, you can arrange the information chronologically, by type, or by column. For example, if you sort "date for indoor seed planting" from earliest to latest, you can generate a list showing what needs to be sowed each week right from the beginning to the end of the season; this is what you will use as a seed plan. In the same way, you can generate a plan for transplanting seedlings outside that will list what is to be done each week of the season.

PROJECT PLANS

These are extremely practical, ground-level tools: setting out a list of tasks to be done, the crops planted, and the results obtained at every growing stage. At Le Rizen we have several project plans that we print out and keep in different-coloured folders to facilitate organizing the work: one each for seeds, planting out,* observations and interventions, orders, harvests, sales.

It is perfectly normal for the work in the field not to work out exactly as it did in the planning stage. This is why we like to keep a column to note what we actually did along with any observations: the dates and actual number of seeds, transplanting and harvest, how insect-resistant different cultivars were, and so on. If you don't keep a project plan, a simple notebook is an excellent record-keeping tool.

These working notes are precious: they help you evaluate your biggest successes, where they occurred in the garden, and at what point in the season. You will also have a much better idea of what to plant the following year and what to adjust so you can constantly improve production.

Essentially, a good growing plan should clearly indicate which vegetables and cultivars need to be sown and transplanted, along with the location, quantity, and timing needed to harvest on the desired date. This a crucial step that facilitates organization, clarifies the seasonal tasks, and saves time.

See the Appendices starting on page 344 for information tables on the fifteen Asian vegetables in this book.

ORDERING SEEDS

Getting ready to place your seed order is an exciting time that makes all the planning work start to feel real! Most seed businesses have an online store where you can compare the different varieties and cultivars on offer and buy them from the comfort of your own home.

OUR TIPS FOR YOUR SEEDS

• Choose seeds that are suited to your local climate. Knowing your hardiness zone and the length of your growing season will help you determine which vegetables are best suited to your climate.

• Given that seed-germination rates drop over time, it's a good idea to do a germination test of any seeds left over from the previous year (see below). We also recommend ordering only the number of seeds you need for the coming season, plus an extra 30 to 50%.

GERMINATION TESTING AT HOME

• Take ten seeds from a packet and place them on a piece of kitchen towel soaked with room-temperature water.

• Fold the kitchen towel over on itself and put it in a sealable bag.

• Close up the bag and leave it in a warm place; for example, on top of the fridge.

• When the seeds have germinated or the number of days to expected germination have passed, open the bag and count how many seeds germinated.

• If five out of ten seeds have germinated you have a 50% germination rate.

• When you come to plant the seeds, you can plant double the amount to compensate for the lower germination rate.

• If you want to wait for your plants to flower so you can harvest seeds for planting the following year, make sure to choose open-pollinated or heirloom seeds. This will produce plants that are true to the one you initially planted, as long as you have respected the distances needed to avoid cross-pollination.* For example, bok choy and mizuna, which are both *Brassica rapas*, might cross-pollinate if grown next to each other.

• If you are focused on yield, uniform fruit, and insect — or disease — resistance, choose hybrid (F1) seeds that have the desired characteristics. But if flavour is your priority, hybrids might not be your first choice, since they are often selected for characteristics other than taste. It's best to try different varieties and cultivars, and to figure out over time which ones best suit your needs.

• Whether you are making the transition to organic or are already certified, choose certified organic seeds if available. At a minimum, ensure the seeds are not genetically modified and untreated.*

SOW 30 TO 50% EXTRA

When you start off, it's a good idea to give yourself enough of a margin to allow for errors that might arise at the different growing stages: poor germination, success rate after transplanting, loss in the field to insects, disease, weather, and so on. It is standard to sow 30 to 50% extra based on your intended harvest to compensate for losses during the growing stages. In market gardening we call this the safety factor.

OTHER PURCHASES AT
THE BEGINNING OF THE SEASON

The beginning of the season is also when we acquire all the necessary equipment to carry out our work: inputs, tools, and infrastructure.

Joining a gardening group in your area is an excellent way of finding used equipment, discovering great local suppliers, or just swapping seeds and tips.

THE FIRST INDOOR SOWINGS

At the end of winter, temperatures gradually start to rise, the days get longer, and the scent of the thawing earth wafts through the air. This is the moment to abandon your desk, put on your rubber boots, and set things in motion with the first indoor sowings!

From our selection of vegetables, only lemongrass is sown indoors in March. Sow all the other vegetable seeds inside in April and early May.

WHY DO WE START SEEDS INSIDE?

Starting seeds in a controlled environment gives them the best conditions in terms of temperature, humidity, and light. Generally speaking, seeds should be kept at a temperature of 77°F (25°C) during germination. After that, the young seedlings need 14 to 16 hours of daylight per day and appreciate temperatures between 68° and 72°F (20° and 22°C) in the day and 59°F (15°C) at night, with relative air humidity of between 65 and 80%.

Several benefits justify the extra effort required for indoor seed-starting: we obtain higher germination rates and healthy young plants that will be more resilient once in the ground. We note as well that with a shorter period in the field, the plants have less pressure from weeds and insects compared with plants sown directly in the garden (direct sowing).

SUCCESSIVE SOWING

If you want to harvest quick-growing plants throughout the season, it's a good idea to use successive sowing techniques. Take, for example, the Shanghai variety of bok choy, which has a growing time of 50 days. If it is sown on April 10, it will be ready for harvesting on May 30. After this date, it will carry on growing and then form a floral bud* before going to seed. You will therefore need to ensure that other seedlings are ready to take over if you want to have a supply of bok choy through to the end of October. At Le Rizen, we plant seven successive sowings of bok choy; in other words, we start bok choy indoors seven times over the course of the season, 21 days apart. If the first sowing is on April 10, the last sowing will be August 14.

WHERE TO START SEEDS?

• At home: Near a bright window with auxiliary lighting, or in the garage with a good source of heat and a full-spectrum (e.g., LED) light

• In a greenhouse, on tables that can be taken away to make room for vegetables in the ground later on

GETTING WELL SET UP FOR INDOOR SEED-STARTING

MULTICELL TRAYS

At Le Rizen, we start our indoor seeds in multicell trays* that we put in our greenhouse. These trays have multiple sections that you fill with seed starting mix and plant seeds in to obtain one plant per cell. On the market, these trays are fairly standard in dimension (10 x 20 inches/25 x 50 cm) and come in different formats, with either 50, 72, 128, or 200 identically sized cells. The higher the number of cells per tray, the smaller the cells and the less time the vegetables can spend there. We commonly refer to the trays by the number of cells they have; for example, "the 72 trays."

CHOOSING THE RIGHT POTTING SOIL

Potting soil is a type of soil that is usually enriched with different kinds of organic matter and is used as a substrate for growing plants.

• **Seed starting soil**: A type of soil that is not overly enriched and used as a substrate for indoor sowing into multicell trays.

• **Potting soil**: A richer soil used to pot up* in bigger pots seedlings of summer vegetables that have to wait until all risk of frost has passed before being transplanted out (shiso, Asian eggplant, Asian cucumber, luffa, and lemongrass).

STEPS TO FOLLOW FOR STARTING ASIAN VEGETABLE SEEDS INDOORS

• For Chinese cabbage, okra, Asian eggplant, Asian cucumber, and luffa, use a 72-cell tray, which allows the plants to grow more before being transplanted directly (for Chinese cabbage) or being potted up into 4- x 4-inch (10 x 10 cm) pots (for the others). Potting up allows the plants to reach a more advanced growth stage, which makes them more resilient once planted out in the field.

• For shiso and lemongrass, which can be difficult to germinate, sow the seeds in a 200-cell tray, or scatter them in a tray with no cells. Later, pot up into 4- x 4-inch (10 x 10 cm) pots.

• For Malabar spinach, we use a 128-cell tray to germinate the seeds indoors. The germination is very slow; they can easily stay in the tray until they can be planted out.

• For the other vegetables in the book, which are plants that we sow frequently, in greater quantities, and which spend less time indoors, use a 128- or 162-cell tray. The plants will be in the cells for only three to four weeks in total: two or three weeks in the greenhouse and up to a week of acclimatizing* (hardening off). After this brief period, they will be ready to plant out in the field.

For successful sowings, follow the instructions on the packet. The general rule is to plant seeds three times deeper than their diameter. With a little practice, you can plant most seeds by hand, rolling them between your finger and thumb to let one at a time drop into each cell. Then, unless indicated to the contrary, cover the tray with soil and make sure it stays damp until germination. Heating mats under the trays can facilitate speedy and uniform growth, particularly for heat-loving plants (Malabar spinach, shiso, okra, Asian eggplant, Asian cucumber, luffa, lemongrass).

HINTS AND TIPS

For small seeds such as amaranth, there are some inexpensive hand tools for seeding that make the task much easier by distributing just one seed at a time once the tool is activated above the cell either by gravity or air pressure.

Don't forget to label your trays and your pots. At Le Rizen, we use name labels with the code we give the vegetable followed by the number of successive sowings. For labels that don't need to last long, you can use wooden sticks and permanent marker: the writing will wear away and the stick will decompose over time. To label plants that will be in the field for a longer time, opt for reasonably durable, weather-resistant plastic labels that can be reused in subsequent seasons.

WHEN TO WATER?

Once the seeds have germinated, water only when the soil starts to dry out. On sunny days, it's best to water between 9 a.m. and 3 p.m., which is when plants most need water. On rainy or cloudy days, it's better to hold off on watering until the soil dries out.

Always use room-temperature water for watering. Watering with cold water, or too much, or with poor drainage through the holes in the bottom of the multicell trays can lead to diseases, such as damping off, or other problems.

On page 346 of the Appendix, see the table titled "Indoor Sowing," which gathers the key information for starting indoor sowings for each of the fifteen vegetables in this book, and in particular the number and dates of successive seedings at Le Rizen, and our advice for germinating.

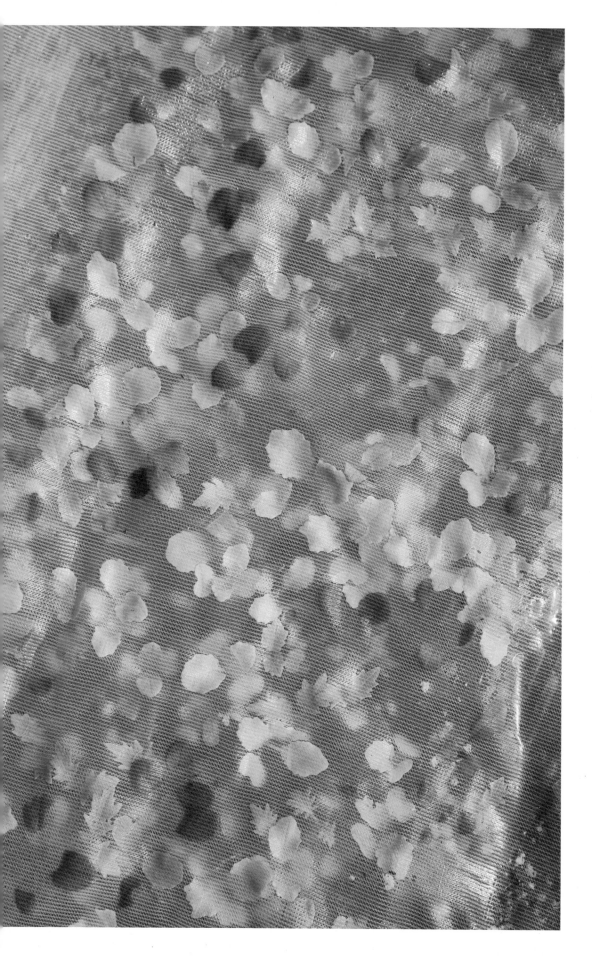

SPRING

春
天

STÉPHANIE'S BURNOUT STORY

Spring is the beginning of vegetable season and of physical labour. This is the time to develop good habits so you don't get exhausted or injured during the season.

In January 2016, among many very emotional personal events, I moved to Frelighsburg to continue my life there. In February, I decided to start growing Asian vegetables by renting a plot of land on a visionary farm that had enormous faith in their potential. I dug the beds with a shovel with the amazing help of my friends and family and members of the farm. We moved the compost with a wheelbarrow. Since I did not study agriculture production, and I had never worked a full farm season, I learned a great deal on the job.

At the same time, I was still working part time for farming organizations. By day I travelled to Montreal, and by evening I went home to water my vegetables in Frelighsburg. I travelled to Cuba and Spain for a few days to take part in international agroecology conferences. I also kept up my social activities whenever I could.

On the farm, I was sleeping in a tent on an inflatable mattress that no longer inflated. I was living off slices of bread and peanut butter.

In February 2017, I felt as though I was sinking. My energy levels were very low, and sometimes I would start crying uncontrollably. I then decided to go for a week-long retreat in the mountains, with myself, a personal diary, a colouring book, and a book that made me smile, cry, and understand what I was experiencing: *The Joy of Burnout*.

Ever since that time, I have carried on reading and doing personal training to learn to listen to myself, to respect my limits, to stop wanting to cram too much into a day, and to switch to a way of life that allows me to be calmer and more serene on a daily basis.

The job of market gardening has lessons to teach me every year, both technical and personal. The path travelled and the obstacles overcome make even more satisfying each harvest that nourishes mouths and souls.

Factors that make market farmers vulnerable to burnout

· Being deeply committed to the job, often based on environmental or social convictions that lead to us investing our entire being in the hope of bringing about positive change in the world.

· Being vulnerable to external factors beyond our control, particularly insects and destructive animals, weather conditions, diseases, accidents, and low prices at the grocery store that don't reflect the work and energy needed to grow and transport the food.

· Very demanding physical work.

· A job in which we often need to wear multiple hats to keep an eye on all facets of the business: growing, sales, deliveries, human resources, mechanics, accounting, construction, landscaping, etc.

· The challenge of finding a balance between work and personal/family life, given the long hours, especially when you are just getting started.

My two tips for preventing overwork

A question of attitude: In my opinion, the most effective way to prevent or overcome burnout is to, every day, align my body, mind, and heart with the different elements of my daily life: work, social, and love life; environment and surroundings; physical and psychological health; finances; and personal and spiritual development. I can measure how closely aligned I am by my level of general satisfaction in each of these areas. Alignment, or balance, is reached when we are completely satisfied with all aspects of our lives. And this degree of satisfaction lies in the small and large decisions we make every minute of our lives; for example, smiling, accepting, appreciating ...

To reach this point, you can choose from a range of tools: breathing, mindfulness meditation, relaxation, healthy eating, physical exercise, sleep, leisure time, social activities, writing a personal journal, neuropsychological exercises, and many more. I believe that everyone should establish their own routine with the type, length, intensity, and timing during the day that suits them.

Take care of body and mind: The body is the most important tool for a market gardener! It is at the start of a significant domino effect: our ability to maintain our physical and psychological health has a much greater effect than we realize on the sustainability of working as a market gardener. And this is intrinsically linked to the viability of our farms, on which rests our collective food sovereignty. It's important to keep in mind that the work is both physically and psychologically challenging — lifting heavy loads, maintaining crouched or bent positions for long periods, accomplishing all tasks effectively in weather conditions varying from heatwaves to frosts, and reacting to unexpected situations out of our control (drought, ravaging insects, diseases, hail, etc.).

It's a shame that no manual or training about gardening and market gardening discusses the importance of warming up at the beginning of the workday or stretching at the end. Perhaps it's because of my former life as a gymnast that I understand the importance of not using my muscles when they're cold. Warming up means giving yourself the best chance of avoiding injury and chronic pain. You often hear that the market gardening season is like a marathon, and that is true. You need to know how to run for eight months without burning out, and then start over year after year. In the agricultural sector, the rate of psychological distress is twice as high as it is in the general population in Quebec. Psychological distress can lead to depression, professional burnout, and even suicide. Whether you grow vegetables or not, I invite and encourage you to cultivate your life as if taking care of a plant: with kindness, a good balance, and gentleness.

SET TO WORK! THE FIRST ROUND OF PLANTING OUT AND PLUNGING YOUR HANDS INTO THE SOIL

After six months of snow, the first time we put our hands back in the earth is one of the most joyful parts of the job: playing outside and getting muddy! Above all, it's important to prepare the ground well to create the best conditions for growing healthy plants.

NOURISHING THE SOIL

Being a substrate that feeds the plant, a rich and fertile soil is essential for growing good vegetables. Whatever method you use to work the soil, you need to aim for a pH of between 5.5 and 6.5, an aerated texture, and the presence of essential minerals in the proportions each plant needs.

To find out the condition of your soil, you can do a soil test to determine its pH level as well as the levels of nitrogen, phosphorus, and potassium. You can either bring soil samples to a specialist soil analysis centre or purchase a home testing kit (available in some hardware stores). Depending on the test results and the agronomic recommendations, if there are any, you can improve the soil with amendments like green manure, compost, manure, and minerals to maintain and enhance the soil quality over the long term.

If you want to grow organic vegetables, you will need to choose your input sources carefully. At Le Rizen, because our vegetables have been certified organic since 2018, our choices about what we use and how often to apply it are regulated by the specifications of our organic certifier.

BASIC AMENDMENTS

Compost rich in nitrogen, potassium, and slow-release phosphorus: Spread when you are preparing the growing surface so that the plants can be nourished by it throughout their growth.

Nitrogen-rich fertilizer: A granular fertilizer such as composted or heat-treated chicken manure or animal or plant flours should be spread at the base of plants when they are planted out, because they need it at this critical stage of growth.

Lime: Add when preparing the growing surface to increase soil pH, if necessary.

Green manures: Buckwheat, pea, clover, rye, oat, and other seeds can be scattered or sown with a seeder over the growing surfaces before or after the main crop. Advantages include reducing weeds, protecting the soil from erosion between two crops, and improving both fertility and soil structure by providing the organic matter that stimulates micro-organism activity in the soil. From April to early September, you can sow green manures on your growing areas, whether with the aim of planting a crop later or simply to cover the soil.

Boron: Boron is a crucial micro-element for the Brassica family. Brassicas are susceptible to developing a boron deficit, which often manifests as a hollow heart. To avoid this, it is recommended to apply a diluted boron solution (follow the manufacturer's instructions) to all brassicas with a pressure sprayer,* and to do this twice during the growing season: once when planting out and once when the floral buds appear (choy sum, gai lan) or when heads start to form (bok choy, mustard greens, Chinese cabbage).

HARDENING OFF

Hardening off is the transition period when the plants leave the comfort of the greenhouse or house behind and gradually get used to the sun, the cooler outside temperatures, and the wind.

We know that young plants started in multicell trays are ready to be hardened off when the roots are well formed in the cell. Allow seven days for hardening off in spring and fall, and one or two in the summer.

EASY OPTIONS FOR HARDENING OFF

· A table outside with plastic-covered hoops or a floating row cover

· A metal-framed car shelter (such as Tempo) covered in greenhouse plastic, ideally with opening sides

· Bring the plants outside on a cloudy day or put them in the shade, and bring them inside if cool nights are expected

PLANTING OUT

Once the young plants are hardened off, they are ready to be taken out of the tray or pot and planted in the great outdoors: it's planting-out season! The trays and pots must be well watered, or even soaked, so that the entire root clump gets a good drink.

At Le Rizen, we plant out the first plants around May 1. The whole team is involved, and we train the new recruits to plant tomorrow's harvest today.

It is always better to plant out on a cool, cloudy morning or before the sun gets too strong.

See the "Planting Out" table in the Appendix on page 347 for the essential details of planting out our fifteen vegetables.

KEY EQUIPMENT FOR PROTECTING YOUR CROPS

In the context of a commercial growing business, there are four essential pieces of equipment if you want to start early in the season and keep going until late, or if you want to limit insect leaf damage: insect netting, floating row covers, hoops, and bags of rocks or sand.

INSECT NETTING

With its very fine gauge, this makes a physical barrier against flea beetles and other predatory insects that can seriously devastate a crop. The net gauge should be chosen depending on what insect you want to keep out. Insect netting stands up to being handled, lets more light through, has a weaker thermal effect, but is more expensive than floating row covers.

To be effective, the net must not have holes in it, and must be fixed so that there is no gap between the ground and the net. At Le Rizen, we set them up when we plant out all our brassica crops (bok choy, choy sum, gai lan, mustard greens, Chinese cabbage) and leave them on until the end of the crop, or until they are tall enough to withstand minor insect attacks. Since our brassica sowings are harvested over several weeks, we close off one end of the net with a shovel of earth at each hoop, and close the other end with a sack of rocks, which lets us quickly uncover and recover the crop.

FLOATING ROW COVERS

These are made of thin fabric that provides crops with a few extra degrees of warmth in early spring and fall, when nighttime temperatures can drop to near-freezing. In addition to protecting the crop from frost and wind, the row covers also speed up growth. For direct sowings, floating row covers maintain soil humidity and allow for a better germination rate.

Tip: If your budget is limited, you can buy a roll of Agryl P12, which is very thin and does duty as both an insect netting and a floating row cover. This is what we started with in the first season at Le Rizen. But handle with care because it rips very easily.

We now install Novagryl P-19, which is thicker, when we plant out our crops.

In spring: Fix the floating row covers to the ground with shovelfuls of soil.

· For the first sowings of chrysanthemum, celtuce, amaranth, and shiso, remove the cover when the temperatures warm up.

· For Malabar spinach, okra, Asian eggplant, Asian cucumber, luffa, and lemongrass, remove the cover when flowers appear or when the plants are restricted by the cover.

In fall: Fix the floating row covers to the ground with shovelfuls of earth on one side and sacks of rocks on the other.

For the last sowings of chrysanthemum, celtuce, amaranth, and shiso, open the covers when you harvest and close again afterward.

HOOPS

Both insect netting and floating row covers are supported by hoops spaced at 5 ft (1.5 m) intervals. They are thin sticks made of steel or plastic, long enough that both ends can be inserted into the soil over the width of the growing area. To give you an idea, think of the arches of a car shelter.

BAGS OF ROCKS OR SAND

These need to be made out of rigid plastic or, even better, rigid fabric that lets water through. They are closed with a tie and are used to keep the nets and row covers closed along the sides. During the harvest you need to move the bags only a little to be able to uncover and quickly recover the crops.

WATERING

It is crucial to water after planting out, especially in warm, dry weather or if there is no rain in the forecast.

You can install an irrigation system in the garden. The two most common kinds are drip irrigation and sprinkling.

DRIP IRRIGATION SYSTEM

This is made of light plastic pipes pierced at regular intervals and installed at the base of the plants.

Advantages:

· Simple — once it's set up, all you have to do is turn on the tap and all the crops will be watered.

· Minimal water consumption since there is no loss to evaporation.

· Reduction of dampness in the foliage that can cause leaf diseases in certain high-risk crops, such as Asian cucumber, and more generally when the nights start to cool down in August. Since organic fungicides are not very effective, drip irrigation systems are ideal for organic gardening.

· Works perfectly if using plastic mulch.

Disadvantage:

· It makes it more difficult to use hand-weeding tools, although there are some specifically developed to solve this problem.

SPRINKLER IRRIGATION SYSTEM

This is made up of several sprinklers connected together and placed at regular intervals in the centre of the area to be watered.

Advantages:

· Allows the garden to be uniformly watered, which is perfect for optimizing germination when direct seeding or for growth during a dry spell.

· Can be moved and used for several crops.

· Helps to repel flea beetles, which hate water.

Disadvantages:

· More laborious to move and manoeuvre.

· Low efficiency in windy spots.

· Not ideal when water supplies are limited because more water is lost (walkways and other non-growing zones are watered pointlessly).

MULCH

Before or after planting vegetables in a bed or field, it's a good idea to protect the soil with plastic or natural mulch (wood chips, straw, leaves, cardboard, or grass cuttings). This is particularly true for vegetables that stay in the garden a long time: Chinese cabbage, Malabar spinach, shiso, okra, Asian eggplant, Asian cucumber, luffa, and lemongrass. In fact all vegetables, even leafy greens, can benefit from mulching.

Advantages:

• Preserves soil humidity, reducing the need for watering.

• Fills in the space that would otherwise be overtaken with weeds, which reduces time spent on weeding under the hot summer sun.

• Protects the soil from erosion that would be caused by water and wind when the ground is uncovered.

• Keeps leafy vegetables clean in rainy weather, acting as a barrier between the soil and the vegetables, which helps when cleaning them.

IMPORTANT CONSIDERATIONS

Be careful with carbon-rich plant-based mulches such as straw, cardboard, dead leaves, ramial chipped wood, and wood shavings, which can cause nitrogen deficiency.

If you opt for plastic mulch, plant cool-weather vegetables with a mulch that is white on the top and black underneath, and hot-weather vegetables with a mulch that is black on both sides.

A downside of plastic mulch is that you will absolutely need a supplemental drip irrigation system because rain and water from sprinklers will not go through the plastic.

Some kinds of mulch, straw in particular, can be costly, while others (dead leaves, cardboard, shredded branches) can be found for free.

SOME TIPS

Once you have planted the crops, don't forget them! Do a full tour of the garden at least once a week so that you can assess the needs of each crop and its stage of growth, and quickly rectify the situation if some of them need water, are being attacked by insects, or are ready to be harvested.

Make notes, and then make more notes! In your planting-out records for each vegetable, list the date, the number of plants, its condition (strong or weak), whether the colour is vibrant or yellowed, whether the leaves are chewed or whole, and so on. This data will be useful for planning the following season because you will know what worked and what needs tweaking.

DISEASES

Good growing practices like drainage; a rotation system; maintaining soil structure, pH level, and level of organic matter in the soil; sufficient fertilization; sufficient irrigation; and control of self-propagating plants (weeds) will prevent numerous infections caused by fungi or bacteria.

Diseases caused by bacteria most likely to affect brassicas are black rot, bacterial spot, and bacterial soft rot. Fungal diseases that most often affect brassicas are alternaria, fusarium wilt, clubroot, blackleg, mildew, and sclerotinia.

As mentioned above, a four-year, or ideally six-year, rotation is the best way of preventing brassica diseases.

Because nature is unpredictable and uncontrollable, we are never safe from disease and ravaging insects, which is why regular monitoring of crops by an agronomist is essential for any market-gardening project that aims to be a livelihood.

SPECIFICS OF COLD-LOVING VEGETABLES

Several Asian vegetables are more flavourful and give better results in spring and fall—that is, in the cooler seasons, when there is no frost and no excessive heat. This is true of leafy greens, including brassicas (bok choy, choy sum, gai lan, mustard greens, and Chinese cabbage), chrysanthemum, and celtuce. It's not impossible to grow them in high summer, but they are usually smaller, less sweet, and less crunchy.

VERY COLD RESISTANT

Once they have reached a semi-mature or mature growth stage, Asian greens can tolerate nights with temperatures hovering around 28° to 30°F (−2° to −1°C) if they are underneath a floating row cover. Some crops can even stay frozen several days in a row and still be good to harvest! Avoid harvesting while the plants are actually frozen; it is better to let them thaw beforehand. Remember that plants grow more slowly in cool weather, and that growth stops more or less completely when there are fewer than 10 hours of sunlight a day. You will need to plan to make sure that the crops have reached maturity before November 1st.

RAPID GROWTH

Several Asian greens reach maturity much faster than other Asian brassicas that need a longer growing time; for example, Chinese cabbage or daikon radish, as well as classic crucifers such as broccoli and cauliflower. To harvest over a longer period, plan on successive sowings throughout the growing season.

INTERMEDIATE LEVEL

Greens, and in particular brassicas, present certain challenges in the garden. They can bolt quickly depending on their genetic makeup and the environmental conditions, particularly low temperatures during the early growing weeks (lower than 50°F/10°C for two or three weeks); long days of sunlight (above twelve to fourteen hours); and different sources of stress (lack of water, excessive water, big temperature variations, heat, flea beetles, etc.).

LOVED BY INSECTS

Insects, particularly flea beetles and caterpillars, go crazy for brassicas. To limit the damage, we always recommend placing insect netting or a floating row cover over brassica crops. In high summer and fall, be on the lookout for aphids, which multiply exponentially under the nets and can destroy a whole crop in just a few weeks. Chrysanthemum and celtuce don't need nets because they are rarely attacked by insects. But they do benefit from floating row covers, which give a few extra degrees of warmth early and late in the season.

CONSTANT IRRIGATION

Brassicas need fertile nitrogen-rich soil that is well drained but retains humidity. Because of their shallow, fragile root system, it is important to handle seedlings without disturbing their roots and to water them little and often. The quantity of water needed depends on a multitude of factors, such as soil type, crop stage, climate, soil structure, and drainage.

IDEAL CROPS TO EXTEND THE SEASON

Asian greens grow very well, perhaps even at their best, in early spring and late fall, or even winter. You can also use shelters to increase the temperature around the plants by a few degrees and thus optimize their growth. A growing number of farms have been experimenting successfully with growing greens under different shelters: unheated greenhouse, cold greenhouse (uninsulated, no heating system), caterpillar tunnel (greenhouse plastic stretched over big hoops covering several beds), and minitunnel (greenhouse plastic stretched over hoops covering just one or two beds). Brassicas are among the most productive vegetables in this context.

FANS OF THE COLD

Since cold-loving vegetables bolt when it is too hot, it's best to grow them with a white plastic mulch, or any other mulch that conserves humidity and soil coolness. If you grow them during the summer, try to find them a semi-shaded spot or place them in the shade of taller plants like runner beans.

SENSITIVE TO WILTING

Cold-loving vegetables will quickly wilt, get floppy, and lose their crunch in sun and heat. Optimize the time of harvesting as well as conditioning and storage techniques to protect the vegetable until it is sold or eaten.

BATTLING INSECTS

Preventing and getting rid of harmful insects is an integral part of vegetable growing. Here is a quick overview of the insects you are most likely to come across when growing our vegetable selection.

FLEA BEETLES

At risk: bok choy, choy sum, gai lan, mustard greens, Chinese cabbage

Crucifer flea beetles and turnip flea beetles are the insects most commonly found when growing brassicas. These are small, shiny, jumping black beetles. They are particularly voracious during hot, dry weather. They munch on the sweetest brassica leaves like bok choy and choy sum, leaving tiny round holes that slowly grow as the leaf grows. Be aware that flea beetle larvae can also do significant damage to the roots of vegetables in the brassica family, such as white turnip and daikon radish.

In organic farming, the insect netting is still the weapon of choice and must be installed immediately after planting out your crops. If you don't have a net, or didn't have time to set it up, and notice that flea beetles are multiplying on a crop, use water to repel them and then immediately set up the net. The key is regular detection and screening so you can act early, before the population gets out of control. Depending on your tolerance levels for leaf damage, you can choose the moment when you should treat with organic pesticides or natural repellent to reduce the flea beetle population.

CATERPILLARS

At risk: bok choy, choy sum, gai lan, mustard greens, Chinese cabbage

Brassicas are preyed upon by various caterpillars, such as the cabbage white, the greater wax moth, the cabbage looper, and the cutworm. The caterpillars eat the leaves, defecate, lay their eggs, and rapidly multiply, causing significant damage. At Le Rizen, caterpillars are mainly a threat to Chinese cabbage, because these stay out in the field for a long time and are deliciously tender and sweet.

Once again, insect netting is the best physical barrier to prevent caterpillar attacks. If you notice caterpillars in your cabbages, you can pick them off by hand and drown them in a bucket of soapy water. As a last resort, it might be necessary to save infested crops by using an organic insecticide based on the bacteria *Bacillus thuringiensis kurstaki* (Btk). This forms small crystals in the insect's digestive system, which end up killing it.

APHIDS

At risk: all vegetables

Aphids are tiny insects measuring just ¹⁄₁₆ to ¹⁄₃₂ inch (1 to 2 mm). Their colour ranges from yellow to green to grey, depending on the species. At Le Rizen, we have noticed that aphids are usually found on the sweetest brassicas: bok choy, choy sum, and Chinese cabbage. Aphid colonies can be found on the underside of the leaves and in the plants' heads, making them difficult to remove. Soaking the greens in an ice bath for a few minutes will get rid of most of the aphids.

They multiply very quickly; infested crops are likely to be decimated within just a few weeks. Predatory insects or parasitoids (if using parasitoids, you must make sure you have properly identified the aphid in question) can be introduced under the nets or in the greenhouse to prevent or try to wipe out an aphid infestation. Because this is not an easy solution, companies specializing in integrated crop management* can help you if you choose this route.

Sometimes the infestation is very localized, so you can pull up and destroy the infested plant to prevent the aphids from spreading to other plants. If the infestation is generalized across the plants, you will often find the aphids on the undersides of outer leaves or in the plants' heads. It might be possible to remove the affected leaves or heads by hand to reduce the population, slow down the infestation, and perhaps save a crop that would arrive at maturity in the next few weeks.

STRIPED CUCUMBER BEETLE

At risk: Asian cucumber

In its adult stage, this beetle measures around ½ inch (0.5 cm) and can be identified by its yellow and black stripes. The striped cucumber beetle can cause irreversible damages to leaves, stems, and fruits of cucurbits. The adults can also transmit the bacteria *Erwinia tracheiphila,* which can provoke leaf wilting. In the spring, installing a floating row cover over the young plants can defend them against the first and most severe wave of striped cucumber beetles and provide a few extra degrees of warmth. There is also a clay-based repellent, permitted for use in organic farming, that can be repeatedly applied on the young plants to protect them.

RED SPIDER MITES

At risk: Asian eggplant, Asian cucumber

Also known as two-spotted spider mites, or *Tetranychus urticae,* red spider mites particularly attack summer crops like Asian eggplant and Asian cucumber. The adult insect is oval in shape, measures 1/48th inch (0.5 mm), and is yellow with two black spots on its shoulders. Leaves infested with spider mites become yellow before drying out and falling off, which reduces the plants' yield.

This acarid proliferates very rapidly in hot, dry conditions, especially in greenhouses or tunnels. If you have an infestation, misting with water has two effects: reducing their proliferation and allowing beneficial insects to survive. An organic option of introducing predatory insects is also recommended to prevent or stamp out a spider-mite infestation.

*Flea beetles have chewed holes
in these choy sum leaves.*

A hole punch is used to pierce plastic mulch before planting out plants.

Above: *Planting out.*
Following pages: *Insect netting, hoops, and floating row covers.*

BOK CHOY

白
菜

BOK CHOY

Also known as: pak choi
Cantonese: 白菜 baak6 coi3 (white | vegetable)
Mandarin: 小白菜 xiǎobáicài (small | white | vegetable),
sometimes called 白菜 báicài (but this can
be confused with Chinese cabbage)

FAMILY: Brassicaceae

SPECIES: *Brassica rapa* subspecies *chinensis*

Bok choy, along with Chinese cabbage, is one of the few Asian vegetables widely known in the West. It comes in all sorts of shapes and colours, from tiny to large and from green to purple. It is delicious, and owes its popularity to its ease of use and versatility in the kitchen. It is easily found in supermarkets, Asian grocery stores, and local organic farms.

HISTORY Originally from the south of China, bok choy has been grown since the fifth century. It is much loved in Chinese cooking and can be found in many traditional dishes, such as the one served during Chinese New Year in Shanghai, which is made of blanched Shanghai bok choy and braised shiitake mushrooms. Bok choy was introduced to the United States at the end of the nineteenth century during the gold rush. Today, it is no longer just a traditional Chinese vegetable.

IN THE SAME FAMILY: **TATSOI**
Also known as: rosette bok choy
塔菜 taap3 coi3/tǎcài (tower | vegetable)
or 塌菜 taap3 coi3/tācài (to fall | vegetable), maybe
because its leaves seem to fall and spread out on
the ground; often preceded by 烏 wū.

SPECIES: *Brassica rapa* subspecies *narinosa*

A cousin of bok choy, tatsoi also resembles it but has a
slightly more pronounced flavour. The green variety, with
its long, thin green stems, makes a pretty rosette shape in
the garden, hence its alternative name. Rainbow tatsoi adds
colour with its wider purple-tinged oval leaves, as well as
a refreshing acidic note when served raw. Although tatsoi
grows less quickly than bok choy, it has the advantage
of being more heat and cold resistant. Prepare tatsoi the
same way as bok choy: separate the leaves individually or
in groups of four or five for cooking.

A beautiful vegetable, bok choy is composed of stems and leaves that are joined at the base like celery. These crunchy, juicy stems are white or green, and its tender veined leaves have a flavour of mild mustard, which softens during cooking.

Bok choy is succulent at every stage of its growth: shoot (also called microgreens), baby, young, mature. However, it is more tender when young rather than large and mature. Although you can eat bok choy's flowering stems,* it is usually harvested before it reaches that stage.

Bok choy comes in several types and sizes, with each one including several cultivars. Here are the three main types of bok choy you might find.

Large bok choy
Cantonese: 大白菜 daai6 baak6 coi3

Can grow from 12 to 18 inches (30 to 45 cm), has wide white stems and large dark green leaves. Harvest when mature — it will still be tender and sweet.

• Joi Choy F1 is a popular and productive cultivar.

Small (baby) or medium (regular) bok choy
6 inches (15 cm) or more, fleshy green stems

• Popular cultivars are Shanghai and Mei Qing F1.

• The Shanghai, the first green-stemmed cultivar to be introduced in the West, is a favourite both in Chinese cooking and at Le Rizen. Harvest when young and tender; it is very robust. Le Rizen grows medium Shanghai bok choy (上海白菜 soeng6 hoi2 baak6 coi3). Baby Shanghai bok choy is very common in grocery stores and particularly appreciated by Chinese communities (上海苗 soeng6 hoi2 miu4).

Mini (dwarf) bok choy
From 3 to 4 inches (8 to 10 cm), with short, thick white stems and slightly curly dark green leaves (奶油白菜 naai5 jau4 baak6 coi3); this is a mature bok choy whose size is naturally very small. It can easily be cooked whole.

In the garden

• At Le Rizen, we opt for successive plantings of Shanghai bok choy so as to obtain big harvests from late May through November.

• Bok choy is ideal for growing in pots because it grows very quickly, takes up little space, and likes a semi-shaded spot in summer.

• To harvest, you can pick off the outside leaves as needed, rather like lettuce, or wait until the plant reaches the desired size and harvest whole or cut it 1 inch (2.5 cm) above the base to allow it to regrow.

• Once harvested, bok choy is very fragile. To handle and wash without damaging it too much, harvest and then lay it on the soil until the crunchy stems soften — from a few minutes to an hour. Then you can bundle two bok choy plants together with an elastic band, making a bunch without harming the stems. Bok choy will easily return to its crunchy state after a cold bath or some time in the fridge.

STORING
Keeps for a few days in a sealed plastic bag or container in the fridge, or for 14 to 21 days after harvest under optimal conditions.

PREPARING
Pull off the stems at the base, then rinse with the leaves. You can also cut the leaves from the stems, if you want. Use the stems and leaves whole, especially the smaller varieties, or cut them in two lengthwise or into 1-inch (2.5 cm) pieces.

NUTRITION

Bok choy is an excellent source of vitamin K and a good source of vitamins A and C. It's also a source of calcium, vitamin B6, and folate. The calcium in bok choy, as with all brassicas (such as choy sum and mustard greens), is more easily absorbed than that in other green vegetables, such as spinach or amaranth, because bok choy is lower in oxalate, a substance that reduces intestinal absorption of calcium. Calcium has a role not only in forming bones but also in muscle contraction.

IN THE KITCHEN

Edible parts	Ways to eat	Ways to cook
• Leaves	• Raw	• Steam
• Stems	• Cooked	• Boil
• Flowering stems	• Pickled/ lacto-fermented	• Sauté/stir-fry
• Flowers	• Dried	• Roast/grill
		• Deep-fry

Bok choy can replace any leafy green, including spinach, Swiss chard, kale, Chinese cabbage, gai lan, or choy sum. Its stems can also replace celery. Bok choy goes well with ginger, soy sauce, sesame oil, and sesame seeds.

RAW

· In salads, use the young leaves whole, or thinly slice or roughly chop the mature leaves and stems, and serve with an acidic vinaigrette.

· The shoots and sprouted seeds can be added to any dish to decorate and add freshness and flavour.

COOKED

We particularly like bok choy cooked, as it becomes milder and more flavourful. Cook it for just 2 to 4 minutes to preserve its crunchy texture and give it a nice shine.

Our favourite cooking methods:

· In the wok! It is delicious cooked Chinese stir-fry-style with ginger or garlic, alone or with other vegetables such as bean sprouts.

· Sautéed in a frying pan and seasoned with nutmeg.

· Roasted in the oven or grilled or steamed, it's the perfect accompaniment to dumplings served with black rice vinegar.

· Works well in rice, noodle, fish, chicken, and meat dishes.

· Added at the end of cooking in soups, hot pots, and stews. Baby bok choy is perfect in noodle soups, and large bok choy works well in soups like our uncle Jean's recipe (see opposite).

Bok choy leaves can be dried and then used during the winter in soups or other dishes, such as meat soups (see "A few Chinese preserves" on page 317). To do this, blanch the leaves with their stems attached for 2 minutes or until the colour brightens, plunge into cold water, drain, then spread out to dry in the sun, low-temperature oven, or dehydrator. To use the dried leaves, soak in water for 2 hours, then stew until tender.

Uncle Jean's bok choy and chicken soup

A simple, tasty recipe with just four steps:

1. In a pot of boiling water, blanch a chicken thigh. Rinse in cold water and discard the cooking water.

2. Fill the pot with water again and bring to a boil. Meanwhile, remove the skin and fat from the chicken.

3. When the water comes to a boil, add the blanched chicken thigh, a small onion cut in half, and a piece of crushed ginger. Reduce the heat to low and let simmer, covered, for 1 hour.

4. Discard the onion. Add some chopped bok choy leaves and diced carrots. Bring to a boil, then cook for 15 to 20 minutes, depending on how tender you like the vegetables. Add salt and soy sauce to taste, and enjoy!

For this recipe, our uncle suggests using large bok choy, but he says you can also switch it up with mustard greens, or use both together. Chayote, which are crunchy, not-too-sweet pear-shaped squashes, are also a great addition to this soup. In fact, according to Jean, you can add pretty much any vegetable you like.

Rainbow tatsoi.

Roasted bok choy

By Caroline

Roasting vegetables is very practical when you want to make several dishes at the same time. Although this method is not very common in Chinese cooking, bok choy lends itself very well to roasting — and it cooks super fast. Caroline developed this simple recipe, which highlights the vegetable's flavour, as a way to optimize meal preparation. For even more flavour, serve with a little sesame or chili oil, or sprinkle some sesame seeds overtop.

Preparation 10 to 15 min • Cooking 3 to 4 min • 4 servings

INGREDIENTS

2 to 5 Shanghai bok choy (12 oz/330g)

1 tbsp (15 mL) canola oil

Salt, to taste

Chili oil, to taste (optional)

METHOD

1. Move the oven rack to the bottom third position. Preheat the oven to 400°F (200°C).

2. Detach the bok choy stems at the base and rinse under water.

3. Using a knife, cut any wide leaves and stems in half lengthways.

4. Place the bok choy on a large baking sheet. Drizzle with oil and toss with tongs until evenly coated. Spread the bok choy out evenly, then roast for 3 to 4 minutes, or until the stems are tender.

5. Salt lightly, and add chili oil (if using).

NOTES AND VARIATIONS

You can replace the bok choy with choy sum or gai lan, adjusting the cooking time as necessary.

Gaspé turbot, lobster, and tatsoi with XO sauce

By Jérémie Bastien

白菜

There is a significant Cantonese influence in this dish, with the XO sauce originating in Hong Kong. Jérémie particularly likes this cuisine because his partner, Lisa, has Cantonese origins. The idea behind the recipe is to elevate the turbot by combining it with lobster. As well as tatsoi, this recipe uses choy sum and gai lan, all simply prepared so as not to distort them. This dish with lobster-stuffed turbot rolled in a seafood wrap is fairly complex to make, so if desired, you could instead cook a turbot fillet in the oven and serve with a lobster tail or the meat from a half-lobster, and a bowl of Asian vegetables with XO sauce. The secret is in the sauce as well as the freshness of the vegetables and seafood.

Preparation and cooking 2 hours • 4 servings • 🍴

INGREDIENTS

4 Gaspé (or local) turbot fillets

1 whole in-season lobster

For the XO sauce

1 tbsp (15 mL) dried scallops

⅓ cup (100 mL) Shaoxing rice cooking wine

2 tbsp (30 mL) dried shrimp

¼ cup (50 mL) vegetable oil

3 cloves of garlic, minced

1.5 oz (45 g) minced fresh ginger
    (approx. 2.5-inch/6 cm piece)

4.5 oz (130 g) banana peppers, diced very small
    (approx. 3 medium peppers)

1½ tbsp (22 mL) fermented black beans, roughly chopped

½ tbsp (7 mL) liquid honey

1 cup (250 mL) pork stock (or other stock)

¼ cup (50 mL) soy sauce (or to taste)

1.7 oz (50 g) prosciutto, cut into very small dice

For the daikon purée

1 small daikon, peeled and cut into ¾-inch (2 cm) cubes

1 yellow-fleshed potato, diced

2 tbsp (30 mL) butter

Salt, to taste

For the seafood wrap

7 oz (200 g) raw shrimp (buy unshelled shrimp)

0.2 oz (6 g) Activa RM (transglutaminase)

¼ tsp (1 mL) salt

For the vegetables

1 bunch of rainbow tatsoi

1 bunch of choy sum

1 bunch of gai lan

3 white turnips, quartered

Vegetable oil (optional)

METHOD

1. For the XO sauce, rehydrate the dried scallops in the cooking wine and the dried shrimp in water.

For the daikon purée

2. In a small saucepan over low heat, combine the daikon and the potato with the butter and a pinch of salt. Cover and cook until the vegetables are tender.

3. Drain, purée in a blender, and season with salt to taste.

For the seafood

4. In a large pot of salted boiling water, cook the lobster whole for 10 minutes, or for perfect results, cook the lobster in separate parts: claws for 2 minutes, tail for 4 minutes, knuckles for 5 minutes. Transfer the lobster to an ice bath to stop the cooking process.

5. Shell the lobster. Keep the meat of the claws for the seafood wrap, and set aside the knuckle and tail meat to stuff the turbot fillets. Reserve the shells.

6. Peel the shrimp, reserving the shells.

7. Make a seafood stock with the reserved lobster's shells, thoracic cage, and feet, as well as the shrimp shells. To make a simple seafood stock, place the reserved seafood parts in a pot, cover with water, and simmer for 45 to 60 minutes. Strain well.

For the seafood wrap

8. In a food processor, purée the shrimp meat with 6 tbsp (100 mL) of the seafood stock (or water), the Activa RM, and salt. Transfer the mixture to a bowl.

9. Roughly chop 5 oz (150 g) of the lobster claw meat, and then stir it into the shrimp mixture.

10. Line a 12- by 12-inch (30 cm x 30 cm) baking sheet with parchment paper. Spread a ½-inch (1 cm) thick layer of the seafood mixture on top of the parchment, then cover with another piece of parchment and gently smooth flat. Steam-cook at 130°F (55°C) or at medium-low heat for 5 minutes. (For more information on steam-cooking, see page 54.)

11. Let cool slightly, and then cut the seafood wrap into four 6- x 6-inch (15 x 15 cm) pieces. Alternatively, you can cook the smaller pieces individually.

For the XO sauce

12. Using your fingers, shred the scallops, reserving the cooking wine, and set aside. Drain the shrimp, and mince with a sharp knife.

13. In a frying pan over medium heat, heat the oil. Add the garlic, ginger, and peppers, and cook until softened.

14. Add the minced shrimp, shredded scallops, and black beans, and cook, stirring occasionally, for 2 minutes.

15. Stir in the cooking wine and then the honey.

16. Add the pork stock, and let simmer for 5 minutes.

17. Season with the soy sauce.

18. Add the prosciutto.

For the stuffed turbot roll

19. Fold each turbot fillet lengthways, and insert a portion of lobster meat (knuckle, or tail cut to the size of a knuckle). Carefully roll up the stuffed turbot in a piece of the seafood wrap. Wrap well in plastic wrap, and poach (cook in water) at 135°F (58°C) for 15 minutes. →

For the vegetables

20. Blanch all the vegetables (see page 54).

21. If desired, sauté the vegetables in oil: 1 to 1.5 minutes for the white turnips and 30 seconds for the greens. Cook in batches to avoid crowding the pan.

22. Reheat the daikon purée and the XO sauce.

To assemble

23. On each plate, assemble:
1 stuffed turbot roll
2 tatsoi stems
2 choy sum stems
2 gai lan stems
1 tbsp (15 mL) daikon purée
1 to 2 tbsp (15 to 30 mL) XO sauce
3 white turnip quarters

NOTES AND VARIATIONS

The Activa RM contains the enzyme transglutaminase, which helps the meat stick together. You can buy it online or from specialized grocery stores, or substitute 1 tsp (5 mL) of arrowroot powder.

Jérémie Bastien

Chef, owner of Monarque restaurant

The monarch, that great migratory butterfly, is a nod to Jérémie's culinary journey. He discovered traditional Asian cuisine travelling the West Coast from San Francisco to Vancouver, and then in Australia via Hong Kong and Japan. He then returned to Montreal to open Monarque with his father. On the menu, as in his recipes in this book, you can find influences from his ten years spent travelling outside of Quebec. Since opening Monarque, he has been buying vegetables from Le Rizen, because he finds the freshness and local connection better than what is available to him in Asian grocery stores. With Le Rizen, he has even discovered vegetable varieties he wasn't aware of, which allows him to travel without going anywhere.

The fish and seafood of Madagascar

Our uncle tells the story of how his father had a cement water basin dug into the ground in which he raised fish bought at the market: tilapia, carp, etc. The fish stayed in the basin for at least two weeks so they were cleansed of all impurities. When it was time to eat them, my uncle's family prepared the fish fillets carefully: the fish had to be sliced very thinly and patted dry, then mixed with vegetables like julienned carrots and turnips, a ginger-and-onion dressing, roasted pistachios, and a drizzle of hot canola oil. Fish prepared in this way absolutely has to be harvested the same day it's going to be eaten.

It is not unusual for our family members to rave about the freshness of the fish and the wide range of seafood when talking about the country they grew up in. Definitely something to dream about!

Rustic sticky rice with bok choy

By Yamei Zhao

白菜

This dish, popular in the south of China, is commonly eaten for lunch or dinner because it is a whole meal in itself. It can be prepared with a variety of ingredients, and is quick and easy to make. This version is inspired by the recipe Yamei's mother often put in her lunchbox for school. It reminds her of the flavours of family mealtimes. Although her mother used any available leftover meat, Yamei uses bacon here. Try it and see how a nice, hot sticky rice dish can be comforting and satisfying.

Preparation 10 min • Cooking 20 min • 4 to 6 servings

INGREDIENTS

1 tbsp (15 mL) vegetable oil

1 yellow onion, diced

2 cloves of garlic, minced

2 to 3 very thin slices of fresh ginger

1 tsp (5 mL) five spice powder

½ lb (250 g) bacon, chopped into ½-inch (1 cm) pieces

1 carrot, cut into half circles

4 cups (1 L) bok choy, cut widthwise into ½-inch (1 cm) pieces

2 cups (500 mL) uncooked sticky rice, rinsed and drained

½ tsp (2 mL) salt

Ground black pepper, to taste

3 cups (750 mL) hot water

2 green onions, green and white parts, thinly sliced

METHOD

1. In a large frying pan over medium heat, heat the oil. Add the onion, garlic, and ginger. Stir in the five spice powder and bacon. Cook for 2 to 3 minutes, stirring occasionally, until the bacon is browned.

2. Add the carrot and then the bok choy. Cook, stirring rapidly, for 20 seconds, or until the colour of the bok choy becomes more vivid.

3. Add the rice and stir well. Add the salt, pepper, and water. Reduce the heat to very low, cover, and cook for 15 to 20 minutes, or until the water has been absorbed and the rice is tender. If needed, add a bit more water while cooking.

4. Stir in the green onions, and then season to taste.

NOTES AND VARIATIONS

· The bok choy can be replaced with any other leafy green.

· The bacon can be replaced with sausage, pork belly, chicken, tempeh, seitan, or soy-marinated tofu.

· For more flavour, add mushrooms or replace the water with stock.

· If you don't have sticky rice or want to make a lighter dish, you can use a short-grain rice such as Arborio.

· Yamei's recipe was initially made with pork belly, which is not as widely available as bacon. Pork belly is the cut used in the famous Cantonese roast pork belly dish.

Yamei Zhao
Rendez-vous Café

Yamei was born in China in the province of Shanxi, studied at Nanjing, and then lived and worked in Shanghai for ten years. Today she is the owner of the Rendez-vous Café, a café-restaurant in downtown Cowansville in the Eastern Townships that is known as a warm, welcoming place. Always smiling, Yamei serves, among other dishes, comforting Asian meals. She is enthusiastic about Chinese culinary culture, and here presents us with one of her favourite recipes.

CHOY SUM

菜
心

CHOY SUM

Also known as: flowering cabbage
菜心 coi3 sam1/càixīn (vegetable | heart)

FAMILY: Brassicaceae

SPECIES: *Brassica rapa* subspecies *chinensis* var. *parachinensis*

Choy sum is one of the mysterious, little-known vegetables found almost exclusively in Asian grocery stores. However, this vegetable is very popular in China, and becomes a firm favourite with many people who are tasting it for the first time. Its flower stalks are exquisite, and its yellow flowers are pretty. Sweeter than bok choy and just as adaptable in the kitchen, choy sum has everything going for it.

IN THE SAME FAMILY: **YU CHOY**

Choy sum is often confused with yu choy (油菜), because they look the same and have a similar flavour. Grown the same way as choy sum, yu choy is slightly more vigorous in the garden, grows straighter, and has shinier leaves. Yu choy seeds have long been used in China as a source of oil for both cooking and lamps, inspiring its Chinese name, which literally means "oil | vegetable."

HISTORY Originally from continental China, choy sum is widely grown there, particularly in the south, where it is very popular, and in Hong Kong. It is mainly grown for its flowering stems, which differentiates it from the other vegetables in the brassica family, whose young flowering stems can be eaten, although the plants are usually harvested before these stems appear.

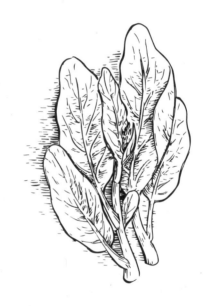

Botanically close to bok choy, choy sum resembles gai lan, although it is more tender, sweeter, and less bitter. Its white or pale green crunchy, juicy stems are more slender than those of gai lan. Its oval leaves have a very mild mustard flavour, and its buds have a delicate broccoli flavour. Its floral stems are at their best when the young yellow flowers are just about to bloom. These flowers are a pure delicacy for the mouth—a floral explosion that is both mustardy and sweet. Depending on the variety and growing conditions, choy sum grows to between 8 and 22 inches (20 and 56 cm) in height.

In the garden

• It is best to stick to two early-spring sowings and two fall sowings, because choy sum is so sweet that flea beetles simply devour it in the summer heat. Whenever you grow it, it will need insect netting at all times.

• At Le Rizen, we like growing cultivar 80, which produces a thick stem, up to 1 inch (2.5 cm) in diameter, and whose first flowering stems are often ready to be harvested between 40 and 55 days after indoor sowing. The smaller varieties will be faster.

• Like bok choy, choy sum can be grown in a pot.

• The first harvest should be when around 10% of the yellow flowers are just starting to bloom and there are plenty of beautiful floral stems in the bud stage.

• We always harvest choy sum by hand to ensure that the stem is crunchy: if the stem bends instead of breaking, it means it is fibrous and you need to break it off higher, where it is still crunchy.

• You can harvest the whole plant, but the flowering-stem technique (see "Harvesting techniques" on page 194) is much better for getting two or three harvests of young floral stems per week for 25 to 40 days. If you regularly use this method to harvest choy sum, the plant will keep producing new shoots. Choy sum is therefore very productive if the cuts from the first harvest are done in the right place and at the right time, and if the harvests are frequent and consistent.

STORING
Keeps for a few days in a sealed plastic bag or container in the fridge, or for 10 to 14 days after harvest under optimal conditions.

PREPARING
Rinse, then cut off base of stems if dry. Cook whole or separate leaves, stems, and flowers. The stems can be cut into 2- to 4-inch (5 to 10 cm) chunks.

NUTRITION

Choy sum is a source of iron and vitamin C. Iron plays an essential role in the formation of red blood cells, which transport oxygen. Iron from plant sources is best absorbed when consumed with vitamin C, which makes choy sum especially useful since it contains both nutrients.

IN THE KITCHEN

Edible parts	Ways to eat	Ways to cook
• Leaves	• Raw	• Steam
• Stems	• Cooked	• Boil
• Flowering stems	• Pickled/ lacto-fermented	• Sauté/stir-fry
• Flowers	• Dried	• Roast/grill
		• Deep-fry

Choy sum is cooked the same ways as gai lan and bok choy. The flowering stems of all brassicas are interchangeable. It goes well with garlic, ginger, soy sauce, and sesame oil.

RAW

• Sprouted seeds, shoots, leaves, stems, and floral stems can be eaten raw; for example, added to salads.

• The flowers are a nice garnish, adding colour, delicacy, and perfume to dishes.

COOKED
Like many vegetables, choy sum is served cooked in Chinese cooking; this means it is more tender, and its flavour is softer and sweeter. A short cooking time allows you to keep its taste and its crunch, and to achieve a beautiful, vivid colour.

Some cooking suggestions:
• Cut it into lengths before stir-frying in a wok.

• Steam-cook it whole or sauté from raw. We present our favourite seasoning method in the recipe for Speedy Steamed Choy Sum (page 131).

• Although choy sum is often served on its own, we also like it in soups and stir-fries with noodles, shrimp, chicken, or meat.

Choy sum soup

Aunt Marie calls this recipe, which was passed on to her by an old friend, "the best soup in the world." That's a lot to live up to! She still loves how flavourful this dish is, despite its extreme simplicity.

In a saucepan, heat a little oil with salt and a small amount of ginger. Gently brown some choy sum, then pour over some water and boil for a few minutes. Enjoy!

Speedy steamed choy sum

By Stéphanie

Ever since Stéphanie started Le Rizen, steamed choy sum (or gai lan) has become her favourite side dish after a good day's work on the farm. Steam-cooking is quick, healthy, and simple. The sauce is made from natural and widely available ingredients, offering a perfect balance between sesame oil, salt, and sweet. Altogether, this dish captures the vegetable's freshness and subtle perfume. And presenting the vegetable whole really celebrates it and always impresses guests.

Preparation 5 min · Cooking 2 to 4 min · 2 servings

INGREDIENTS

1 bunch of choy sum (7 oz/200 g)
1 tbsp (15 mL) sesame oil (or other oil)
1 tbsp (15 mL) soy sauce or tamari
1 tbsp (15 mL) pure maple syrup

METHOD

1. Fill a saucepan with ½ inch (1 cm) of water. Bring to a boil over medium heat.

2. Place the whole choy sum in a vegetable steamer (or you can braise it straight in the pan; see page 54).

3. Place the steamer in the pan, cover with the lid, and cook for 2 or 4 minutes (2 minutes directly in the water or 4 minutes in the steamer), until the stems are tender but still have some crunch.

4. Using tongs, transfer the steamed choy sum to a plate. Drizzle sesame oil, soy sauce, and maple syrup overtop.

5. Eat hot, with fingers or chopsticks.

NOTES AND VARIATIONS

Choy sum can be replaced with gai lan, broccoli, or any other vegetable that needs to be cooked. Cooking time will vary depending on the vegetable.

Cantonese fried rice with choy sum

By Marie Wang

菜心

Marie's mother, our paternal grandmother, has a reputation as an excellent cook, from what we've been told. She ran a hotel-restaurant in Ambatondrazaka in Madagascar, where she used to help with the ovens whenever she could. Marie has given us this recipe for fried rice that her mother, Monique, gave her. It's a rather special recipe: her mother perfected it over time, and she was so proud of it, according to her daughter, that she was constantly giving people the recipe and talking about it. Marie hopes that this recipe will continue to be passed down from generation to generation.

Preparation 30 min • Cooking 30 min • 4 servings

INGREDIENTS

7 oz (200 g) choy sum, stems and leaves separated,
    chopped into ½-inch (1 cm) pieces

7 oz (200 g) Chinese barbecue pork (char siu), thinly sliced

4 cups (1 L) cooked white rice,
    prepared the day before and refrigerated

½ tbsp (7 mL) soy sauce or tamari

2 green onions, thinly sliced

5 tbsp (75 mL) vegetable oil

Salt, to taste

For the shrimp

7 oz (200 g) shrimp, shelled and deveined

¼ tsp (1 mL) salt

⅛ tsp (0.5 mL) granulated sugar

2 cloves of garlic, crushed

2 tbsp (30 mL) rice cooking wine

For the eggs

2 large eggs

1 tbsp (15 mL) water

For the sauce

2 eggs

1 tbsp (15 mL) water

1 tbsp (15 mL) soy sauce or tamari

METHOD

1. For the shrimp: Add the salt, sugar, and shrimp to a bowl of cold water. Let soak for 30 minutes at room temperature. Drain, and then set aside.

2. For the eggs: In a small bowl, using a fork or small whisk, beat together the eggs, water, and a pinch of salt. Set aside.

3. For the sauce: In another small bowl, using a fork or small whisk, beat together the ingredients for the sauce along with a pinch of salt.

4. Heat a wok over high heat. Add 1 tbsp (15 mL) of oil and a pinch of salt. Sauté the choy sum stems for 2 minutes, stirring constantly, and then add the leaves and continue cooking for 3 minutes. Set aside in a large dish.

5. Over medium-high heat, pour the beaten eggs into the wok and let them cook like an omelette for 2 minutes per side. Transfer the omelette to a board and cut it into slices ½ to ¾ inch (1 to 2 cm) long and ¼ inch (½ cm) wide. Set aside in the large dish.

6. Heat the wok to medium heat, then add 1 tbsp (15 mL) of the oil and stir-fry the pork for 5 minutes. Set aside in the large dish.

7. In the wok, over high heat, add 1 tbsp (15 mL) oil and stir-fry the shrimp with the garlic for 5 minutes. Add the rice cooking wine and stir. Transfer the shrimp to a board and cut into small pieces. Transfer the shrimp and cooking juices to the large dish.

8. In the wok, over medium heat, add another 2 tbsp (15 mL) oil, then the rice, and stir. Add the sauce, and stir well for 3 minutes. Add the ingredients from the large dish, and stir well for 5 minutes (being careful not to crush the rice). Add the soy sauce and combine.

9. To serve, divide among serving bowls and sprinkle with green onions.

NOTES AND VARIATIONS

· The choy sum can be replaced with gai lan or frozen peas.

· Char siu is a great Cantonese classic made with pork (especially pork shoulder or butt) marinated in a sweet barbecue sauce and then roasted. You can buy it in grocery stores in Chinese neighbourhoods or substitute marinated firm tofu (see recipe below) or roast pork tenderloin.

· For an authentic taste, a wok is ideal, but this recipe can also be made in a frying pan.

· For a vegan version, replace the shrimp, pork, and eggs with edamame and a block (16 oz/454 g) of firm tofu, marinated (see recipe below), and omit the eggs from the sauce.

MARINATED TOFU by Marie Wang

Preparation 10 min • Cooking 30 min • Rest overnight • 4 servings

Ingredients

1 block (16 oz/454 g) firm tofu,
    cut into ½- x ¾-inch (1 x 2 cm) sticks

For the marinade

¼ cup (60 mL) soy sauce or tamari

2 tbsp (30 mL) water

4 tsp (20 mL) sesame oil

4 cloves of garlic, minced

4 tsp (20 mL) minced fresh ginger

½ tsp (2 mL) chili paste (e.g., sambal oelek)

Method

Day before

1. Put the tofu in a bowl.

2. In a small bowl, whisk together the marinade ingredients. Pour over the tofu and gently mix together.

3. Cover and marinate in the fridge overnight.

To cook

4. Move the oven rack to the centre position. Preheat the oven to 375°F (190°C).

5. Line a baking sheet with parchment paper to prevent the tofu from sticking. Spread out the tofu. Cook in the oven for 30 minutes, turning halfway through.

From Marie-Thé to Marie Wang

Marie-Thérèse Wang was born in 1958 in Madagascar. She spent a lot of time in her parents' flower garden — it really belonged to her mother, who worked in it every morning. Marie-Thé, as she was affectionately called, particularly liked the loquat and its big yellow two-stoned fruit. To her tongue, it tastes somewhat like peach but is even sweeter. Later, much later, in a grocery store far from her native country, here in Canada, she would buy them and always find them too sour — just not as sweet as they were in her memory.

In the garden, there were also strawberries, and hens that produced nothing but an incredible racket. When she couldn't stand the noise any longer, Marie-Thé would race back inside the house. If she was lucky, it would be one of the rare days when her mother was making dessert. The room would be filled with the scents of baking, and the little girl would remember the beautifully soft custard tarts that, just the other day, had brightened up an otherwise dull afternoon. As always, she would notice how her mother approached her task, aiming for perfection rather than treating it as a banal household chore.

Sometimes, her father would take her and her brother into the big city. What a feast all day long! Restaurant for lunch, ice-cream kiosk, and even pizza for dinner. They generally ate so much during the day that they almost didn't have any room left for this dish, which was very rare in Madagascar. Marie-Thé loved those moments when she experienced the pleasure of discovering new flavours from previously unknown places for the first time.

Marie Wang is our father's sister, and hardly anyone still calls her Marie-Thé. She is the aunt who is always talking to us about food, who takes us to great restaurants, who pushes on us pastries that she has made or bought, who spends hours cooking delicious meals or fancy desserts, barely taking a minute to sit down and eat. It's hard to believe, but despite her passion for food, she confirms that she hasn't always had a passion for cooking. It was only after she got married that she became interested in the art of cooking, and she started phoning her mother to ask how to do this or that. And if our aunt loves sugar, she loves fried food with a pure, unconditional love, particularly sambos (*sambôsy* in Malagasy), a doughnut stuffed with a mix of ground meat, green onions, and curry powder, inspired by Indian samosas. We notice in Marie a trait that she herself noticed in her late mother — an intense curiosity that drives her to find the perfect recipe. These two women are models of perseverance in life in general as well as in the kitchen.

We can confirm without a doubt that Aunt Marie is one of the women who has passed down to us the love of discovering and cooking new flavours. Even today she is very involved in our lives, as well as being a retiree who is very involved in her community. Her willingness to participate in her nieces' book project led her to share a few of her delicious recipes.

GAI LAN

芥
蘭

GAI LAN

Also known as: Chinese broccoli
芥蘭 / 芥兰 gaai3 laan2/jièlán (mustard | ?)
In Mandarin also called: 芥藍 / 芥蓝 jièlán (mustard | ?)

FAMILY: Brassicaceae

SPECIES: *Brassica oleracea* var. *alboglabra*

HISTORY Introduced in China a long time ago, gai lan probably came from the Mediterranean, where the much better known broccoli has been grown since antiquity. Gai lan probably has a common ancestor with broccoli.

Gai lan, better known as Chinese broccoli, is another great staple of Chinese cooking. It's what you find in dim sum restaurants, served with oyster sauce. Just like broccoli, it is crunchy and has elegant floral buds, but it is sweeter, and its juicy young stem does not need to be peeled. Gai lan is growing in popularity, but while we wait for it to be more widely available in stores, why not dedicate a spot to it in your garden or in a pot on your deck? You will appreciate its productivity as well as its resistance to insects, cold, and heat.

A variety of broccoli resembling rapini and choy sum, gai lan has a delicate broccoli flavour. Its flowering stems are harvested just before its small yellow or white flowers appear. Its wide, thick leaves are fleshy and turn a beautiful deep green when cooked. One gai lan plant can grow up to 17.5 inches (45 cm) tall and just as wide, depending on the cultivar and the spacing between plants.

In the garden

• Growing gai lan is similar to growing choy sum — but even easier because it is less prone to flea beetle and aphid attacks.

• Although it is possible to harvest gai lan throughout the season, at Le Rizen we opt for two successive sowings in early spring and two successive sowings in fall to obtain the best results.

• At Le Rizen we love the Green Pearl cultivar, whose first flowering stems are often ready to harvest 55 to 70 days after the date of indoor sowing. The harvests can then take place for 30 to 80 days, depending on the temperature and your patience for harvesting the thinnest stems as time goes by.

• Gai lan is an excellent alternative to broccoli grown in pots. It takes up less space, is ready more quickly, and is productive over a longer period of time.

• You can harvest the young plants whole or use the flowering-stem technique (see "Harvesting techniques" on page 194), just as you do with choy sum. The big difference is that with gai lan, you always harvest the flowering stem before the flowers open.

STORING
Gai lan keeps for a few days in a sealed plastic bag or container in the fridge, or for 10 to 14 days after harvest in optimal conditions.

PREPARING
Gai lan is prepared and used just like broccoli. Rinse it, and then cut off the base of the stems if dry. Peel the stems if the skin is tough. Use whole or cut the stems into 3- to 4-inch (7 to 10 cm) strips or slice them diagonally. The thicker stems can be cut in half lengthways to speed up cooking.

NUTRITION
Gai lan is an excellent source of vitamin K and a good source of folate. It's also a source of fibre, calcium, vitamin A, vitamin C, and riboflavin. Riboflavin (vitamin B2) helps the body produce energy from the nutrients found in the foods we eat.

IN THE KITCHEN

Edible parts	Ways to eat	Ways to cook
• Leaves	• Raw	• Steam
• Stems	• Cooked	• Boil
• Flowering stems	• Pickled/ lacto-fermented	• Sauté/stir-fry
• Flowers	• Dried	• Roast/grill
		• Deep-fry

Gai lan is cooked the same way as choy sum, which it can easily replace in recipes. It can also replace several other green vegetables, including broccoli (just take care to adjust the cooking time depending on the size of the vegetable). Gai lan goes well with garlic, ginger, chili, Asian sauces, and lemon juice.

RAW
• Sprouted seeds, shoots, flowering stems, and flowers add crunch and character to salads.

• You can also blanch gai lan before adding it to salads.

• Just as you do for kale, you can soften gai lan by hand-massaging it with lemon juice.

COOKED
Like choy sum, gai lan is especially delicious cooked. Its flavour when cooked is sweeter and its colour brighter. Cook it for just a few minutes to keep the stems' crunchy texture.

Our favourite ways to prepare gai lan:
• Traditionally, gai lan is briefly boiled whole until tender (1 to 2 minutes), and then served with oyster sauce and fried garlic.

• Steam, roast, or grill on the barbecue. You will find our favourite gai lan seasoning in the Grilled Gai Lan recipe (see page 143).

• It is really good sautéed on its own with ginger or with other vegetables, noodles, shrimp, chicken, or meat. Stir-fried with thin strips of beef, it's a great option for replacing the broccoli in beloved beef and broccoli stir-fry. When you sauté it, you can add a little water or light rice cooking wine for aroma and to help cook the stems before adding the leaves.

Uncle Jean's tip

To bring out the flavour of gai lan even more when stir-frying, our uncle suggests adding stock and cognac or sugar. "When you stir-fry gai lan, put some stock on top, put the lid on, bring it back to a boil, and there you have it!"

Grilled gai lan

By Stéphanie

With its fleshy stems, gai lan is great for grilling. In addition, oiled and grilled gai lan leaves are reminiscent of the famous fried spinach leaves served at the Chinese buffets we loved so much when we were young. It's the ideal recipe for a summer potluck because you can prepare the sauce in advance and then just put the oiled gai lan in a large bowl. When you arrive, simply grill it, pour over the sauce, and enjoy in good company.

Preparation 5 min • Cooking 4 to 6 min • 2 servings

INGREDIENTS

1 bunch of gai lan (7 oz/200 g)
1 tbsp (15 mL) canola oil
1 tsp (5 mL) sesame oil
1 tbsp (15 mL) soy sauce or tamari
1 tbsp (15 mL) pure maple syrup

METHOD

1. Preheat the barbecue to 300°F (150°C).

2. Place the gai lan in a large bowl. Drizzle with the canola oil and use your hands to make sure all of the leaves are well coated.

3. Place the prepared gai lan on the upper rack of the barbecue and cook for 2 minutes. Turn over and cook for another 2 to 3 minutes, or until the stems are tender but still a little crunchy and the leaves are crispy without being burnt.

4. Using tongs, transfer the gai lan back to the bowl. Drizzle with the sesame oil, soy sauce, and maple syrup. Using tongs, mix well.

5. Enjoy hot, with fingers or chopsticks.

NOTES AND VARIATIONS

You can replace the gai lan with choy sum, celtuce, broccoli, or any other vegetable that lends itself to grilling.

Lightly braised gai lan with miso and pancetta

By Dana Cooper

芥
蘭

Ever since she discovered gai lan, Dana has been cooking it this way. She makes her own pancetta, an Italian charcuterie meat, from local Berkshire pig pork belly that she seasons and marinates for 10 days, then dries for a month. The marriage of pancetta with gai lan and miso is absolutely perfect. In addition, the technique Dana uses to braise the gai lan is quick and easy. Stéphanie, who has been hearing Dana sing the praises of this recipe for years, can now testify: it truly is an irresistible dish.

Preparation 5 min · Cooking 10 min · 4 servings

INGREDIENTS

2 bunches of gai lan (14 oz/400 g)
¼ cup (60 mL) pancetta, cut into small pieces (¼ x ¾ inch/0.5 x 2 cm)
⅓ cup (75 mL) water
4 tsp (20 mL) white miso paste
1 tbsp (15 mL) unsalted butter (optional)

METHOD

1. In a frying pan over medium-low heat, cook the pancetta for about 3 minutes to render the fat. Add the gai lan and stir until well coated in fat.

2. Add the water to the pan. Cover with the lid and cook for 3 to 4 minutes, or until the gai lan is tender.

3. Remove the lid. Gently stir the miso into the liquid at the bottom of the pan (if there is no liquid left, add a little water). Gently stir the gai lan until coated in sauce. For a slightly silkier sauce, stir in the butter (if using).

NOTES AND VARIATIONS

· You can replace the gai lan with choy sum, bok choy, Swiss chard, or any other green.

· For a different flavour, add minced garlic in step 1, taking care not to burn it.

· Dana uses pancetta because she loves the crispness and the umami, but you can substitute bacon or a combination of smoked tofu and minced garlic.

Dana Cooper
Fraîche!

Dana Cooper is a foodie who is as committed to her community of Sutton in the Eastern Townships as she is to her business, Fraîche! The latter shares local products and her cosmopolitan cooking knowledge. She loves discovering flavourful vegetables from other parts of the world, and Le Rizen has introduced her to several. She is delighted to share a few recipes she has developed based on these discoveries.

Gai lan with sizzling oil (*Biang biang gai lan*)

By Félix Antoine Parenteau

芥蘭

This recipe is inspired by a famous noodle dish from northwest China: *biang biang mian*. Replacing the noodles with gai lan makes for a lighter yet still flavourful dish. This dish requires an interesting technique: sizzling oil. The oil is heated to a high temperature, and then poured over the aromatics right on the serving plate.

Preparation 10 min • Cooking 20 min • 2 servings •

INGREDIENTS

1 bunch of gai lan (5.5 oz/160 g)
Salt, for blanching
⅓ cup (75 mL) canola oil

For the aromatics
1 tsp (5 mL) Korean chili flakes (*gochugaru*)
1 tsp (5 mL) puréed garlic (use a Microplane)
1 tbsp (15 mL) green onion, green part only, finely sliced

For the aromatic soy sauce
6 tbsp (75 mL) soy sauce or tamari
2 tbsp (30 mL) granulated sugar
1 tbsp (15 mL) black rice vinegar
1 dried bay leaf
1 whole star anise
1 thick slice fresh ginger (0.5 oz/10 g)
1 green onion, white part only

METHOD

1. In a small saucepan, stir together all of the ingredients for the aromatic soy sauce. Bring to a boil, reduce the heat, and simmer gently for 10 minutes, or until the sauce is syrupy and reduced by a half. Strain through a fine-mesh sieve and transfer to a sealed container.

2. Blanch the gai lan by plunging it first into salted boiling water for 1 minute and then into a bowl of ice-cold water.

3. Once the gai lan is cool, remove it from the ice bath and, using your hands, wring it gently to remove as much water as possible. Using a knife, cut the thickest stems lengthways.

4. Lay the gai lan on a plate. Pour over 2 tbsp (30 mL) of the aromatic soy sauce. Sprinkle with the chili flakes, garlic, and green onion.

5. In a small saucepan, heat the oil until it reaches 400°F (200°C) or starts smoking. Very carefully, taking care not to splash, pour the very hot oil over the aromatics on the plate.

6. Serve immediately.

NOTES AND VARIATIONS

• You can switch out the gai lan for asparagus, green beans, choy sum, or bok choy. Black rice vinegar can be replaced by balsamic vinegar. Korean chili can be replaced by any other chili that is flavourful and not overly hot, such as Aleppo or Espelette pepper.

• You won't need all the aromatic soy sauce. Any left over will keep for a long time in the fridge. It's delicious with dumplings, wontons, or over a simple bowl of rice.

Félix Antoine Parenteau
Sauce Prune

Chef and owner of Sauce Prune, an Asian grocery store as well as a counter selling prepared meals in Cowansville, Quebec, the self-taught Félix Antoine is devoted to Asian cuisine. To him, Le Rizen's vegetables are a canvas on which he explores tastes and textures, allowing him to help people in the Eastern Townships discover Chinese gastronomy even while using local ingredients.

MUSTARD GREENS

芥
菜

MUSTARD GREENS

Also known as: Chinese mustard, Indian mustard, leaf mustard, mustard cabbage
芥菜 gaai3 coi3/jiècài (mustard | vegetable)

FAMILY: Brassicaceae

SPECIES: The term "mustard greens" usually refers to different varieties of the species *Brassica juncea* (the best known being brown mustard, also known as Chinese mustard or gai choy) and, more broadly, to a group of leafy vegetables with a spicier flavour, such as mizuna (*Brassica rapa* subspecies *nipposinica*) or Tokyo Bekana (*Brassica rapa* subspecies *chinensis*).

HISTORY Popular in Asia, especially in China, Japan, and Korea, mustard greens are also eaten in Africa, Italy, and the southern United States, especially in African-American cuisine. Originally from the Himalayas in Central Asia, this vegetable spread across China, India, and the Caucasus. Brown mustard is the most commonly grown variety, for its seeds as much as for its leaves. It could be a cross between a variety of cabbage (*Brassica rapa*) and black mustard (*Brassica nigra*).

Best known for its seeds, which make the famous condiment, mustard is also eaten as a vegetable in many parts of the world. Its leaves have an amazing variety of shapes, colours, and piquancy, ranging from a gentle mustard flavour to the heat of wasabi. Ideal for adding some zing to salads and stir-fries, the leaves also make great pestos. You can find the young leaves in various mesclun mixes, and the mature leaves are sold in Asian grocery stores.

IN THE SAME FAMILY: **MIZUNA**
Also known as: mizuna greens, mizuna mustard
水菜 seoi2 coi3/shuǐcài (water | vegetable)

Mizuna is considered a Japanese vegetable even though it probably originated in China. It is found in Japanese cooking, including in salads and garnishes. It's used for its slightly spicy flavour, which is reminiscent of arugula without being too strong, and its pretty leaves, which are vivid green, very fine, and laced at the edges. Its slender stems are juicy, which probably explains its Chinese name.

IN THE SAME FAMILY: **TOKYO BEKANA**
Tokyo Bekana is in the same subspecies as bok choy. Its large pale green leaves are slightly curly, and its white stems, thinner than bok choy stems, are crunchy and juicy. Its flavour is mild and peppery, while its leaves are very tender.

Mustard leaves can have a mild or strong flavour, combined with a slight bitterness. Their taste depends on the variety and other factors, such as stage of maturity and growing conditions. For example, the leaves are more tender and mild when they are harvested in spring or fall or when harvested young. Depending on the variety, the leaves are sometimes big or long, curly or lacy, green or purple, producing a fabulous mix of greenery. Some have a thick, wide stem, such as head mustard or dai gai choy, which literally means "big | mustard | vegetable" and is very commonly used in Chinese cuisine. We recommend trying a few kinds to find the ones you like best. Depending on the variety and the space they have, mustard greens can reach 17.5 inches (45 cm) in diameter if allowed to reach maturity.

In the garden

· In our experience at Le Rizen, mustard greens are one of the least attacked brassicas; we still keep them covered with a net at all times.

· As there are a large number of varieties of mustard greens, we suggest that you obtain a packet of mixed mustard seeds. At Le Rizen we grow a mix of spicy mustards, a mix of mild brassicas that includes mild mustards, and mizuna.

· Mustard greens grow very well in pots, window boxes, and garden beds. The greens benefit from semi-shade in full summer.

· The simplest and most productive harvesting technique is cutting the whole plant when it is mature. To produce attractive bunches or bouquets, you can pick some leaves individually by hand or use the cut-and-come-again harvesting technique, removing the leaf above the base of the stem to allow new leaves to grow. You can also leave some plants to flower, because the flowering stems are edible and add a nice crunch to dishes.

STORING
Keeps for a few days in a sealable plastic bag or container in the fridge, or from 10 to 14 days after harvest in optimal conditions.

PREPARING
Rinse, then use the leaves whole. You can also cut them into strips or chunks.

NUTRITION
Mustard leaves are an excellent source of vitamin K. They are also a good source of vitamin C as well as fibre, calcium, iron, magnesium, copper, vitamin A, and vitamin B6. They also contain glucosinolates, which could have a protective effect against certain types of cancer.

IN THE KITCHEN

Edible parts	Ways to eat	Ways to cook
• Leaves	• Raw	• Steam
• Stems	• Cooked	• Boil
• Flowering stems	• Pickled/ lacto-fermented	• Sauté/stir-fry
• Flowers	• Dried	• Roast/grill
• Seeds		• Deep-fry
• Roots		

Mustard greens are used in the same way as spinach and may be used as a substitute, adding a zesty note to your cooking. They go well with garlic, onion, ginger, Asian sauces, and pork. To soften the bitterness, add a sweet ingredient to the dressing or sauce.

RAW
· The leaves, flowering stems, shoots, and sprouted seeds are delicious in salads, sandwiches, and burgers. We enjoy eating the leaves in a sandwich with an over-easy egg, thin slices of cheese, and a little butter, or in a salad with a hardboiled egg and an acidic dressing.

· The leaves are excellent in pesto, especially mizuna leaves.

· The flowers also brighten up salads.

Mustard greens can be pickled or lacto-fermented, including the stems and roots. The varieties with fleshy stems and roots are often lacto-fermented (see page 317).

COOKED
· To soften the strong flavour, the leaves can be cooked or mashed with pulses or potatoes.

· Cook the leaves briefly (1 or 2 minutes) but avoid cooking in an aluminum or iron pot or they might turn black.

Our favourite ways to use mustard greens:
· Add at the end of cooking to soups, stews, and stir-fries; for example, a gingery bone broth with salmon and diced tofu.

· Stir-fry alone or with other vegetables, fish, chicken, or meat.

· Steam-cook, then flavour with sesame oil and soy sauce.

· Blanch, then incorporate into dishes like lasagne or a savoury pie.

· Dress in oil, salt, and pepper, then grill on the barbecue and season with lemon juice and red chili flakes.

The leaves and shoots can also be dried and later added to soups. The flower buds and the flowers can be cooked like the leaves. The seeds can be dry-roasted or fried with oil and used as a spice, particularly in Indian cooking.

Spicy mustard greens.

Mizuna.

Japanese sesame salad (*Goma-ae*)

By Rébecca Brilvicas-Pinsonnault

芥菜

Goma-ae is a side dish typical of traditional Japanese cooking, served with sushi or grilled fish or any other grilled meat or vegetable. Having a soft spot for mizuna and spicy mustard, Rébecca highlights these two ingredients in a simple recipe. It is delicious, and stands out for its beautiful presentation as well as for its characteristically Japanese simplicity.

Preparation 10 min · Cooking 5 to 10 min · Resting 5 to 10 min (or up to 24 hr) · 4 to 5 servings

INGREDIENTS

1 bunch of mizuna (10 oz/275 g)
1 bunch of spicy mustard (10 oz/275 g)
Salt, for blanching

For the dressing
¼ cup (60 mL) toasted sesame seeds
2 tbsp (30 mL) granulated sugar
¼ cup (60 mL) soy sauce or tamari

For the garnish
Toasted sesame seeds (optional)
Edible shoots or flowers (optional)

METHOD

1. Blanch the greens by plunging them first into salted boiling water for 2 minutes and then into a large bowl of ice water. Drain and press dry with a towel.

2. Roughly grind the sesame seeds. In a large bowl, whisk together the dressing ingredients. Add the greens, and toss until well coated. Let rest for 5 to 10 minutes (or up to 24 hours in the fridge).

3. Lay out the salad on a chopping board, with the leaves and stems parallel. Using your hands, press them together and make a cylinder about 3 inches (8 cm) wide. Cut it widthwise into 4 or 5 equal portions.

4. Serve as an appetizer or a side dish on individual plates, and garnish with the toasted sesame seeds and edible shoots or flowers.

NOTES AND VARIATIONS

You can replace the mizuna and the spicy mustard with any leafy green or vegetable of your choosing; for example, bok choy, tatsoi, choy sum, gai lan, or spinach. Classic vegetables such as julienned carrot and green or yellow beans can also be used (just skip step 3).

Rébecca Brilvicas-Pinsonnault

Cooking is a passion Rébecca has devoted herself to since she was very small. She was introduced to Japanese culture at a young age, and this became a source of inspiration to her, both in the kitchen and in visual arts. Based in Sutton, she joyfully supports Le Rizen, whose vegetables and other products inspire her magnificent creations.

Nabe with miso and butter

By Rébecca Brilvicas-Pinsonnault

芥菜

The word *nabemono*, or just *nabe*, means "pot-au-feu," and is a dish that is served during cold weather in Japanese households. There are as many kinds as there are regions in Japan, since the essence of nabe is using local, in-season products: root vegetables and fresh vegetables, stock made from local meat, miso, or even soy beverage. Some nabe contain only meat or fish, while others are vegetarian. This recipe is ideal for sampling several Asian vegetables at the same time. It's also the first meal Rébecca enjoyed with her hosts on her first trip to Japan. Connections formed around the donabe (the stewpot) and quickly turned into beautiful friendships. Without a doubt, there is something incredibly comforting and convivial in the act of gathering together around a table to share a gently bubbling dish.

Preparation 30 min • Cooking 30 min or longer • 6 to 8 servings

INGREDIENTS

For the homemade dashi (broth)
2 or 3 large chunks of kombu seaweed
3 tbsp (45 mL) bonito flakes (or 4 dried shiitake mushrooms)

For the stock
2½ tbsp (37 mL) red miso paste
2 tbsp (30 mL) white miso paste
¼ cup (60 mL) saké
2½ tbsp (37 mL) mirin
1 tbsp (15 mL) light soy sauce or ½ tbsp (7 mL) dark soy sauce
4 cups (1 L) homemade dashi (recipe follows; or instant dashi or stock of your choice)

For the nabe
2 medium potatoes, peeled and chopped into 1½-inch (4 cm) cubes
¼ or ½ Chinese cabbage, cut into wide 1½- to 2½-inch (4 to 6 cm) strips, the thinner part of the leaves separated from the thicker part
1 piece of daikon (4 to 6 inches/10 to 15 cm), thinly sliced
1 package (5 oz/150 g) of enoki mushrooms (or a large handful of the mushrooms of your choice), stems removed
1 small bouquet per person of mizuna and/or spicy mustard and/or edible chrysanthemum, chopped to lengths of 4 to 6 inches (10 to 15 cm)
3½ to 10½ oz (100 to 300 g) salmon fillet, skin removed and cut into large pieces
3½ to 10½ oz (100 to 300 g) pork belly, cut into ½-inch (1 cm) thick and 2-inch (5 cm) long slices
8 to 16 oz (225 to 454 g) medium-firm tofu, cut into large cubes or ¾- to 1¼-inch (2 to 3 cm) slices
2 tbsp (30 mL) butter, sliced

For the last course (*shime*)
Cooked Calrose rice
2 to 4 eggs, beaten
Or: cooked Asian noodles of your choice
Shichimi togarashi, to taste (optional)

METHOD

1. In a pot of boiling water, cook the potatoes until nearly tender. Set aside.

2. Meanwhile, pour 4 cups (1 L) of water into a saucepan. Add the kombu and let soak for 5 minutes. Place the pan of soaked kombu over medium heat, and heat the water until it bubbles without coming to a boil. Transfer the kombu to a plate, reserving the water. Add the bonito flakes to the hot water, and let simmer until the stock is fragrant.

3. In a bowl, combine all of the ingredients for the stock.

4. Prepare the ingredients for the stew and lay everything out in dishes on the table.

To serve

5. Set up an induction plate or portable stove in the centre of the table. Put a large pot on it, and turn to medium-high heat. Pour in the bowlful of stock ingredients.

6. When the stock starts to bubble, add the thicker parts of the cabbage and daikon, then cover. When the stock bubbles again, add the rest of the cabbage and the mushrooms. Cover and let simmer for a few minutes. Add the salmon, pork, and tofu. When they are cooked through, add the leafy greens and the butter, then turn off the heat.

7. Serve the ingredients for the nabe with the stock, and enjoy. Season with shichimi togarashi for a little spice.

8. When only stock (around ⅓) and a few ingredients are left, make the final course. Turn on the heat to medium. Add the cooked rice (two-thirds of the volume of the stock) and stir. Once the stock comes to a boil, gradually pour in the beaten eggs. Turn off the heat, cover, and let cook to the desired consistency. (In Japan, this dish is often called "Japanese risotto.") Alternatively, you could add Asian noodles and season to taste.

NOTES AND VARIATIONS

• The quantity and the type of ingredients for the nabe are simply suggestions. Give your imagination free rein and cook whatever is in the fridge. You can choose a combination of salmon, pork, and tofu, or just one of these items.

• For a vegan version, replace the butter with coconut cream or oil, and the eggs with scrambled soft tofu.

• For the potatoes, it is better to use a variety that keeps its shape during cooking; for example, Yukon Gold.

• Kombu seaweed is a large brown ribbon-shaped kelp with a salty, smoky flavour.

• Bonito flakes are dried, fermented smoked fish, with an umami and slightly salty taste. Like kombu, it's a basic ingredient for making dashi, a Japanese stock made from dried ingredients (seaweed, mushrooms, fish). The bonito flakes can be replaced with more kombu or dried mushrooms (shiitake, for example), or even left out altogether.

• Shichimi togarashi is a Japanese spice blend known for its citrusy flavour and a spicy taste that stays in your mouth for a long time. It can be replaced by dried ground chili or hot sauce.

EDIBLE CHRYSANTHEMUM

茼
蒿

EDIBLE CHRYSANTHEMUM

Also known as: chrysanthemum greens,
garland chrysanthemum, crown daisy
茼蒿 tung4 hou1/tónghāo (similar to | wild grass)
In Cantonese also called: 唐蒿 tong4 hou1 (? | wild grass)

FAMILY: Asteraceae

SPECIES: *Glebionis coronaria*
(or formerly *Chrysanthemum coronarium*)

HISTORY Originally from the Mediterranean region, edible chrysanthemum grows across Europe, Africa, and Asia. An ornamental plant in the West, it is eaten as a vegetable in Asia, including in China and Japan, and is a very popular leafy green in Japan.

Few people outside Asian communities know of the existence of this species of chrysanthemum whose leaves are commonly eaten. It has a unique floral flavour, reminiscent of the perfume of ornamental chrysanthemums, with just a hint of bitterness. Edible chrysanthemum is mainly found in Asian grocery stores. Several seed companies also offer organic varieties of this chrysanthemum. Try it out for yourself and see how easy it is to grow, whether in a window box or a garden.

Edible chrysanthemum is mainly cultivated for its beautiful lacy leaves, which taste somewhat similar to parsley or celery. Slightly bitter and tangy, its flavour is more pronounced when the leaves are mature or overcooked. You can also eat the crunchy and refreshing young stems, which are milder in flavour. Its pretty daisy-like flowers are perfect for garnishing meals or decorating your home.

In the garden

• The chrysanthemum is one of the easiest Asian vegetables to grow in the garden: it grows well and is usually not attacked by insects, nor is it susceptible to disease. Its only downside is that it bolts quickly in the summer, so grow it in the spring or fall only. You can also plant it in the garden or in a pot in a semi-shaded spot.

• The Garland variety is very popular, and usually the one we grow at Le Rizen. Tiger Ear is also an excellent choice.

• Chrysanthemum is harvested when it is 4 to 6 inches (10 to 15 cm) tall, and is cut whole from the base. The flowering-stem method (see "Harvesting techniques" on page 194) can also be used, but the new growth is generally not as tender and abundant as the first growth. Always harvest before the flower buds open — after this the stems become fibrous and the leaves too bitter.

STORING
Keeps for a few days in a sealed plastic bag or container in the fridge, or for 14 to 21 days after harvest in optimal conditions.

PREPARING
Remove the tough stems. Rinse and use the leaves and young stems, either whole or roughly chopped.

NUTRITION
Chrysanthemum leaves are a good source of manganese and folate. They are also a source of fibre, potassium, iron, copper, vitamin A, and B-group vitamins (thiamin, riboflavin, vitamin B6, and folate). Thiamin (vitamin B1) helps the body produce energy from carbohydrates, and prevents nerve and heart problems arising from a vitamin deficiency.

IN THE KITCHEN

Edible parts	Ways to eat	Ways to cook
• Leaves	• Raw	• Steam
• Young stems	• Cooked	• Boil
• Flowering stems	• Pickled/ lacto-fermented	• Sauté/stir-fry
• Petals	• Dried	• Roast/grill
		• Deep-fry

Chrysanthemum is cooked the same way as mustard greens or spinach. It goes well with garlic, sesame, rice vinegar, and soy sauce. To soften the bitterness, add honey or maple syrup.

RAW
• The shoots, leaves, young stems, and flowering stems are all excellent in salads, alone or mixed with other greens or vegetables. They can be mixed with tomatoes, bean sprouts, and crumbled tofu, or with a creamy Asian sesame dressing (see page 56).

• The flower petals can also be enjoyed, setting aside the bitter heart, and used to garnish soups, salads, and stir-fries. Dried petals can be rehydrated in warm water before use.

COOKED
A short cooking time will soften the bitterness of the leaves, while a longer cooking time will accentuate it. Cook for 1 minute maximum.

Our favourite ways to prepare it:
• The Japanese way: blanched and then marinated in a sauce (ohitashi) or a sesame-based dressing (goma-ae).

• The Chinese way: roughly chopped, then added to a chicken stock with slices of fresh ginger.

• Added at the end of any recipe, including soups, hot pots, stews, and vegetable, fish, poultry, or meat stir-fries.

• In stir-fries, the leaves and young stems go well with bamboo shoots, sugar snap peas, and bean sprouts, or with chicken or pork, then seasoned with sesame oil and soy sauce.

The dried leaves can be placed in the bottom of a bowl before adding a hot broth.

NOTE
Edible chrysanthemum is a different species from that found in the popular chrysanthemum tea served in Chinese restaurants. The chrysanthemum used for this infusion is the florist's chrysanthemum (*Chrysanthemum morifolium*), which is widely used in traditional Chinese medicine.

Chrysanthemum-stuffed crêpes (*Bings*)

By Anita Feng

蒿
蒿

In China, a *bing* is a stuffed crêpe often eaten for breakfast or grabbed on the go from a street vendor. It's usually filled with meat, but here Anita suggests an egg-based vegetarian version, which she discovered in a hotel in Chengdu, the capital of Sichuan province. According to her, this recipe deserves to be widely known and will earn many fans.

Preparation 50 min • Cooking 30 min • 8 servings

INGREDIENTS

Dough
2¼ cups (560 mL) all-purpose flour
    + extra to flour work surface
1 tsp (5 mL) granulated sugar
¾ tsp (3 mL) instant yeast
¾ cup (200 mL) warm water
1 tbsp (15 mL) canola oil + extra to cover
    and manipulate the dough

Chrysanthemum
1 lb (500 g) edible chrysanthemum, leaves and tender stems
¼ tsp (1 mL) baking soda

Filling
A little canola oil
4 medium eggs, beaten
2 tbsp (30 mL) soy sauce or tamari
1 tbsp (15 mL) oyster sauce
1 tbsp (15 mL) sesame oil
1 pinch of granulated sugar
1 pinch of salt

For cooking
2 tbsp (30 mL) canola oil

Sauce (optional)
Black rice vinegar
Chili oil

METHOD

For the dough

1. In a bowl, combine the flour, sugar, yeast, and water. Mix until the dough comes together, then add the oil and mix again. Using your hands, shape the dough into a ball and knead until smooth. Place it in the bowl and lightly drizzle with oil. Cover with a clean kitchen towel and set aside for 30 to 40 minutes to rest, or until the dough doubles in volume.

For the chrysanthemum

2. In a saucepan, boil just enough water to blanch the chrysanthemum. Stir in the baking soda, then plunge the chrysanthemum in the boiling water for about 30 seconds. Using a slotted spoon or colander, transfer the chrysanthemum to a bowl of ice water. Remove the leaves from the ice bath and, using your hands, squeeze dry.

3. Finely chop the chrysanthemum.

For the filling

4. In a frying pan, heat a little oil, and then scramble the eggs. Transfer to a large bowl.

5. Add the chopped chrysanthemum and the rest of the filling ingredients. Stir well, and then set aside.

For the buns

6. Flour a work surface and oil your hands to avoid the dough sticking to them. Roll the dough on the work surface to form a sausage shape, then divide it into eight equal pieces.

7. Knead each piece lightly to form a ball, and then flatten with a rolling pin to obtain a 6-inch (15 cm) disk.

8. For each disk, place about 3 oz (80 g) of stuffing in the middle. Fold the edges of the dough in, toward the centre, keeping the dough from touching the filling (otherwise sealing the crêpe will be difficult), and pinch and twist the edges in one direction to form a tight seal.

9. Place each crêpe seal-side down on a floured work surface, then flatten gently with a rolling pin or your hand until the crêpe is about 4 inches (10 cm) across or ¾ inch (2 cm) thick.

To cook

10. Heat the oil in a large frying pan over medium heat. Gently place 2 or 3 *bings* in the pan and cover. Brown for 5 to 6 minutes on each side. Repeat with the remaining *bings*, adding more oil to the pan as necessary.

For the sauce

11. If desired, serve with a sauce of equal parts black rice vinegar and chili oil.

NOTES AND VARIATIONS

· You can replace the chrysanthemum with napa cabbage, the eggs with scrambled tofu, and the oyster sauce with hoisin sauce.

· The addition of baking soda in the boiling water is a common practice in Chinese cooking. It helps to preserve the colour of the green vegetables. It also softens the texture, modifies the flavour, and increases vitamin loss. Its use is optional.

Anita Feng, J'ai Feng

Anita was born in Panama and grew up in the city of Guangzhou (also called Canton) until the age of ten. She dived headfirst into Chinese cooking when the restaurant her parents owned in Montreal found itself without a chef. In the kitchen, she found a medium for sharing and enjoying Chinese gastronomy and culture. Her journey inspired her to train in China, where she drew inspiration from regional culinary traditions. Once back in Montreal, she breathed new life into them with high-quality seasonal ingredients, including Asian vegetables from Le Rizen. The result is a very refined contemporary Chinese cuisine, skilfully marrying flavours and textures, and leaving your taste buds wanting more.

Maple-sautéed chrysanthemum

By Caroline

This recipe is the result of the same process that has produced many other stir-fries: improvisation with ingredients on hand and the inspiration of the moment. It was one of Caroline's first culinary experiments with this vegetable when she discovered it at Le Rizen. The tomato adds juice and freshness, while the maple syrup perfectly balances the chrysanthemum's slight bitterness. This dish goes well with grilled meat and rice (or other grain).

Preparation 10 min • Cooking 5 min • 3 to 4 servings

INGREDIENTS

1 bunch (11 oz/320 g) of fresh chrysanthemum

1 tbsp (15 mL) canola oil

1 yellow onion, cut into ¼-inch (5 mm) slices

1 clove of garlic, minced

1 tbsp (15 mL) minced fresh ginger
(a piece about ½ inch/1 cm thick)

1 diced tomato

2 tbsp (30 mL) pure maple syrup

For the sauce

1 tsp (5 mL) cooking liquor or light rice cooking wine

1 tsp (5 mL) rice vinegar

1 tsp (5 mL) sesame oil

½ tsp (2 mL) soy sauce or tamari

METHOD

1. Place the chrysanthemum on a chopping board. Cut the leaves into ½-inch (1 cm) wide strips, and the stems into ½-inch (1 cm) pieces. Separate leaves and stems.

2. In a small bowl, whisk together the ingredients for the sauce. Set aside.

3. In a large frying pan over medium-high, heat the oil. Add the onion, and cook for 2 minutes, until softened and slightly golden. Add the garlic and ginger, and cook for 15 seconds.

4. Add the stems, and sauté for 1 minute. Add the leaves, and cook, stirring, for 45 seconds, just until they wilt.

5. Add the maple syrup, and stir for 10 seconds. Add the tomato and the sauce, and stir for another 10 seconds.

6. Serve in a sharing plate.

NOTES AND VARIATIONS

• The chrysanthemum can be replaced with mizuna; reduce the amount of maple syrup by half.

• You can also swap out the rice vinegar for apple cider vinegar and the cooking liquor for vegetable stock.

Chrysanthemum pesto noodles with edamame

By Caroline and Patricia

Chrysanthemum is perfect in pesto, since it is not too bitter when raw and has generous foliage. With this recipe, our intention was to suggest an Asian version of pasta with pesto, and we think this is the perfect blend of flavours!

Preparation and cooking 35 min · Makes 4 servings or 1 cup (250 mL) pesto

INGREDIENTS

2 cups (500 mL) shelled frozen edamame

9 oz (250 g) rice noodles (⅛ inch/3 mm wide)

For the pesto

9 cups (2.25 L) rinsed chrysanthemum leaves

1 to 2 cloves of garlic, minced

1½ tbsp (22 mL) minced fresh ginger
(a piece about ⅔ inch/1.5 cm thick)

2 tbsp (30 mL) toasted sesame seeds

1½ tbsp (22 mL) rice vinegar

1 tsp (5 mL) soy sauce or tamari

½ tsp (2 mL) fresh lime juice

½ tsp (2 mL) pure maple syrup

⅓ cup (75 mL) canola oil

Freshly ground black pepper, to taste

METHOD

1. Put the edamame in a pot with 4 cups (1 L) water. Bring to a boil, reduce the heat, and simmer for 5 to 7 minutes, or until the edamame are tender. Drain, then set aside in the pot.

2. In a large pot, bring 10 cups (2.5 L) of water to a boil. Add the noodles and stir with chopsticks or tongs to separate. Simmer for 5 minutes, until the noodles are tender. Drain, then set aside in the large pot.

3. While the edamame and noodles are cooking, finely chop the chrysanthemum, garlic, and ginger. Put in a bowl, then add the sesame seeds, rice vinegar, soy sauce, lime juice, maple syrup, and a little black pepper. Mix with a fork. Gradually add the oil while stirring with the fork.

4. Add the pesto and the edamame to the noodles, then stir gently with a spatula or chopsticks.

5. Garnish with raw vegetables (quartered cherry tomatoes, grated carrot, finely sliced radish, etc.) or serve with raw vegetables on the side.

NOTES AND VARIATIONS

You can replace the chrysanthemum with mizuna and use a food processor to make the pesto.

It's never too late (to learn to cook)

Our father, Henri, is one of those people who never learned to cook as a teenager or young adult. The only thing his mother taught him was how to cook rice in the rice cooker! When our father arrived in Sherbrooke, alone, he was entirely reliant on the CEGEP cafeteria and then the university cafeteria. For a while, if the cafeteria was closed on the weekend, he would order a large pizza and divide it between Saturday's and Sunday's meals. When he became a father, he was responsible for getting groceries, making breakfast, and barbecuing, and our mother made lunches and dinners.

When our mother died, our father had to roll up his sleeves. He took some cooking classes at a community centre and quickly realized that there was nothing complicated about following a recipe. Our father had always loved stews, and this didn't change, even after his classes: minimal effort for satisfying and plentiful results. He even got innovative, making congee with pigs' feet in the slow cooker! He also makes excellent wok stir-fries with Asian vegetables from Le Rizen.

Today, he still cooks whenever we visit him, planning out menus for special occasions, learning from our aunt Dany how to cook Chinese dishes, and making sandwiches for the Saturday farmers' markets (where he religiously helps Stéphanie), and he remains attentive to our preferences and tips.

We are proud and moved to witness our father's incredible capacity to adapt, and to receive all the love he shows us in the form of delicious homemade meals.

CELTUCE

萵
筍

CELTUCE

Also known as: stem lettuce, asparagus lettuce, Chinese lettuce

萵筍 / 萵笋 wo1 seon2/wōsǔn (lettuce | bamboo shoot)

FAMILY: Asteraceae

SPECIES: *Lactuca sativa* var. *angustana*

HISTORY Originally from China, celtuce has been grown there, for its stem, for a long time. It would have been introduced into the United States at the end of the nineteenth century by missionaries returning from China. The English name celtuce was first used by a seed company in the States, possibly to refer to a lettuce with a crunch like celery.

Celtuce is another vegetable that is practically unknown outside Asian communities but that deserves a place in our cooking repertoire. Initially it grows like a lettuce, and then its stem starts lengthening and it starts to resemble a mini palm tree. Prized for its crunchy stem, it is perfect in crudités and practical for picnics and snacks on the go. It is mainly found in Asian grocery stores. The stem and leaves are usually sold separately, the leaves under the name AA choy or AA 菜 and the stem as wo sun or any of celtuce's other names.

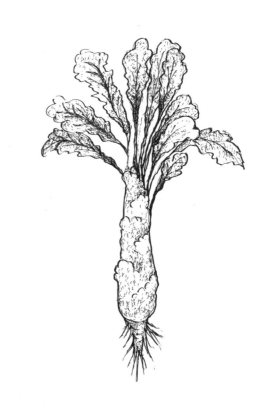

Although celtuce is actually a lettuce variety in the same family as Boston, leaf, and romaine, it is very different. In the garden, leaves look similar to romaine and grow along the length of the stem. In the grocery store, when the side leaves are removed, the long thick stem ends in a clump of leaves. Its green, translucent, crunchy yet tender stem has a mild flavour reminiscent of lettuce, celery, asparagus, cucumber, and walnut. The young leaves are sweet like lettuce. Although the leaves become bitter when they mature, they are still edible.

In the garden

· In the garden, celtuce is grown almost exactly the same way as lettuce. However, you do need to allow more space per plant, about 12 inches (30 cm), even in a pot.

· In the summer heat, several cultivars we have tried bolt before the stem is as thick or as long as you would find in an Asian grocery store. At Le Rizen, we have obtained the best results with the cultivar Spring Tower, which is sown in April and May.

· Choose a soil that retains humidity, and water regularly. Once the stem starts to grow, water more moderately to avoid splitting the stem.

· When you notice that several leaves have formed, and the stem is ¾ to 1¼ inch (2 to 3 cm) in diameter, you can harvest your first leaves from the base. This practice yields excellent soft, creamy salad leaves, and it also stimulates the plant's growth and the formation of a thick stem.

· To harvest the entire plant, wait until the stem has reached a diameter of ¾ to 2 inches (2 to 5 cm) and the plant measures 12 inches (30 cm) tall, then cut the stem as close as possible to the ground using a sharp knife. Celtuce must be harvested before the flowers open: the appearance of the buds is your last chance to harvest before the vegetable turns bitter.

STORING

Keeps for several days in a sealed plastic bag or container in the fridge, or for 10 to 14 days after harvest in optimal conditions.

Note: For improved storage of harvested celtuce, pluck the leaves off the stem, leaving the upper leaves attached.

PREPARING

Celtuce is prepared the same way as broccoli. Rinse the stem and leaves, then detach the leaves from the stem at the leaf base. Peel the stem if fibrous, then slice on the diagonal, julienne, or grate. To slice diagonally, cut the stem in two lengthways, then cut slices on the diagonal about 1⁄32 inch (2 mm) thick. Chop the leaves roughly.

Note: Young celtuce does not need peeling, but the stem becomes fibrous with age.

NUTRITION

Celtuce is a good source of manganese. It also contains vitamin A, vitamin C, and folate, a vitamin found in the form of folic acid in supplements, which is necessary for developing cells in the body and is particularly important during pregnancy for the growing fetus.

IN THE KITCHEN

Edible parts	Ways to eat	Ways to cook
● Leaves	● Raw	● Steam
● Stems	● Cooked	● Boil
	● Pickled/ lacto-fermented	● Sauté/stir-fry
		● Roast/grill
	● Dried	● Deep-fry

Celtuce is used the same way as celery. It goes well with garlic, chili pepper, lemon, and vinegar.

RAW

· The stem is delicious served raw or in salads, seasoned with a spicy dressing, while the young leaves can be served raw in salads.

· In China, the stem is often pickled (see the delectable recipe for Quick-Pickled Celtuce on page 183).

COOKED

Cook the stem the same way as asparagus. Cook for 3 to 4 minutes maximum so it is tender with a little crunch. In Sichuan, celtuce stem often replaces bamboo shoots.

Our favourite ways to prepare it:
· Roasted in the oven or on the barbecue, in batons marinated quickly in oil, soy sauce, vinegar, maple syrup, and ground Korean chili.

· Sliced diagonally then stir-fried in the wok with garlic.

· Julienned and stir-fried with julienned pork and wood ear mushrooms, and a garlic sauce — a traditional dish from Chengdu, the capital of Sichuan province.

Other ideas for cooking:
· Stir-fried alone or with other vegetables, fish, poultry, or pork with garlic, hot pepper, pepper, soy sauce, or oyster sauce.

· Blanched then served with a creamy sauce, or cooked au gratin, covered with sauce, breadcrumbs, or grated cheese.

· In China, it is also added to soups.

The leaves can be briefly stir-fried in the wok and are excellent added to soups at the end of cooking. You can also blanch them or steam-cook them, then season them with a sesame-based dressing (goma-ae).

Dungeness crab with celtuce, mint, goat yogurt, oxalis

By Jérémie Bastien

萵苣

Jérémie particularly likes the flavour and crunchy texture of celtuce. In this recipe, it adds a lot of freshness and goes very well with the delicate crab meat. The combination of goat yogurt, with its creamy texture and tart flavour, cucumber, and mint is reminiscent of Mediterranean cooking. This is a flavourful dish with the unique signature of the Monarque restaurant. Although it is possible to simplify this elaborate recipe, if you take on the challenge of cooking it, you will learn to master several techniques.

Day before: Preparation 2 min • Rest overnight

Same day: Preparation and cooking 1 hr 45 min • Rest 6 hr
4 servings

INGREDIENTS

1 celtuce stem
Salt, for blanching
7 oz (200 g) fresh Dungeness crab meat (or Nordic shrimp)
20 wood sorrel leaves (or sorrel)

Mint vinegar jelly

½ cup (125 mL) white balsamic vinegar
¼ bunch (0.5 oz/15 g) mint
¼ tsp (1 mL) granulated sugar
¼ tsp (1 mL) agar-agar

Cucumber jelly

6 tbsp + 2 tsp (100 mL) Asian cucumber juice
    (or other type of cucumber)
4 tsp (20 mL) white soy sauce
3 leaves of gelatin (or ½ tsp/2 mL powdered gelatin)

Seafood crackers

1 oz (25 g) raw shrimp meat
2 tbsp (30 mL) seafood stock
2 tbsp (30 mL) hot water
⅓ cup (75 mL) + ¼ cup (60 mL) tapioca flour
½ tsp (2 mL) salt
Vegetable oil, for frying

Mint oil

1 cup (250 mL) vegetable oil
2 bunches (4 oz/120 g) mint, leaves detached from stems

Whipped goat yogurt (optional)

2 cups (500 mL) goat yogurt
2 tbsp (30 mL) white balsamic vinegar
0.05 oz (1.5 g) xanthan gum
Salt, to taste

METHOD

For the mint vinegar jelly

The day before

1. Infuse the white balsamic vinegar with the mint overnight in the fridge.

The same day

2. Sieve the liquid in a saucepan to remove the mint, and then add the sugar.

3. Bring to a boil, and then sprinkle in the agar-agar.

4. Reduce the heat and cook for 2 minutes, until the agar-agar has dissolved.

5. Sieve again (optional) and pour into a sealable container.

6. Set in the fridge for 4 to 6 hours, then transfer to a blender and blend until it becomes a runny jelly.

For the cucumber jelly

7. Seed the cucumber to make a greener, tastier jelly, and then extract the juice with a juice extractor.

8. Season with the white soy sauce.

9. Heat some of the soy cucumber juice mixture and dissolve the gelatin in it, and then mix with the rest of the liquid. Pour into a sealable container and refrigerate until set (4 to 6 hours).

For the seafood crackers

10. Mix together the seafood stock, hot water, tapioca flour, and salt to form a paste.

11. Transfer this mixture to a food processor, add the shrimp meat, and blend until smooth.

12. Spread out into a ¾-inch (2 cm) thick layer between two sheets of parchment paper placed in a glass or stainless steel container around 5 inches (12 cm) across. Steam-cook at 195°F (90°C) (medium-low heat) for 45 minutes.

13. Chill for 15–30 minutes, and cut into julienne strips.

14. Place in a dehydrator or an oven preheated to 120°F (50°C) for 1 hour, or until you get a pliable plastic texture.

15. Deep-fry at 375°F (190°C) until puffed.

For the mint oil

16. Blanch the mint leaves and chill them in an ice bath.

17. Press the leaves firmly between your hands to extract as much water as possible.

18. Transfer to a blender, add the vegetable oil, and mix until smooth, and then pour through a coffee filter.

For the celtuce

19. Cut the celtuce stem into 1¼-inch (3 cm) strips and, using a cylindrical pastry cutter, shape the flesh into ½-inch (1 cm) diameter cylinders. Alternatively, peel the celtuce stem and shape lengthways to obtain narrow cylinders.

20. Transfer the celtuce cylinders to a saucepan of boiling salted water, and blanch for 1 minute. Transfer to an ice bath to stop the cooking process.

For the whipped goat yogurt

21. Whisk together the whipped goat yogurt ingredients in a bowl until the xanthan gum is well hydrated.

22. Transfer to a whipped cream dispenser with two N_2O cartridges to produce an aerated texture. →

To assemble

23. On each plate, assemble:

1.7 oz (50 g) crab meat

5 tsp (25 mL) cucumber jelly, to spread over the crab meat

5 pipette dots of mint vinegar jelly, to spread on the crab meat

3 cylinders of blanched celtuce

1 whirl (1 tbsp/15 mL) whipped goat yogurt

1 tsp (5 mL) mint oil

2 seafood crackers

5 wood sorrel leaves

NOTES AND VARIATIONS

· The celtuce can be replaced with Asian or English cucumber.

· The seafood crackers can be replaced with shop-bought prawn crackers. These chips are a snack we enjoy occasionally, to go with crispy skin chicken at Chinese restaurants.

· The whipped goat yogurt can be replaced with goat yogurt.

· The white soy sauce can be replaced with a smaller amount of regular soy sauce (the cucumber jelly will be darker).

· Jérémie uses creeping wood sorrel (*Oxalis corniculata*), whose leaves are purple and flowers yellow. This perennial plant, which grows very well in a pot, is known for its slightly sour leaves that taste like sorrel and are usually divided into three clover-like leaves. It can be replaced with sorrel.

Quick-pickled celtuce

By Anita Feng

萵筍

During her travels in Sichuan province in 2017, Anita had the experience of cooking celtuce in several ways. In this recipe, this undervalued vegetable, generally enjoyed in stir-fries, is quick pickled and spiced Sichuan-style. This easy and original recipe is ideal for brightening up salads or serving with noodles.

Preparation 10 min · Cooking 5 min · Resting 30 min + overnight Makes one 2 cup (500 mL) Mason jar · ❱❱

INGREDIENTS

1.8 lb (800 g) celtuce, peeled and cut into batons
Salt, to draw out the moisture

Marinade
2 cups (500 mL) water
1 cup (225 mL) white vinegar
3 tbsp (45 mL) soy sauce
2 tbsp (30 mL) granulated sugar
1 tsp (5 mL) salt
2 Thai (bird's-eye) chilis, sliced

METHOD

For the marinade
1. Combine the marinade ingredients in a saucepan and bring to a boil. Remove from the heat and place in the refrigerator to cool down.

To quick pickle
2. Put the celtuce into a bowl, and add a generous pinch of salt. Set aside for 30 minutes to let the salt draw out the moisture. Drain, and transfer the celtuce to a 2 cup (500 mL) Mason jar.

3. Pour the prepared marinade into the jar, cover with the lid, and refrigerate overnight. The pickled celtuce keeps in the fridge for up to a week.

NOTES AND VARIATIONS

· Instead of celtuce, you could use radish, daikon, or kohlrabi.

· For a less spicy version, you could reduce or omit the Thai chilis.

Celtuce leaf and dried cranberry salad

By Stéphanie

Preparation 10 min · 4 servings

INGREDIENTS

Leaves from 1 celtuce (5 to 10)
Leaves from ½ a Boston lettuce
2 small white turnips (or radishes)
Raw sunflower seeds, to taste
Dried unsweetened cranberries, to taste

For the dressing
¼ cup (60 mL) olive oil
4 tsp (20 mL) organic apple cider vinegar
2 tsp (10 mL) liquid honey
2 tsp (10 mL) grainy mustard
½ tsp (2 mL) ground turmeric
½ tsp (2 mL) ground ginger
Salt and pepper, to taste

METHOD

1. In a dry frying pan over medium heat, toast the sunflower seeds, stirring occasionally, until browned. Set aside.

2. In a small bowl, whisk together all of the ingredients for the dressing.

3. Rinse the celtuce and Boston lettuce leaves under cold running water, and then dry in a salad spinner or with a kitchen towel.

4. Cut the leaves into ½- to ¾-inch (1 to 2 cm) squares or into strips.

5. Cut the white turnips in half, and then into thin slices.

6. Divide the leaves, white turnips, sunflower seeds, and dried cranberries evenly between four plates. Drizzle with the dressing. Serve.

SUMMER

夏天

HARVEST TIME

In a market-garden season, harvest days are among the most important. Every minute and every action count to preserve the greatest freshness of the vegetables you have been taking care of since sowing the seeds. Although it is a stressful time, these days are extremely satisfying because this is the moment when you are literally harvesting the fruits of your labour.

THE GOLDEN RULE

The moment of harvest and the post-harvest operations (washing, packaging, storing, and transportation) are all determining factors in how long the vegetables will keep. First, harvest early in the day any greens that wilt quickly, then finish up with more resistant vegetables such as fruit vegetables and lemongrass, which can be harvested in the afternoon. In addition, for greens as well as other vegetables, the ideal is not to leave them out in the sun too long. As soon as possible, put the bins of harvested vegetables in the shade with a lid, so that the sun and wind cannot dry out the leaves, and then into a bath of ice water — except for fruit vegetables and lemongrass — and finally in the fridge.

BASIC EQUIPMENT AND INFRASTRUCTURE FOR HARVESTING
To harvest and store vegetables, we use plastic bins pierced with a hole in each corner of the bottom (use a drill and a ½-inch/1 cm diameter drill bit) to let any excess water drain off.

WASHING STATION
Set up the washing station somewhere covered or in the shade near your fridge or the cold room where you will store the vegetables. Here are the essentials:

- Tub or large rigid container supported on a wooden structure at an ergonomic height
- Drinking water
- Multipurpose table near the tub to sort and weigh the vegetables, hold the bins for the clean vegetables, and wrap the vegetables as required
- Hose for washing the bins
- Wooden pallets or low slatted table to dry the cleaned bins

BEST TIME OF DAY AND WEEK AT LE RIZEN FOR HARVESTING OUR FIFTEEN ASIAN VEGETABLES

	MONDAY	TUESDAY	WEDNESDAY	THURSDAY	FRIDAY
Morning	Choy sum Gai lan Asian cucumber		Bok choy Mustard greens Chrysanthemum Choy sum Gai lan Shiso Amaranth Celtuce Malabar spinach Asian cucumber	Chinese cabbage*	Choy sum Gai lan Asian cucumber
Afternoon**	Okra Asian eggplant Luffa		Okra Luffa Lemongrass		Okra Asian eggplant Luffa

Some vegetables absolutely must be harvested three times a week, while others can be harvested just once per week.

Harvest when mature, and as early as possible in the day.

** Harvest in the afternoon if you don't have time in the morning. The morning is always better.

HARVESTING TECHNIQUES

Generally speaking, Asian vegetables are harvested the same way as other vegetables. The big difference is that among these Asian vegetables, there is a very wide range of leafy greens. These can be harvested in several ways, but it is important to know that the technique you choose will have an impact on the quality and quantity of subsequent harvests.

Here we set out the four main harvesting techniques for the fifteen Asian vegetables presented in this book. We will help you understand which technique to choose.

AT WHAT STAGE SHOULD I HARVEST THE GREENS?

It is not always easy to spot the ideal moment to pick leafy greens, since they can be harvested at different stages, depending on preference.

Most often we find Asian vegetables in mesclun blends as baby leaves. They can also be harvested at the shoot or sprout stage.

At Le Rizen, we make the conscious decision to harvest leafy greens when they are mature or semi-mature, for two main reasons. First, we want to achieve each seed's full potential. Imagine a baby mizuna leaf beside a mature mizuna with multiple stems and weighing up to several kilos. It's incredible to think of the number of additional mouths you can feed by just waiting a few weeks for the plant to develop naturally.

Second, the great advantage of growing leaves until they are mature is that you can assemble them in beautiful bouquets, or bunches, and secure them with an elastic band. When using an elastic band, be sure to make just enough twists to hold the stems in place without cutting off the circulation in the stems, which damages them. This method allows the bunches to be handled easily, and allows us to sell them to our customers, chefs, and zero-waste grocery stores without any plastic packaging.

To make bunches of bok choy, tatsoi, and Malabar spinach, we surround the stems with a twist of biodegradable rubber bands size 32. To make bunches of the other vegetables, we tie their stems just below the leaves with two twists of elastic band size 18.

HARVESTING THE WHOLE PLANT

This is the basic technique for harvesting greens if you want to harvest only once when the plant is mature or semi-mature.

You can do this in two ways:

WITHOUT ROOTS

This technique is the simplest, cleanest, and easiest. Using a well-sharpened knife, cut at the lower stem, under the plant, where the roots and leaves meet.

TOOL: A large cabbage knife, which looks like a small machete with a diagonal pointed blade. This tool allows you to cut by pushing the oblique blade toward the vegetable rather than pulling. This makes harvesting easier.

VEGETABLES TO USE THIS TECHNIQUE ON: bok choy, Chinese cabbage, celtuce

Also possible for: choy sum, gai lan, mustard greens, chrysanthemum, amaranth, shiso

WITH ROOTS

With your hands positioned underneath the plant, lift gently to harvest with its roots. Shake off the excess soil, then wrap up the leaves with the clump of earth in a plastic bag. This technique will help keep the plant fresh longer.

TOOL: hands

Top: Harvesting a whole plant without roots.
Bottom: Harvesting a whole plant with roots.

FLOWERING STEM

This technique is a little more complex but has the advantage of yielding multiple harvests from the same plant. This is the main technique used to harvest choy sum and gai lan, which are grown specifically for their flowering stems.

The flowering stem is the part of the plant that has a stem, leaves, and a bud or flower. Did you know that the flowering stems of all edible brassicas are delicious? They are tender and sweet when young. As the flower develops and produces seeds, the stem becomes fibrous until eventually it is too tough to eat. Typically, you should harvest the stem when the flower is at the bud stage. The exception to the rule is choy sum, which is most enjoyed when its yellow flowers start to bloom, since it is particularly flavourful.

WHERE TO CUT?

For the first cut, trim the main flowering stem above the third or fourth true leaf above the base. Do not count the two fake leaves, or cotyledons,* situated at the very base of the plant, which fall off once the plant grows. You will notice that at every place where stem and leaf meet, there is a small shoot. Be careful not to tear it as you harvest, because you will lose a precious flowering stem you can harvest later.

For vegetables with a thick main stem, such as gai lan, it is advisable to use a knife for the first cut. The first stem is usually the thickest and firmest, so precise harvesting by hand is difficult and risks damaging regrowth if the cut is not made in the right spot. After this, the stems will be thinner, and it will be easier to harvest by hand.

To harvest by hand, hold the plant where the stem meets the leaf with one hand, to protect the future shoot that will regrow there. With the other hand, cut the flowering stem just above the junction. With time you will be able to do this movement with one hand by protecting the shoot between your third finger and your palm, and breaking off the flowering stem with your thumb and index finger.

Once the shoots left on the plants have become lateral stems, you can either harvest the lateral stem whole or cut it above the first leaf to produce another harvest on this lateral stem.

TOOLS: Hands, knife, or pruning shears

VEGETABLES TO USE THIS TECHNIQUE ON: choy sum (hands), gai lan (knife for the first cut, then hands), chrysanthemum (hands), amaranth (hands), Malabar spinach (pruning shears or knife), shiso (pruning shears)

NOTE

It's better to leave just two to four shoots on the plant. That will prevent the plant from becoming exhausted and will allow you to obtain a further reasonable harvest. In fact, if you leave too many shoots, the plant will tire itself out producing a lot of new stems; these will be thinner. On the other hand, if you don't leave enough shoots and leaves, the plant won't have enough energy to keep growing.

CUT-AND-COME-AGAIN

This technique is also applicable to leafy greens and consists of cutting the young or mature leaves while leaving the plant's heart in the middle intact. The cut-and-come-again technique consists of cutting almost the whole plant above its growth point — in other words, taking care to leave about 1¼ inch (3 cm) above the base of the plant and making sure to preserve the little leaves at its heart. These will grow again and the plant will regenerate, leading to a second and even third harvest. You can also cut mature bok choy and wait for it to fully grow back. This is the ideal technique if the number of plants is limited and you want to maximize each plant; for example, if growing in pots.

TOOL: A small serrated knife (e.g., a steak knife) or smooth knife (e.g., an Opinel knife) to make a nice sharp cut.

VEGETABLES TO USE THIS TECHNIQUE ON: mustard greens

Also possible for: bok choy, Chinese cabbage, chrysanthemum, amaranth

VARIATION

It is also possible to harvest the outer leaves as they reach the desired size, leaving the centre leaves, which will then become the outer leaves. This technique allows you to harvest a small number of greens every few days. However, you will obtain an abundant yield in this way only if you wait for the plant to reach maturity.

Top: Harvesting the floral stem.
Bottom: Cut-and-come-again technique.

PEDICEL CUTTING

Fruit vegetables need to be harvested with pruning shears. Cut at the pedicel (in other words, the part that links the fruit to its stem). You can also harvest with your hands, snapping where the pedicel is attached to the stem. When you harvest, it's important to handle the fruit delicately so as not to damage it; if you do, it will not keep for as long. Avoid picking Asian cucumbers when the plants are wet (from rain or watering); the presence of water while you are handling the plants can encourage the development of bacterial disease.

TOOL: Pruning shears, hands

VEGETABLES TO USE THIS TECHNIQUE ON: okra, Asian eggplant, Asian cucumber, luffa

WHAT ABOUT LEMONGRASS?

Harvest lemongrass by pulling on each stalk just above the root, or with the root. Refer to the lemongrass section below for more details.

Consider wearing gloves when handling okra, Asian eggplant, and Asian cucumber, which can all prick; lemongrass can cut skin.

PRESERVING VEGETABLE FRESHNESS

To fully enjoy fresh vegetables and reduce food waste, we encourage you to use the optimal storage technique for each vegetable. In this way, you will fully honour your work and that of everyone who took care of the vegetables from seed to harvest.

FOR LEAFY GREENS
Bok choy, choy sum, gai lan, mustard greens, Chinese cabbage, edible chrysanthemum, celtuce, amaranth, Malabar spinach, shiso

To ensure optimal storage of the leafy greens, it is important to make sure they are moist before putting them in the fridge or the cold room.

Greens harvested in cold or rainy weather are beautifully crunchy and can be stored in the cold immediately. On the other hand, if they are harvested in warm weather, the leaves tend to soften. They can also wilt on the way home from the market or the grocery store, especially if bought without packaging. In this situation, revive them in cold water, a simple and proven method that will ensure the leafy greens last a long time.

To do this, fill a large bowl with very cold water and submerge the leafy greens for a few minutes. Then shake them off over the sink and put them in a sealable container lined with a kitchen towel or paper towel. It's important to seal the container with a lid since the fridge will quickly dry out vegetables exposed to the air, even in the vegetable crisper. Brown paper bags are not the best for storage because they absorb the leaves' moisture, which causes them to wilt more quickly.

On the farm, we plunge our leafy-green bouquets in cold water, head down in the bath, then gently swish them around, holding them by their elastic band. Moving them in the water allows you to wash away any soil residue as well as any insects lodged between the leaves. Then we just shake the greens over the bath to remove the excess water, keeping some water droplets on the leaves for storage. We place them in lidded plastic bins with holes in the bottom so that the excess water can drain away.

LABEL WELL TO AVOID PROBLEMS

Before placing the bins or bags of vegetables in cold storage, we label them with the vegetable code and the harvest date, using masking tape and a permanent marker, or even chalk marker, to write directly on the bin.

PERFECT TEMPERATURE

Place a thermometer in your fridge or cold room. It should always show a temperature of between 32° and 39°F (0° and 4°C), ideally between 32° and 34°F (0° and 1°C). If stored like this from the moment they are picked, the greens will usually stay nice and crisp for 10 to 14 days. Although the literature suggests storing shiso at a temperature of 50°F (10°C), we have always washed and stored it in the cold room like the other leafy greens and have excellent results storing it for 14 days without any trouble.

FOR FRUIT VEGETABLES
Okra, eggplant, cucumber, luffa

It is not necessary to rinse fruit vegetables before storing them in the fridge. However, Asian eggplant and Asian cucumber can be soaked in cold water if soft or if harvested in warm weather.

Wrap the fruit vegetables in a kitchen towel or paper towel before storing them in a bag or sealable plastic bin. This stops condensation from dripping onto the skin, which will make them deteriorate more quickly.

Fruit vegetables keep best at warmer temperatures, between 44° and 55°F (7° and 13°C) (see "Preserving" on page 345 to find out the exact temperatures for each vegetable). At this temperature, okra will keep for 5 to 10 days after harvest, eggplant for 7 to 10 days, cucumber for 10 to 14 days, and luffa for 7 to 14 days.

If you do not have a cold room at these temperatures, don't worry: fruit vegetables will keep for several days even in the fridge or in a cool room. You can place a thick cover, such as a sleeping bag, over the plastic bin or a towel on the bag to help keep them warm by a few extra degrees.

LEMONGRASS

Lemongrass keeps between 10 and 14 days from harvest at an optimal temperature of 35° to 42°F (2° to 6°C) in a sealable bin or bag placed in the fridge or a cold room.

Top: Pedicel cutting.
Bottom: Harvesting lemongrass.

THE PARTICULARITIES OF HEAT-LOVING VEGETABLES

Thanks to the climate in southern Quebec, we can—with the help of some basic equipment—grow vegetables that are usually found in tropical regions: fruit vegetables (okra, Asian eggplant, Asian cucumber, luffa), leafy greens (amaranth, Malabar spinach, shiso), and aromatics (lemongrass).

HEAVY FEEDERS

VEGETABLES: okra, Asian eggplant, cucumber, luffa, lemongrass

Because of our cold season, and given that these vegetables don't survive when the mercury drops below freezing, we grow these plants as annuals.

We categorize them as demanding because they have high nutrition needs, and it is only after having absorbed a lot of nutrients from water and the soil that the plants will produce fruit at the end of their life cycle. This means that you will need to adequately fertilize these crops when you plant them, and irrigate them regularly. These plants also benefit from high sun exposure to maximize the potential for photosynthesis and avoid the diseases that develop if the leaves are wet too frequently. By doing this, Le Rizen has obtained excellent yields of these fruit vegetables and herbs out in the field. They are very heat-loving and will be even more productive if grown under a caterpillar tunnel or in a greenhouse.

TOLERANT LEAFY GREENS

Several Asian vegetables such as amaranth, Malabar spinach, and shiso tolerate heat well and are also not very susceptible to insect attacks. At Le Rizen, two successive sowings of Malabar spinach at the beginning of the season and three of amaranth and shiso spread across the season give us enough to harvest every week from June to September. These greens are less likely to flower prematurely and are slower to wilt in the sun's heat than the greens that prefer cooler temperatures. By growing these summer greens we can increase the number of greens to enjoy during the warmer season.

A LITTLE HELP EARLY AND LATE IN THE SEASON

From the end of May to early June, when all risk of frost has passed, we plant out the heat-loving vegetables in the field and systematically set up the floating row covers. At the end of the summer, we also cover the final sowing of amaranth, Malabar spinach, and shiso. To learn more about floating row covers, see "Planting out" on page 94.

CONSERVING HEAT AND SOIL MOISTURE

For vegetables that spend a long time in the garden, such as Malabar spinach, okra, eggplant, cucumber, luffa, and lemongrass, it is recommended to install a geotextile (a porous covering of woven plastic that allows rain through) or black plastic over the growing surface, and to cut a hole in the material where you want to insert the plants. The black colour allows more warmth to accumulate around the tropical plants, which need as much heat as possible to produce decent yields. In your backyard, rocks can even be placed around the plants, which benefit from the heat the rocks absorb during the day. You can also mulch with straw or other materials to retain moisture in the soil and prevent weeds from competing with the plants.

Right: Asian eggplant.
Next page left: Okra.
Next page right: Asian cucumbers.

Asian cucumber plants.

AMARANTH

莧
菜

AMARANTH

Also known as: Chinese spinach
莧菜 / 苋菜 jin6 coi3/xiàncài (amaranth | vegetable)

FAMILY: Amaranthaceae

SPECIES: There are several species; the ones eaten most often are *Amaranthus tricolor*, *Amaranthus cruentus* (red amaranth), and *Amaranthus blitum* (purple amaranth)

HISTORY Originally from tropical regions of America, Africa, and Asia, amaranth is now found all over the world. Its seeds are eaten as a cereal, which was a staple food for pre-Columbian peoples, while its leaves are enjoyed as a vegetable, especially in Asian, African, and Antillean cuisines.

Amaranth, well known in the garden as an ornamental plant or a weed, is much less well known as a food, whether in its cereal or vegetable form. However, amaranth grown for its leaves is a great substitute for spinach, which cannot tolerate the summer heat. Very popular in Asia, amaranth is cooked in the same way as spinach; it is usually preferred cooked or lacto-fermented so that its leaves are silkier. You can find it in Asian or African grocery stores.

Although the leaves of all species of amaranth are edible, some are grown specifically for their leaves. These are better for eating as a vegetable. Depending on the species, the leaves are green, purple, or a combination of green and purple. Their flavour is reminiscent of spinach or Swiss chard, and can be stronger depending on the variety and the stage of development. The young juicy stems have an asparagus-like flavour.

In the garden

· Amaranth is a very hardy plant that grows really well in the garden. It is not usually attacked by insects, although it can be vulnerable to large flea beetles when the weather is very hot and dry.

· It likes a light, sandy fertile soil but will nevertheless tolerate a more clay, slightly acidic soil. Once planted, it can tolerate heat and drought well. Caution: over-fertilizing makes the leaves tough.

· Seed companies offer several species of amaranth, which can be found in the vegetable or ornamental sections of their catalogues. Choose a cultivar for its leaves. We like the Red Leaf cultivar (*Amaranthus tricolor*) for the beauty of its purple and green leaves.

· Amaranth can also be grown in a pot. Since it has long roots, it's best to use a container 6 to 12 inches (15 to 30 cm) deep.

· At Le Rizen, we harvest amaranth by hand using the flowering-stem technique once it has grown to a height of 8 to 12 inches (20 to 30 cm), always before the flower buds appear. For the first harvest, we prefer to cut only the main stem, leaving the lower two or three leaves. From each leaf that we leave, secondary stems will grow.

· This way, you can harvest amaranth over 3 to 5 consecutive weeks before the plants flower and the stems become too fibrous. Using the cut-and-come-again technique, you can also cut it off completely 1¼ inches (3 cm) above the base, and then let it grow again.

· Once harvested and washed, amaranth keeps very well and doesn't wilt much in the sun, hence its Greek name *amarantos*, which means "which does not wilt."

· If you allow amaranth to flower and spread its seeds over the soil, it will naturally reseed itself the next season. To prevent it from becoming invasive, cut the plants before the flowers turn brown and dry.

STORING
Keeps for a few days in a sealed plastic bag or container in the fridge, or for 10 to 14 days after harvest in optimal conditions.

PREPARING
Rinse the leaves and stems. Mature or thick stems can be tough: remove them, peel, or trim off about ¾ inch (2 cm) at the end. Then cut the stem into 2-inch (5 cm) sticks, and cook the stems before the leaves. The latter can be used whole, cut, or chopped.

IN THE KITCHEN

Edible parts	Ways to eat	Ways to cook
• Leaves	• Raw	• Steam
• Stems	• Cooked	• Boil
• Seeds	• Pickled/ lacto-fermented	• Sauté/stir-fry
	• Dried	• Roast/grill
		• Deep-fry

Amaranth can be used like spinach, which it can also replace. It goes well with garlic, ginger, and lemon.

RAW
· The sprouted seeds and the young leaves can be added to salads, and the young shoots, often purple, add colour to mesclun.

· To soften the leaves, massage with lemon juice or oil the same way you would for kale. In Taiwan, the leaves are often rubbed to soften them.

COOKED
Amaranth is often cooked, as it becomes much more tender. It cooks quickly; just a few minutes is enough.

Our favourite ways to prepare it:
· Added at the end of cooking, in soups and stews, such as a clear broth, a congee, or a curry.

· Steam-cooked, or braised in its own juice (without adding any liquid), then seasoned with a sauce made from sesame oil, soy sauce, and rice vinegar.

· Browned in a little oil, then drizzled with lemon juice, or sautéed in a wok with Chinese chives or garlic.

· Another idea is to stir-fry ginger and garlic in a wok, add amaranth, salt, and pepper, and cook, covered, for 3 to 4 minutes over low heat, then drizzle with a little sesame oil.

These cooking methods are popular in Chinese and Asian cooking, but it is also possible to cook amaranth in other ways. A popular dish in Antillean cooking is callaloo, in which roughly chopped amaranth is stewed for 5 to 10 minutes with other ingredients such as tomatoes, onions, and chilis.

As for the seeds, pop them like popcorn or cook them like a grain.

Note: The purple leaves will colour any dish, such as white sauces, congee, or clear broths.

NUTRITION Amaranth leaves are an excellent source of vitamin K, a good source of manganese, and a source of several other vitamins (vitamin A, vitamin C, riboflavin, vitamin B6, folate) and minerals (potassium, calcium, iron, magnesium, zinc, copper). They contain as much iron as spinach. Copper aids in the formation of red blood cells and protects the body against damage caused by oxidation.

Soups and fruits

When we were children, dinners were made according to a very Cantonese plan: soup as a starter, a main course, at least one side vegetable, and fruit for dessert. After all, this is the same thing our parents experienced in Madagascar.

Our mother always made vegetable soup. Most of the time, it was a broth comprising a leafy green, sliced carrots, and diced potatoes. Soup is an important part of Chinese cooking; in Guangdong province, it is often clear like our mother's, almost like stock. Although it is eaten at the end of a meal in the majority of regions in China, Cantonese families prefer it at the beginning, and sometimes eat it again at the very end.

At our house, cooked desserts were usually reserved for special occasions such as birthdays. On normal days we just ate some fruit. And now and again, if avocados were on sale at the grocery store, we enjoyed a delicious dessert of puréed avocado with sugar and a hint of Grand Marnier. Even in Chinese restaurants, it is common to serve orange quarters at the end of a meal.

Amaranth soup

By Yvonne Yau

莧
菜

In the south of China, people drink a lot of soup, whether at breakfast, lunch, or dinner, in summer and in winter. One of Yvonne's favourite soups is amaranth soup with its beautiful pink colour. When she was younger and started her period, her mother made her this soup and added some pork liver, telling her that it would feed her blood. Yvonne serves this soup both as an appetizer and as a side dish. It's a simple recipe that can easily be made entirely from local ingredients. Ask at a local farm where they raise animals on pasture if you can have bones and offal; these parts are unpopular yet very nourishing.

Preparation 10 min • Cooking 10 min • 4 servings

INGREDIENTS

2 bunches (16 oz/450 g) of *Amaranthus tricolor*
    or any purple-leaf amaranth, leaves and stems
1 tbsp (15 mL) olive oil
2 slices of fresh ginger ($\frac{1}{16}$ inch/2 mm thick)
1 cup (250 mL) bone or vegetable broth
3 cloves of garlic, minced
¼ tsp (1 mL) salt
1 green onion, cut into ¼-inch (5 mm) slices

METHOD

1. Separate the amaranth leaves from the stems. Cut the tender part of the stems into ½-inch (1 cm) pieces and throw away the tough parts.

2. Heat a frying pan over medium heat. Add the oil and stir-fry the ginger until it starts to smell good. Add the amaranth stems and stir-fry for 2 minutes. Add the leaves and stir-fry for 1 minute. Add the stock, cover, reduce the heat, and simmer for 3 to 5 minutes, or until the stems and leaves are tender.

3. Add the garlic, stir, and turn off the heat. Season with salt and stir.

4. Garnish with sliced green onion.

NOTES AND VARIATIONS

• Amaranth leaves can be replaced with spinach, bok choy, or Swiss chard.

• You can use water instead of stock; if you do, replace the salt with 1 tsp (5 mL) white miso paste.

Yvonne Yau

Originally from Hong Kong, Yvonne grew up in British Columbia, where she met a Québécois downhill skier who convinced her to share his life living between Whistler and Sutton. At the Sutton market she was overjoyed to find Stéphanie's organic Asian vegetable stall, and the two women became friends. Yvonne is a true epicure, always searching for the perfect balance between pleasure, nourishment, and health. She adores culinary adventures, buying as close as possible to the source, and farm-to-table meals.

Lentil and amaranth dhal (*Thotakura pappu*)

By Guillaume Lozeau

In India, the word *dhal* is used to refer to several kinds of lentils as well as to the stewed dishes made from them. Lentil dishes made with leafy greens are very popular all over India. This dish is one of the favourites at Le Super Qualité, a well-loved snack bar in Montreal. The recipe is typical of the province of Andhra Pradesh, which is known for its delicious, spicy vegetarian cuisine.

Preparation and cooking 1 hr • 6 to 8 servings •

INGREDIENTS

1 cup (250 mL) red lentils

½ tsp (2 mL) ground turmeric

¼ tsp (1 mL) fenugreek seeds

7 oz (200 g) amaranth, leaves and stems, finely chopped

3 tbsp (45 mL) tamarind paste

3 green Thai (bird's-eye) chilis
    (or 1 jalapeño or serrano pepper), thinly sliced

2 tsp (10 mL) salt

3 tbsp (45 mL) clarified butter (ghee)

½ cup (125 mL) chopped fresh cilantro

3 tbsp (45 mL) sunflower oil

2 tsp (10 mL) cumin seeds

2 tsp (10 mL) brown (or black) mustard seeds

4 dried red chilis

10 curry leaves

1 tsp (5 mL) asafoetida

METHOD

1. Rinse the lentils in a bowl of water. Drain, then repeat twice more, or until the water runs fairly clear.

2. In a pot, combine the lentils, 3 cups (750 mL) water, turmeric, and fenugreek. Bring to a boil, then reduce the heat to medium, cover, and cook for 45 minutes, or until the lentils are tender. Remove from the heat.

3. Using a blender, blend the contents of the pot. Add the amaranth, tamarind paste, green chilis, and salt. Put the pot back over the heat, and bring to a boil. Simmer for 10 minutes, until the amaranth stems are very tender. Stir in the clarified butter and fresh cilantro. Turn off the heat.

4. In a small frying pan over medium heat, heat the oil. Add the cumin seeds, mustard seeds, and red chilis. Stir to coat all the ingredients in the oil. Once the mustard seeds start to pop (after about 20 seconds), stir in the curry leaves and asafoetida (make sure the curry leaves come into contact with the hot oil). Pour immediately over the lentils.

5. Serve with rice or naan.

NOTES AND VARIATIONS

• You can replace the amaranth with spinach (cook for around 5 minutes) or arugula (no need to cook).

• Tamarind is a pod-shaped fruit that grows in tropical regions. Its pulp is somewhat like dried dates, and the taste is slightly bitter, sweet, and sour. You can find it as a paste (dilute with a little water) or pressed into a block (soften with hot water, and then pass through a sieve). The tamarind pulp in the recipe can be replaced with the juice of three lemons, but note that the result will be slightly different and you might need to reduce water slightly at step 2.

• You can buy clarified butter or make your own. Melt butter in the microwave or in a pan on the stove, use a spoon to skim off the white foam that forms on the surface, then pour the oil into another container, leaving behind the whey or white liquid at the bottom of the pan (you keep only the yellow oil). Clarified butter can withstand much higher temperatures than regular butter.

• Asafoetida is the dried resin of giant fennel, a perennial from central Asia. Its unpleasant smell disappears during cooking, leaving behind a flavour reminiscent of onion or garlic (it can thus replace these aromatics). Often used in Indian cooking, asafoetida perfumes vegetables, fish, and sauces.

• Curry leaf is the leaf of an Asian shrub, called curry tree, with an herby, slightly citrusy flavour. It is used as an aromatic in India and Southeast Asia to add flavour to soups and curries. It can be omitted in the recipe or replaced with 1 or 2 dried bay leaves.

Guillaume Lozeau
Le Super Qualité restaurant

Guillaume is the co-owner and chef of the colourful Indian snack bar Le Super Qualité, one of the rare spots in Montreal where you can find authentic food from the south of India. Guillaume has travelled extensively in South and Southeast Asia, and has been inspired by, and learned to master, different culinary traditions. He loves introducing people to new dishes and flavours, which is exactly what he does in this book with two typically South Indian recipes.

莧
菜

Amaranth romazava-style

By Jean-Louis Thémis

Romazava (pronounced *roomazav*) is the national dish of Madagascar. It's a stew, traditionally made from zebu meat (zebu are humped cattle) and Brede mafanes (a leafy vegetable that causes a tingling sensation in the mouth). Romazava can be cooked with all kinds of vegetables; here Jean-Louis makes this gem of Malagasy cooking with amaranth leaves.

Preparation 15 min • Cooking 1 hr 15 min • 4 servings

INGREDIENTS

2 tbsp (30 mL) vegetable oil

1 lb (500 g) beef shoulder or shank, cubed

Salt and pepper, to taste

1 onion, thinly sliced

2 cloves of garlic, minced

1 tbsp (15 mL) minced fresh ginger

1 tbsp (15 mL) tomato paste

2 bunches (1 lb/500 g) of amaranth, leaves only, roughly chopped

METHOD

1. In a deep pan over high heat, heat the oil, then stir-fry the beef cubes for about 5 minutes. When the cubes are nicely browned, season, add the onion, garlic, and ginger, and then the tomato paste.

2. Just barely cover the ingredients with water, and simmer over medium heat for 1 hour, or until the meat is tender. During cooking, occasionally skim the foam off the surface with a spoon.

3. Add the amaranth leaves. Stir well, cover, and simmer for 10 more minutes.

4. Serve with rice (*vary* in Malagasy) and a condiment such as pickled eggplant or a tomato rougail.

NOTES AND VARIATIONS

• The amaranth can be replaced with spinach or watercress.
• In the islands of the Indian Ocean, leafy greens served cooked are called "bredes" (as opposed to lettuces, leafy greens that are eaten raw in salads).

Tomato rougail

By Caroline

Preparation 10 min • Makes 2 cups (500 mL) •

INGREDIENTS

3 very ripe tomatoes, diced

2 green onions, green parts only, thinly sliced

1 tbsp (15 mL) canola oil

½ green Thai (bird's-eye) chili, finely minced

Salt, to taste

METHOD

1. Combine all of the ingredients in a bowl.

2. Refrigerate for 1 hour, and then serve.

Jean-Louis Thémis
Cuisiniers sans frontières and Parti culinaire du Québec

Jean-Louis Thémis, also known as Chef Thémis, is the founder of Cuisiniers sans frontières and the Parti culinaire du Québec. According to him, gastronomy should not be limited to its playful side but elevated to a philosophical and political level. He grew up in Madagascar when the island was still a French colony, with a Greek grandfather and a Malagasy mother; fusion is therefore at the foundation of who he is and what he cooks. In this book he offers two recipes that are well known in Madagascar, reinvented with our Asian vegetables.

莧
菜

MALABAR SPINACH

潺
菜

MALABAR SPINACH

Also known as: basella, Ceylon spinach, Indian spinach
潺菜 saan4 coi3/cháncài (flow | vegetable)
In Mandarin also called: 木耳菜 mù'ěrcài
(wood | ear | vegetable)

FAMILY: Basellaceae

SPECIES: *Basella alba* or *Basella rubra*

HISTORY Probably of Indian origin, Malabar spinach has been grown in China for a long time. Enjoyed in India and now widely spread across the tropics, it was introduced to Europe in the early nineteenth century. Red Malabar spinach produces shiny little red fruits, traditionally used in China as food colouring or craft dye.

Malabar spinach is an intriguing vegetable. Like okra, it contains a gelatinous substance called mucilage that becomes viscous on contact with water and feels like foam in the mouth. When lightly fried or steamed, its texture is more like that of spinach. Malabar spinach has a great deal of potential in vegan and gluten-free cooking because of its thickening properties. Outside Asian grocery stores, where you can find it fresh, you'll find it in pots in garden centres. You will enjoy growing this vegetable, both outside and inside, for its beautiful vines, its low maintenance, and its heat tolerance.

Although its young leaves and stems have a mild spinach flavour, Malabar spinach belongs to a completely different family. It is identified by its slightly sour taste, similar to sorrel, and by its thick shiny leaves. This climbing plant can reach between 10 to 20 feet (3 to 6 m) in height in the tropics, where it is a perennial. The two most common varieties are green Malabar spinach, somewhat shorter with its citrusy leaves and stems, and red Malabar spinach, whose long stems and small leaves, both red-tinted, have a fruity flavour.

In the garden

• Malabar spinach takes 2 to 3 weeks to germinate, which is why it is recommended to start seeds indoors. After the germination stage has been successfully navigated, the rest of the growing process will be very easy — once it has been planted outside in the spring, it requires very little attention and is not usually attacked by insects, and the harvest period for a single plant can stretch from early July to the arrival of frosty nights in the fall.

• The ideal soil for growing Malabar spinach is slightly acidic, moist, and fertile. However, it can also tolerate poor soil.

• Red Malabar spinach, with its bunches of edible berries, is especially pretty grown in a pot indoors, on a balcony, or on a patio. Malabar spinach can climb or trail. When the plant reaches the top of its climbing support, such as a fence or a trellis, cut the top off the main stem, also called the growth point, to encourage the growth of its lateral stems. It is also possible to let the plants trail on the ground, taking care to harvest long stems regularly so that they don't take over the whole garden.

• Whether it is climbing or trailing, you can harvest young shoots and large leaves. It's best to leave lateral stems until they have grown to at least 5 inches (13 cm) in length before picking them.

• There is also a growing method that keeps the plants short, removes the need for support, and facilitates harvesting. We have tried this method with success. It consists of making two successive sowings two weeks apart. They are then planted out in the garden, again two weeks apart. When the first plants have grown to 12 inches (30 cm) tall, harvest the top section of the plant (main stem, leaves, and some lateral stems), making sure to leave at least the bottom third intact. Then alternate harvesting between the two sets of plants, since you need to wait for one to three weeks before you can harvest from the same plant again. After the second cut, you must not be afraid to cut low enough to encourage the growth of large leaves, but always take care not to cut off the first two basal leaves and never remove all of a plant's stems and leaves.

• You can take a cutting of Malabar spinach. Just cut the top part of the stem to a length of 3 to 5 inches (7 to 15 cm), remove the leaves at the base, plant it in a pot, and then overwinter it in a warm, sunny place in the house. The following summer, the plant can either be kept as a houseplant or planted outside again.

STORING

Keeps for a few days in a sealed plastic bag or container in the fridge, or for 10 to 14 days after harvest in optimal conditions.

PREPARING

Rinse the leaves and the stems, and remove any tough ends from the stems. You can also remove the main ribs of the mature leaves if they are too tough. Use the leaves whole or roughly chop leaves and stems.

IN THE KITCHEN

Edible parts	Ways to eat	Ways to cook
• Leaves	• Raw	• Steam
• Stems	• Cooked	• Boil
• Red berries	• Dried	• Sauté/stir-fry
		• Deep-fry

Malabar spinach is used the same way as spinach: raw, or more often cooked. It goes well with garlic, ginger, coconut milk, and nutmeg.

RAW

• The shoots, young leaves, and young stems can all be added to salads.

• Malabar spinach can also be dried and powdered, and then used to replace certain binding agents, such as eggs, chia or flaxseeds, and guar or xanthan gum, which are used in many recipes, including soups, omelettes, vegan waffles, and veggie pâtés.

COOKED

Because of its mucilage, Malabar spinach can replace okra to thicken soups and stews. Limit its cooking time to a few minutes so that it doesn't become too viscous.

Our favourite ways to prepare it:

• Delicious sautéed with only garlic and salt, or added to a quiche, omelette, veggie pâté, or veggie burger.

• Blanched for 2 minutes, puréed, and then incorporated into sweet and savoury recipes such as spreads, dips, pies, and cakes, which will then have a pretty hint of green.

• Steam-cooked and then seasoned with oyster sauce and fried garlic, like many other Asian greens.

• Added to curries and dhals, or placed in a bowl and covered with hot broth.

• In China, it is stewed in bone broth or water with slices of ginger, crumbled tofu or ground pork, and an egg.

• It can be dipped in batter and fried like pakoras.

NUTRITION Malabar spinach is an excellent source of vitamin A and vitamin C, and a good source of manganese and folate. It's also a source of other vitamins (riboflavin, vitamin B6) and minerals (potassium, calcium, magnesium, copper). Magnesium is important for nerve and muscle health and bone development.

Left: *Red Malabar spinach vines.*
Above: *Green Malabar spinach is squatter and fleshier.*

Malabar spinach stir-fry with ginger and Sichuan pepper oil

By Mong Chi Chong

In Chinese cooking, not too much thought goes into cooking vegetables: stir-fry them with a few aromatics to make their flavour pop. Chi uses Malabar spinach leaves harvested from her own garden to make this easy and satisfying recipe, which she enjoys with a simple bowl of rice.

Preparation 5 min • Cooking 8 min • 4 servings • 🌶

INGREDIENTS

16 oz (450 g) red Malabar spinach leaves
3 tbsp (45 mL) vegetable oil
2 tbsp (30 mL) minced fresh ginger
2 tbsp (30 mL) water
1 tsp (5 mL) green Sichuan pepper oil
½ to 1 tsp (2 to 5 mL) salt

METHOD

1. In a frying pan over medium heat, heat the oil. Stir-fry the ginger for about 45 seconds.

2. Add the spinach and stir-fry for 3 minutes to keep it from sticking.

3. Add the water, and then the Sichuan pepper oil and salt. Cook until the spinach is tender without being soggy.

4. Serve with rice.

NOTES AND VARIATIONS

Sichuan pepper oil is oil infused with Sichuan peppercorn. The kind made from green Sichuan peppercorn has a herbier aroma than the one made from red peppercorn.

Mong Chi Chong

Chi has been Stéphanie's friend since 2007; she is practically part of the family. She is a massage therapist who specializes in Asian massages in Quebec City, and is extremely generous, curious, and creative. She has initiated Stéphanie into several aspects of Asian culture, teaching her Cantonese, sharing stories and traditions, and accompanying her on her journey to being more zen on a daily basis. She is also devoted to growing Asian vegetables in her yard, including Malabar spinach, which inspired this recipe.

Malabar spinach and black-eyed peas curry (*Valchebaji ani gule*)

By Guillaume Lozeau

This recipe is from the magnificent coastal region of Malabar, which borders the provinces of Karnataka and Kerala in southwest India. It highlights black-eyed peas, a pulse that is usually cream-coloured or sometimes red, brown, black, or yellowish green, and that has a spot like an eye at the point where it joins the plant. For Guillaume and Le Super Qualité team, this recipe is a perfect example of the genius of South Indian cooking, which manages to transform humble ingredients into dishes that are affordable, nutritious, and delicious.

Preparation and cooking 1 hr 30 min • Soaking 12 to 24 hrs
6 to 8 servings •

INGREDIENTS

1 cup (250 mL) black-eyed peas

1 cup (250 mL) fresh or frozen coconut

2 tbsp (30 mL) coconut oil

1 yellow onion, diced

4 cloves of garlic, finely minced

1 tomato, finely diced

1 bunch (5 oz/150 g) of Malabar spinach roughly chopped

½ tbsp (7 mL) ground chili

½ tbsp (7 mL) salt

¼ tsp (1 mL) asafoetida

Spices

1 tbsp (15 mL) coriander seeds

2 tsp (10 mL) cumin seeds

½ tsp (2 mL) whole black peppercorns

¼ tsp (1 mL) fenugreek seeds

METHOD

1. Rinse the peas in a bowl of water. Drain, then rinse once more, or until the water runs clear. Soak the peas in water for 12 to 24 hours (the beans will need at least double their volume of water). Drain.

2. In a saucepan, bring 3 cups (750 mL) water to a boil. Add the peas, return to a boil, and then reduce the heat to medium. Simmer the beans, covered, for 1 hour, or until they are tender and soft.

3. Meanwhile in a frying pan, dry-roast the spices. When they are fragrant and the seeds have turned a little darker, they are ready. Take care not to burn them. Let them cool completely, and then grind in a mortar or spice mill. Set aside.

4. Once the beans are cooked, strain them and keep the cooking liquid. Use this liquid to grind the coconut in a blender, making it as smooth as possible.

5. In the empty saucepan, over medium heat, heat the coconut oil. Stir-fry the onion and garlic until the onions are translucent. Add the ground coconut, beans, spices, tomato, Malabar spinach, ground chili, salt, and asafoetida. Bring to a boil, and then cook gently for 10 to 15 minutes, or until the spinach is tender and the tomatoes are starting to fall apart. If the mixture is too thick, add just enough water to reach a pouring consistency.

NOTES AND VARIATIONS

· Malabar spinach can be replaced with spinach or Swiss chard.

· The asafoetida can be omitted without any significant effect to the final result. (See page 215 for more info on asafoetida.)

· The coconut can be replaced by coconut milk by reducing the amount of water used in the recipe.

SHISO

紫
蘇

SHISO

Also known as: perilla, beefsteak plant, Chinese basil
紫蘇 / 紫苏 zi2 sou1/zǐsū (purple | perilla)

FAMILY: Lamiaceae

SPECIES: *Perilla frutescens*

HISTORY Originating in Asia, shiso is widely used in Japan, especially in sushi dishes. Although it is not used in modern Chinese cooking, shiso is mentioned in ancient Chinese recipes, in which it was eaten as a vegetable and in soups.

Shiso is a popular herb in Japan. Its flavour is reminiscent of cumin, coriander, cinnamon, and anise. The abundant and aromatic leaves are used for decorating and scenting fish, meats, rice dishes, and salads. We love purple shiso, which makes a splendid pink lemonade. In the garden, we appreciate the rusticity and beauty of the different forms of shiso, which reseeds naturally and can be integrated as a perennial into ornamental arrangements.

NUTRITION

Shiso leaves are an excellent source of vitamin K as well as a source of manganese and vitamin A. Vitamin A helps us see in the dark and helps maintain a healthy skin.

Shiso is an annual plant that can reach a height of 35 inches (90 cm), with beautiful large leaves that can measure 3 inches (7.5 cm) across, often with lacy edges and colours varying between purple, bronze, or green. Green shiso is milder and more citrusy than purple shiso. The ribbed leaves, slightly firmer than basil, are eaten most often, but you can also eat the pretty spear-shaped flowers, the seeds, the sprouts, and the shoots. The shiso used in Japanese cooking is more precisely a variety of perilla (var. *crispa*), and comes in many forms and colours. There is also a variety used in Korean cooking (*Perilla frutescens*) and another that grows in Japan's mountains (var. *hirtella*).

In the garden

· Shiso grows well and is generally not susceptible to insect attacks; it is an herb that can be easily grown in the garden or in a pot. Undemanding with regard to soil fertility, it can grow in slightly acidic but well-drained soil.

· Just like basil, shiso likes full sun and will not tolerate frost, but it is hardier than basil and is better at withstanding cold nights.

· The biggest difficulty is the germination stage, which can take up to 21 days and often results in a disappointing germination rate. To improve this rate, choose newer seeds and use a heat mat to keep the trays at a temperature of 68°F (20°C). In addition, just gently cover the seeds with soil, because they need light to germinate.

· We have observed that shiso plants benefit enormously from being potted up, and their growth will be stronger if the plants already measure 6 inches (15 cm) when planted out.

· At Le Rizen, we have loved every kind of shiso we have tried. Green shiso and red shiso are classics, and we also enjoy hojiso shiso, whose large leaves are green on top and purple underneath.

· We start harvesting shiso when it has grown to a height of 8 to 10 inches (20 to 25 cm). To do this, you can pull up the entire plant, or just pick off the larger leaves with your fingers. At Le Rizen, we use the flowering-stem technique, which is often used for harvesting regular basil: use pruning shears to snip the main stem just above the two lateral stems. This technique allows you to obtain several harvests before the plant flowers. We have been able to harvest from the same plants from early July to mid-September. The flowering-stem technique increases the length of time the leaves can be stored after harvesting. When the flower buds appear, you can still harvest, but the leaves will be slightly more bitter.

· If you leave the shiso, it will flower and scatter its seeds, reseeding itself naturally the following season. To avoid it becoming invasive, cut the plants before the flowers turn brown and dry, or let just a few plants go to seed.

· It is fairly easy to gather shiso seeds to use them for sowing the following season. All you have to do is cut the stems when the flower is dry, just before the seeds are blown away by the wind. Put the stems head down in a paper bag and keep them in an airy, warm, dry place. When everything is fully dry, shake the bag; the seeds will fall off the plant and gather at the bottom of the bag. Remove the stems, and then pour the contents of the bag onto a tray tilted toward you. Shake the tray gently so that the seeds fall to the bottom while the other debris stays at the top. Store the seeds in a sealed jar and sow the following year.

· Once fall arrives, you can dig up your shiso plants and pot them, bring them indoors, and place them on a sunny windowsill, then take them back outside in the spring.

IN THE KITCHEN

Edible parts	Ways to eat	Ways to cook
● Leaves	● Raw	● Boil
● Seeds	● Cooked	● Deep-fry
● Flowers	● Pickled/ lacto-fermented	
	● Dried	

Shiso makes a good replacement for basil, and adds a wonderful aroma to many dishes. Green shiso is ideal for delicate dishes like salads and wraps, while purple shiso is perfect for adding colour and zest to fish, meat, marinades, drinks, and desserts.

RAW
Shiso is best eaten raw because it loses its flavour when cooked.

Our favourite ways to prepare it:
· Chop the leaves just before serving to conserve all the flavour, and then add to cold tofu, raw fish, or even steak. Shiso also adds flavour to salads and goes well with cucumber and thinly sliced cabbage. You can also use the shoots.

· Use the whole leaves to wrap chunks of cooked fish, pork, or beef. Add them to sushi (as in shiso maki, made with chilled rice with vinegar added and shiso, wrapped in a sheet of dried seaweed), or spring rolls. They can also be used to make pesto.

· The purple leaves tint marinades, such as pickled ginger or pickled Japanese plums (umeboshi). Marinate a few leaves in rice vinegar to flavour it, or steep them in water with lemon juice and sugar to make a delicious lemonade, perfect for hot summer days.

· Both the flower buds and flowers can season and decorate dishes. The seeds can be ground and then used as a substitute in the Japanese seven-spice mix called shichimi togarashi.

COOKING
Even though it is best eaten raw, shiso can also be cooked. Add at the end of cooking to soups such as ramen or to stews, or serve in tempura (dipped in flour or batter, and then fried).

The leaves can be dried and later used in stocks, soups, teas, or lemonades. To dry the leaves, hang a few bunches by the stems (see also "Extending the life of vegetables" on page 314).

STORING
Keeps for a week in a sealed plastic bag or container in the fridge, or for 7 to 14 days after harvest in optimal conditions.

PREPARING
Prepare and use shiso like an herb: rinse the leaves on the stems, and then remove the leaves.

Laotian meat salad (*Laap*)

By Maxime Chanhda-Tremblay

紫蘇

Maxime's love for *laap* comes from his Laotian culture — his Thai grandparents started their family in Laos before moving to Quebec. This traditional Laotian dish of spiced ground meat, usually served cold with sticky rice, is easy to prepare and works with all protein sources. The *laap,* or *larb,* is usually made with mint rather than shiso, but both of these herbs bring a wonderful freshness to this dish.

Preparation 20 min • Cooking 10 min • Resting 30 min
4 servings •

INGREDIENTS

1 to 2 tbsp (15 to 30 mL) vegetable oil

1 lb (500 g) ground pork

½ cup (125 mL) uncooked sticky rice
(the recipe will use 2 tsp/10 mL roasted sticky rice flour)

1 French shallot, thinly sliced

3.5 oz (100 g) long beans, thinly sliced

2 tbsp (30 mL) mắm nêm fish sauce (rather than nước mắm)

Juice of 2 limes (about ¼ cup/60 mL)

Ground black pepper, to taste

Shiso (or mint) leaves, to taste

Cilantro leaves, to taste

Bean sprouts, to taste

1 Thai (bird's-eye) chili, thinly sliced (optional)

For serving

Chinese cabbage leaves

Slices of Asian cucumber

METHOD

For the meat

1. Heat a wok over medium-high heat. Pour in the oil, then brown the pork until cooked through. Set aside in a bowl in the fridge.

For the toasted sticky rice flour

2. In a wok (or cast-iron frying pan) over medium heat, dry-toast uncooked sticky rice, stirring regularly until the grains are dark golden. Let cool completely, and then use a mortar and pestle or spice mill to grind it into flour.

For the salad

3. Once the pork is chilled, add the shallots and long beans, then stir well. Add 2 tsp (10 mL) (or to taste) of the toasted rice flour, as well as the fish sauce, lime juice, and black pepper. Mix well and adjust seasoning as required.

4. Roughly chop the shiso and cilantro leaves, then mix them with the salad. Add the bean sprouts. For a traditional spicy flavour, add the Thai (bird's-eye) chili.

5. Serve on a cabbage leaf with slices of cucumber. Sprinkle with toasted sticky rice flour.

NOTES AND VARIATIONS

• As a starter, this Laotian salad is served simply on a cabbage leaf with sliced cucumbers. As a main dish, enjoy it with jasmine rice or, even better, with steam-cooked sticky rice.

• The ground pork can be replaced by ground chicken, strips of beef, or Nordic shrimp. It can also be switched out for fresh shiitake mushrooms: allow at least three times the quantity of meat.

• The long bean, or yardlong bean, resembles a very long green bean and can reach 12 to 35 inches (30 to 90 cm) in length. It is used the same way as green beans: its flavour is similar to the latter, while its texture is denser and crunchier, even after cooking. It can also be replaced with asparagus.

• The roasted sticky rice flour is the key to this recipe! You will have leftovers — store in a sealed container for several weeks.

Maxime Chanhda-Tremblay
Épicerie Chanhda

Maxime is half Thai and half Québécois. He has always been surrounded by Asian cooking, having grown up with a restaurant-owning mother and an aunt who owned an Asian grocery store where he often helped out. As a teenager, as he was helping people find Thai basil, he never expected to take up the family culinary torch. Since then, he has created a restaurant he named after himself, Chanhda, and then took over the Lao-Indochine Asian grocery store in Quebec City. His journey means that he appreciates the work of other passionate people who, like Stéphanie, work to spread their culture of origin. It's important for him to support a farmer who practices a different — and environmentally respectful — form of agriculture.

Spring rolls with shiso and duck

By Dana Cooper

紫蘇

Spring rolls are simple yet magnificent, appetizing, and as fun to cook as they are to eat. Since duck is a rich, expensive meat, Dana prepares it here with flavours that are pronounced enough that she can use the duck sparingly. According to her, the duck really benefits from a touch of sweetness, which the vegetables in this recipe bring. In addition, shiso, whose taste can be reminiscent of mint, works very well with sweet ingredients. The flavours of the duck and the shiso are perfectly highlighted in this dish, which is beautifully decorated with edible flowers. It's the perfect dish for a dinner party, since the rolls can be sliced up and served as a starter or with other sharing dishes.

Preparation 30 min • Cooking 30 min • Resting 1 hr 10 min • Makes 4 to 5 rolls

INGREDIENTS

1 duck breast

4 to 5 medium rice wraps

2.5 oz (75 g) rice vermicelli

Crunchy vegetables such as sugar snap peas, carrots, Asian cucumbers

4 to 5 medium (2-inch/5 cm) shiso leaves

10 to 25 edible flowers, whole or petals (optional)

Spice mix

1 star anise

1 tsp (5 mL) whole black peppercorns

½ tsp (2 mL) fennel seeds

½ tsp (2 mL) whole allspice, or ¼ tsp (1 mL) ground allspice

1 tsp (5 mL) salt

METHOD

1. In a mortar or spice mill, finely grind the star anise, peppercorns, fennel seeds, and allspice (if using whole). Transfer to a bowl, add the salt and ground allspice (if using), and mix well. Set aside.

2. Score the top of the duck breast into squares, cutting through the skin and the fat, but not the flesh. Turn over the breast, and then rub the meat and the inside of the cuts with the spice mix so that it sticks. Cover, and then refrigerate for at least 1 hour and up to 6 hours.

3. In a cast-iron pan, brown the duck breast. First cook the fatty side for 20 minutes over medium-low heat, and then the meat side for 5 to 10 minutes. At a few points during the cooking process, scoop up the fat and the cooking juices, and pour them over the breast.

4. While the duck breast is cooking, prepare the vermicelli and the vegetables:

a. Cook the vermicelli according to the package instructions.

b. Cut the vegetables into thin strips with a sharp knife or mandolin. Note: Sugar snap peas can be used whole — remove the string simply by snapping the top part of the pod and pulling on the string. Remove and discard the seeded part of the cucumber, and keep the skin and flesh.

c. Thinly slice the shiso leaves into ¼-inch (0.5 cm) wide strips, or keep them whole for prettier presentation.

5. When the duck breast is cooked to your taste, let it rest for 10 to 15 minutes, and then cut it against the grain into ¼- inch (0.5 cm) thick slices.

6. Assemble the rolls:

a. In a large bowl of warm water, soak a rice wrap for 10 seconds, and then gently place it on a damp kitchen towel.

b. Place the shiso and flowers horizontally in the centre of the rice wrap, and then add the vegetables, vermicelli, and a few slices of duck. Make sure not to overfill the rolls.

c. To form a roll that will hold together well, fold over the bottom of the wrap to cover all the ingredients, then fold over the two sides, and then roll up into a cylinder.

d. Repeat with the rest of the ingredients.

7. Place the rolls on a long plate or chopping board.

If you are making the spring rolls ahead, roll them individually in plastic wrap so that the rice sheet does not harden or crack.

NOTES AND VARIATIONS

• For beautiful rolls, choose a combination of colourful, crunchy vegetables. Avoid juicy vegetables, which will make the rolls soggy. Other vegetable possibilities include snow peas, lettuce, radish, daikon, turnip, and kohlrabi.

• The duck can be replaced with firm tofu cut into batons. Coat well in the spice mix and cook until browned on all sides.

• Tip: For a more stable wrap and to avoid any cracking during assembly, soak a second rice wrap, and then place its left edge in the centre of the first wrap so you end up with two overlapping wraps. Then add the fillings.

• Dana, always looking for ways to reduce packaging in the kitchen, has come up with rolls that are flavourful without sauce. They can be served as is to fully appreciate the freshness and flavour of the ingredients. You can even add the spicy crispy bits from the frying pan.

Shiso and lychee sorbet

By Marie Wang

紫
蘇

Our aunt Marie is a specialist in, and lover of, desserts. She completed several patisserie classes in France, and loves tasting the latest creations of famous chefs. Her creativity and talent for inventing new desserts have impressed several of them. It's not surprising, then, that for this book she concocted two dessert recipes featuring our Asian vegetables.

For the shiso syrup
Preparation 5 min • Cooking 5 min, resting overnight

For the sorbet
Preparation 10 min, resting 2 hrs • Freezing 30 to 45 minutes

Makes ¾ cup (180 mL), or 2 to 3 popsicles

INGREDIENTS

For the shiso syrup
⅔ cup (150 mL) water
½ cup (125 mL) sugar
7 or 8 large purple shiso leaves

For the sorbet
1 can (18 oz/500 g) canned lychees
2 tbsp (30 mL) fresh lime juice
3 leaves (or to taste) purple shiso, thinly sliced (chiffonade)

METHOD

The day before

1. In a saucepan, boil the water and sugar until the sugar has dissolved. Add the shiso leaves, and then chill overnight in the fridge.

The same day

2. Drain the lychees in a colander and give them a quick rinse under running water.

3. Transfer the lychees to a food processor or blender, and then add the lime juice and ¼ cup (60 mL) of the chilled shiso syrup (discard the leaves beforehand, reserve the rest of the syrup for serving). Mix until smooth.

4. Add the thinly sliced shiso leaves, and fold in using a wooden spoon.

5. Refrigerate for at least 2 hours, and then transfer to an ice-cream maker and process for 30 to 45 minutes, depending on the manufacturer's instructions. (To make popsicles, pour into moulds or shot glasses, insert sticks, then freeze.)

6. To serve, drizzle with a little of the reserved shiso syrup.

NOTES AND VARIATIONS

• Shiso can be replaced with lemongrass, either two locally grown stems with leaves or three leafless stems if bought from a grocery store, cut into ¾ inch (2 cm) chunks and infused for 1 hour for the syrup.

• Lychees are small fruits around the size of apricots, with juicy, sweet pearl-white flesh and a fruity-floral flavour that is reminiscent of strawberry, rose, and muscat. The shell and stone are removed when the fruit is preserved, so canned lychees are ready to eat.

Laou family meal with friends, Madirokely beach.

A chef's vision

The book is frozen, but man is living

— *Chinese proverb*

Our uncle Jean was a chef. He actually followed in the footsteps of his own father, who was an informal chef in the Chinese community of Antsirabe in Madagascar. People would gather together on weekends to socialize and play mah-jong, the classic Chinese board game, and the task of feeding all these mouths would alternate between families. When it was our uncle's family's turn, his father was sometimes too busy playing mah-jong, so he'd summon his son to take charge. The young Jean had to manage by copying what he had seen his father do. This is how his chef's career started at the age of fifteen.

Today our uncle is retired, but he continues to cook with as much passion as ever. He has a lot to say about food! He is also the go-to person in matters of cooking for the whole extended family, and he has his very own culinary approach. For example, all his recipes are in his head: he has never written them down and has no wish to do so. The quantities are never fixed but evaluated in the moment, on the spot, depending on his taste. Even for measuring out water for cooking rice, he goes by eye rather than by using tricks involving a finger or palm. And if he shares a recipe, he prefers it to be spoken and in person.

According to Yu Zhou, a Chinese gastronome, notions of vagueness and learning by observing are characteristic of Chinese cooking's oral tradition and are rooted in Chinese philosophy. Zhou recounts that at the end of the 1980s, the culinary know-how of Shanghai's best-known restaurants was transmitted orally, with nothing ever having been committed to paper. Books of Chinese recipes, at least the ones that are now a little dated, are very comfortable with this vagueness: "a few pieces of," "a little," or "a tiny bit."

Our uncle does not claim that his way is best; it's just his way. Everyone should find their own way. He remains convinced that you cannot learn to cook by following recipes to the letter: "You have to make a dish, change a few things to your taste, then make it again the next day and change different things, then three days later, then the week after that, and then a month later. You can't abandon something that has yet to be perfected! I am still searching. Even at the age of eighty."

OKRA

秋
葵

OKRA

Also known as: gumbo, lady's fingers
秋葵 caul kwai4/qiūkuí (fall/harvest | herbaceous plant
with big flowers)
In Cantonese also called: 羊角豆 joeng4 gok3 dau2
(goat | horn | bean)

FAMILY: Malvaceae

SPECIES: *Abelmoschus esculentus*

HISTORY Okra, whose other name, gumbo, comes from the Angolan word *ki-ngombo*, was originally from Africa. It grows in hot tropical or temperate regions, and is eaten in Africa, Asia, South America, the Antilles, the southern United States, and some Mediterranean countries.

Okra has surprisingly sticky flesh, which, like flaxseeds or seaweed, becomes slightly viscous when it touches water. This makes it perfect for thickening soups and sauces. Okra is eaten in several regions around the world. It's a key ingredient of the famous Louisiana gumbo, a stew made of okra and a mix of vegetables, meat, or seafood. Okra is available fresh or frozen in some supermarkets, in specialized grocery stores of the communities that eat it, and from farms growing African or Asian vegetables. You will see that there are many ways of handling okra so that it is succulent without being too slimy.

NUTRITION

Okra is an excellent source of manganese and vitamin K. It's also a good source of thiamin and folate, as well as fibre and several minerals (potassium, calcium, magnesium, zinc, copper) and vitamins (vitamin C, niacin, vitamin B6). Like eggplant, okra contains mainly soluble fibre and antioxidants. Potassium, which is found in several vegetables, plays an important role in nerve and muscle function, helping the heart and other muscles to contract. A diet high in potassium and low in sodium is good for preventing high blood pressure.

Okra belongs to the same family as hibiscus. Its large pale yellow flowers are impressive and can be eaten raw or cooked. Incredibly, its fruit grows upward, as the cap is attached to a pedicel located under the pod. As with eggplant, all parts of the okra pod can be eaten except for the pedicel and cap. Its flavour is fairly neutral, somewhat like that of green beans. Its flesh is tender and divided into alveoli that contain small round edible seeds. Green or red, okra's thin skin is smooth or downy. Red okra turns green during cooking. By the end of the season, out in the field in a temperate region, an okra plant can measure up to 5 feet (1.5 m).

In the garden

· As a tropical plant, okra produces the most fruit in hot, humid weather. At Le Rizen, we obtain excellent harvests with the Jambalaya F1 (green okra) and Carmine F1 (red okra) cultivars. The widely grown Clemson Spineless is a very productive, open-pollinated cultivar.

· Considering that six to twelve plants are needed to feed a family of four, okra is not the best for growing in pots. That said, you can still have an ornamental plant to admire and to taste a few flowers and leaves.

· Harvesting okra demands patience and discipline. Because the fruits are the same colour as the stems and leaves, they can be completely hidden. Keep your eyes open and be sure to lift the leaves to see what is hiding underneath.

· In our climate, okra harvests follow a bell curve. Be prepared to harvest 1 or 2 fruits per plant, 3 times a week, when the young plants start producing from around mid-July. As the plants grow, the harvest becomes more abundant, and you will be able to harvest up to 8 fruits per plant toward the end of August. This abundance will continue until cold nights arrive, slowing down fruit production.

· Using pruning shears, cut the pedicel when the okra pods measure 2 to 4 inches (5 to 10 cm) long. Beyond 4 inches (10 cm) the fruit usually becomes too fibrous to eat. If this happens, remove the old okra pods from the plant as soon as you notice them so as not to pointlessly use up the plant's energy.

· We recommend harvesting and handling the okra with gloves and long sleeves, because the leaves and fruits have little hairs that can irritate the skin.

· To find out if okra is still good to eat, bend it gently with your fingers. If it bends easily, it is still tender, but if you feel a degree of resistance it is starting to become fibrous.

· Moisture makes okra slimy and turn brown more quickly. Avoid harvesting when it's raining, do not wash it, and make sure it is very dry before storing.

STORING
Keeps for 2 to 3 days wrapped in a paper towel inside a plastic bag and stored in the fridge, and for 5 to 10 days after harvest in optimal conditions.

PREPARING
Peel the cap in a cone shape or cut on its base line. It can also be removed when eating the okra. Use okra whole or sliced in soups and stews.

IN THE KITCHEN

Edible parts	Ways to eat	Ways to cook
• Young leaves	• Raw	• Steam
• Flesh	• Cooked	• Boil
• Skin	• Pickled/	• Sauté/stir-fry
• Seeds	lacto-fermented	• Roast/grill
• Flowers	• Dried	• Deep-fry

Okra goes well with tomato, onion, bell peppers, eggplant, and corn, as well as curry, hot peppers, coriander, oregano, lemon, and vinegar.

RAW

· It can be eaten whole as a crudité.

· It is not very sticky if pickled or lacto-fermented whole.

· Its shoots and young leaves can be added to salads.

· Its flowers can be used to decorate salads and hors d'oeuvre platters. They can also be stuffed with cream cheese, salmon mousse, or tartare, the same way day lilies can.

COOKED
Okra can replace eggplant, but it cooks more quickly. It becomes discoloured on contact with iron and copper, so avoid cooking utensils that contain these metals.

To prevent the okra from becoming too sticky and to keep it crunchy on the outside and silky on the inside, opt for methods that allow you to cook the okra whole or to cook it only briefly.

Whole: Cook for a few minutes at a high temperature.

· Delicious roasted for a few minutes in the oven or grilled on the barbecue.

· Dipped in batter then deep-fried.

· Steam-cooked for 5 minutes.

· Blanched, and then served with a dressing or added to a salad.

Chopped: Cook briefly.

· Sliced on the diagonal, then stir-fried in a frying pan over high heat for 3 to 4 minutes, or until browned.

· Oven-roasted: Cut in two lengthways, drizzled with oil, and seasoned with spices, herbs, and salt and pepper.

To thicken soups and stews, add it whole or sliced 10 minutes before the end of cooking.

The flowers can be coated with batter and then fried, like zucchini flowers.

If the okra has become too big and fibrous: Don't throw it out! Cut it lengthways, remove the seeds, and cook them like green peas. The rest of the fruit can be dehydrated, and then ground into a powder and used as a thickening ingredient in African, vegan, gluten-free, or allergen-free recipes.

*The okra cap can be removed by peeling it conically (**above**)*
*or cutting it along the line at its base (**right**).*

Crispy roasted okra
(*Kurkuri bhindi*)

By Stéphanie

In Hindi, *kurkuri* means "crispy" and *bhindi* means "okra." In India, okra is often battered and fried, served as a starter in restaurants or sold at foodstands as a snack. In this recipe, roasting dries out the okra and leaves it crunchy — just as tasty and less fatty than deep-frying. The choice of flours and spices to coat the okra depends on what you have on hand. The combination here comes from Karine and Visou, Stéphanie's good friends, who cooked some Le Rizen okra like this at a foodie schoolmates reunion.

Preparation 15 to 30 min • Cooking 20 to 25 min
Resting 10 min • 2 servings

INGREDIENTS

8.5 oz (250 g) okra
1 tbsp (15 mL) sunflower oil

For the batter
2½ tbsp (37 mL) chickpea flour
2 tbsp (30 mL) rice flour
1 tsp (5 mL) tandoori powder
1 tsp (5 mL) garam masala
1 tsp (5 mL) five spice powder
¼ tsp (1 mL) ajwain (optional)
1 tsp (5 mL) salt
2 tbsp (30 mL) sunflower oil
1 tbsp (15 mL) apple cider vinegar

For the dip (green coconut chutney)
2 cups (500 mL) loosely packed fresh cilantro, tender stems and leaves
1 cup (250 mL) loosely packed fresh mint leaves
1 tsp (5 mL) cumin seeds or ground cumin
2 cloves of garlic
2 tsp (10 mL) ground ginger
    (or a ¾-inch/2 cm piece of fresh ginger)
2 tbsp (30 mL) fresh lemon juice
⅔ cup (150 mL) coconut milk
¼ tsp (1 mL) salt
1 tsp (5 mL) ground flaxseeds, to thicken

METHOD

1. Rinse the okra under running water, and dry completely with a kitchen towel. It can also be rinsed the day before and left to dry overnight on a towel.

2. Using a knife, peel off the caps conically (or remove the whole cap by cutting along the line at its base), and then cut the okra into quarters lengthways.

3. Place the okra in a large bowl. Add all of the ingredients for the batter and, using your hands, mix well but gently. Set aside for 10 minutes.

4. Meanwhile, place the oven rack in the centre position, and preheat oven to 400°F (200°C).

5. Prepare the dip. Place all of the ingredients in a blender and purée until smooth. Set aside.

6. Oil a large baking sheet. Place the battered okra in one layer on the baking sheet.

7. Roast for 20 to 25 minutes, or until the okra is golden and nicely crunchy. If it is still not crisp by this point, increase the oven temperature to 425°F (220°C) and cook for another 5 minutes. Remove the sheet from the oven and let the okra cool for 5 minutes.

8. Transfer the crispy okra to a serving plate and enjoy hot, with the dip.

NOTES AND VARIATIONS

· The okra can be replaced with any firm vegetable, such as gai lan, celtuce, sugar snap peas, beans, or radishes.

· The spices can be replaced with anything you have at home. You can also make your own Indian spice mix with a selection of the following ingredients:

For tandoori: turmeric, chili, mustard, fenugreek, onion, garlic, ginger, fennel, cumin, black pepper, cinnamon

For garam masala: black pepper, cumin, cardamom, cinnamon, mace, cloves

· In the same family as cumin and caraway, ajwain has a pronounced aroma and a flavour reminiscent of thyme. It can be replaced with a larger quantity of thyme.

· Some other dips to go with crispy okra:

Raita (yogurt flavoured with diced cucumber and onion, cumin, chili, salt, and sugar)

Hummus (chickpea purée, tahini, lemon juice, olive oil, garlic)

· Aioli or mayonnaise flavoured to taste.

秋葵

Lacto-fermented okra

By Le Rizen and Jean-Philippe Villemure

Lacto-fermentation allows you to capture the green colour and the crunchy texture of okra, while also giving it the characteristic flavour of pickles eaten with burgers or sliced up in salads. This very simple dish will keep for several months in the fridge so you can enjoy okra throughout the winter.

Preparation 30 min • Resting 2 to 3 weeks • Makes 3 cups (750 mL)

INGREDIENTS

18 medium okra (10 oz/300 g)
2 cups (500 mL) water
1 tbsp (15 mL) coarse non-iodized salt

Optional

1 vine or oak leaf
Aromatics, to taste (e.g., fresh diced onion,
    thinly sliced garlic)
Spices, to taste (e.g., coriander, cumin, caraway seeds)

METHOD

1. Rub the okra with a paper towel or kitchen towel to remove the fuzz on the surface.

2. Peel the okra caps conically or remove the cap by cutting along the line at its base, avoiding exposing the seeds. Place the okra vertically in a 3-cup (750 mL) Mason jar, leaving ¾ to 2 inches (2 to 5 cm) of headspace (fermenting will increase the volume of the preparation).

3. Add the vine or oak leaf, the aromatics, and the spices.

4. In a bowl, stir the salt into the water until dissolved.

5. Cover the okra with the prepared brine.

6. Seal the lid, but not too tightly (so that the carbon dioxide can escape). Place in a container or on a plate in case any juice leaks out of the jar.

7. Set aside to ferment for 2 to 3 weeks in a cool, dry place. Do not open the jar — contact with oxygen can make the okra go mouldy. Check regularly (more often if it is hot) and clean any juice that comes out of the jar. Will keep in the fridge for up to 6 months.

NOTES AND VARIATIONS

• The okra can be replaced with green beans or sugar snap peas.

• The vine or oak leaf helps the okra keep its crunch.

Jean-Philippe Villemure

Jean-Philippe is the culinary genius who developed the main processed products Le Rizen sells, including the kimchi range, which has many fans. His unbridled enthusiasm for everything to do with food, his countless kitchen experiments, and his creativity mean that everything he concocts is completely irresistible. Stéphanie has found Jean-Philippe to be the ideal accomplice in culinary adventures, whether it's spending an afternoon frying vegetables, making tomato sauce to store, or trying new restaurants in the region.

秋葵

Okra with mushrooms

By Iscra Nicolov

Refreshing and colourful, this recipe transports us to the northeastern Mediterranean region. It lends itself very well to summer meals in the garden or yard, or picnics, because it can be made the night before and served cold with easily transported accompaniments, such as yogurt, nuts, bread, olives, and cheese.

Preparation 10 min • Cooking 15 min
Rest overnight or for a few hours • 6 servings

INGREDIENTS

1 lb (500 g) okra

3 tbsp (45 mL) olive oil

1 cup (250 mL) minced French shallots (or yellow onions)

4 cloves of garlic, thinly sliced

1 cup (250 mL) thinly sliced mushrooms
    (delicious with golden oyster mushrooms)

½ cup (125 mL) dry white wine

¼ cup (60 mL) finely chopped fresh parsley
    leaves (flat or curly)

Salt and pepper, to taste

1.5 lb (600 g) large cherry tomatoes, sliced
    (or 4 red tomatoes)

For serving

Olive oil, coarse salt, freshly ground black pepper, to taste

METHOD

1. Rinse the okra under running water. Using a knife, peel the caps conically (or remove the cap by cutting along the line at its base). Make sure you do not expose the inside of the pod or the okra will become slimy during cooking.

2. In a large frying pan over medium heat, heat the oil and brown the shallots. Add the garlic and the mushrooms. Cook for 5 minutes, stirring occasionally.

3. Add the okra, white wine, parsley, and salt and pepper. Without stirring, place the tomatoes on top. Cover, reduce the heat to low, and cook for 10 minutes, or until the okra is somewhat tender with some crunch remaining.

4. Let cool, then cover and refrigerate for a few hours or overnight.

5. Before serving, drizzle with olive oil and season with coarse salt and freshly ground pepper.

6. Serve cold or warm with plain yogurt and bread.

NOTES AND VARIATIONS

You can replace the wine with the water used to blanch vegetables.

Iscra Nicolov

Iscra is the biggest consumer of Le Rizen's okra. Every season she buys so much that she had to buy a freezer to store it for the winter. This piqued Stéphanie's curiosity. What recipe could be behind this huge okra reserve? The mystery is revealed here: a dish inspired by a book that Iscra brought with her from Bulgaria when she immigrated to Canada thirty years ago. She shares it with us as a way to help bring together the culinary knowledge of different cultures.

ASIAN
EGGPLANT

茄子

ASIAN EGGPLANT

Also known as: Chinese eggplant, Japanese eggplant, Asian aubergine
茄子 ke2 zi2/qiézi (eggplant | noun suffix)
In Cantonese also called: 矮瓜 ai2 gwaa2
(small sized | squash)

FAMILY: Solanaceae

SPECIES: *Solanum melongena*

HISTORY Originally from tropical Asia, eggplant has been grown in Asia for more than 2,500 years, particularly in China and India. It was grown and spread by the Arabs and Persians, and introduced to Italy in the fourteenth century.

In recent years, Asian eggplant has begun to appear alongside regular aubergine in supermarkets and organic grocery stores. We especially like its sweet flavour and its melt-in-the-mouth texture when cooked. This kind of eggplant has very few seeds, does not need to be sweated, and cooks quickly. Very adaptable, it can also stay firm depending on the cooking method. Its long shape offers unique culinary possibilities.

Long and slender, Asian eggplant is an eggplant variety with thin skin, lilac or dark purple in colour (not to be confused with white eggplant, which is also long in shape). Tender and not very bitter, it is flavourful when cooked, since it takes on all the flavours and liquids from cooking.

In the garden

- In addition to the tips offered earlier on how to retain heat around plants, we suggest choosing cultivars known to be productive in your region. At Le Rizen we obtain abundant yields with the Orient Express F1 cultivar (dark purple).

- Growing eggplant in a pot is possible if you start the seeds indoors and then transplant each to a 4-gallon (15 L) container, and provide sufficient fertilization, full sun, and regular watering without flooding.

- The fruit is ready to be harvested when it is 8 to 12 inches (20 to 30 cm) long and 1½ to 2 inches (4 to 5 cm) in diameter. You can also go by its appearance: its skin should be shiny and firm without being hard. If you press on the fruit with your finger, the dent it forms should spring back.

- It's best to harvest with pruning shears and gloves because the pedicel is prickly.

STORING

Keeps for around a week wrapped in a kitchen towel then placed in a sealable plastic bag or container in the fridge, or for 7 to 10 days after harvest in optimal conditions.

PREPARING

Rinse the eggplant under running water, and remove the pedicel. Like regular eggplant, it turns brown quickly: cut immediately before using or douse with lemon juice.

NUTRITION

Asian eggplant is a source of fibre, copper, manganese, vitamin K, and folate. Its mainly soluble fibres can help reduce blood cholesterol and control blood sugar levels, which can be important for diabetes or high cholesterol. Eggplants also have antioxidant compounds that will protect against cell damage.

IN THE KITCHEN

Edible parts	Ways to eat	Ways to cook
• Flesh	• Raw	• Steam
• Skin	• Cooked	• Boil
• Seeds	• Pickled/ lacto-fermented	• Sauté/stir-fry
	• Dried	• Roast/grill
		• Deep-fry

Asian eggplant is used in the same way as regular eggplant. It's best cooked, although it can be eaten raw. It goes well with ingredients like garlic or spices.

RAW

- Serve in salad by cutting into four lengthways, and then into ¼-inch (0.5 cm) thick slices; season with an olive oil and lemon dressing.

- Can be pickled or lacto-fermented, or even dehydrated to make chips (see "Extending the life of vegetables" on page 314).

COOKED

Stuffed Asian eggplant is a classic of Chinese cooking.

- At dim sum restaurants, it is filled with minced shrimp, steam-cooked, and served with an oyster-sauce base.

- Our mother used to make one of our favourite dishes: She would stuff Asian eggplants with seasoned ground pork, and then batter and deep-fry them. We devoured these crunchy, melt-in-the-mouth bites with Worcestershire sauce, and particularly loved what we called "croque-croque" — the crunchy bits of fried leftover batter.

Other ideas for cooking:

- Asian eggplant can easily replace other kinds of eggplants used in a multitude of recipes; for example, in curries or baba ganoush (eggplant and tahini dip).

- Delicious slathered with a miso-based sauce and oven-roasted or grilled.

- Stir-fried on its own or with other vegetables, pork, chicken, or crumbled firm tofu.

- One flavourful Cantonese recipe is a stew of Asian eggplant cut into sticks that are fried and then stir-fried with pork, salted fish, and a sauce made of soy sauce, black rice vinegar, and sugar.

- In China it is also enjoyed boiled. Our uncle Jean makes an eggplant soup that he simmers very gently with pork bone broth, ginger, a large onion, and salt or soy sauce.

Tip: To keep the eggplant from absorbing too much oil, slice it diagonally widthways, alternating the angle to produce triangles. Place the triangles skin-side down on a lightly oiled baking sheet, and then dry-roast until half-cooked before stir-frying.

Asian eggplant achar

By Jean-Louis Thémis

茄
子

Achar is a South Asian pickle that is also found in Indian Ocean islands, including Madagascar. It's a condiment, half-way between chutney and coleslaw, in which blanched and spiced vegetables are macerated in vinegar. In Madagascar, it is served with grilled meats and stews. Our aunts and uncles often make it for family potlucks with delicious homemade sambos. Usually made with cabbage, carrots, and green beans, achar can be made with a range of vegetables or even fruit. Here, Jean-Louis offers an Asian eggplant–based version, having been inspired by their shape and colour.

Preparation 25 min • Cooking 15 min • Makes about 5 cups (1.2 L)

INGREDIENTS

2 Asian eggplants (1 lb/500 g), cut lengthways into batons (2½ inches/7 cm long and ½ inch/1 cm wide and thick)

1 tbsp (15 mL) coarse salt, to sweat

250 mL (1 cup) olive oil

1 tbsp (15 mL) curry powder

1 tbsp (15 mL) mustard seeds

1 tbsp (15 mL) whole pink peppercorns

1 large sprig of fresh thyme

2 dried bay leaves

1 large onion, thinly sliced

3 cloves of garlic, minced

1 tbsp (15 mL) grated fresh ginger

1 green bell pepper, cut into sticks

1 red bell pepper, cut into sticks

⅔ cup (150 mL) white wine vinegar

Salt, to taste

METHOD

1. Put the eggplants in a colander in a sink (or on a dish) and sprinkle with the salt. Let drain for 2 hours.

2. Using the palms of your hands, press hard to remove as much water as possible from the eggplants.

3. In a saucepan, boil enough water to cover the eggplants. When it reaches a boil, blanch the eggplants for 30 seconds and transfer back to the colander. Let drain and set aside.

4. In a wok over medium heat, heat the oil. Add the curry powder, mustard seeds, pink peppercorns, thyme sprig, and bay leaves, and then add the onion, garlic, and ginger. Stir well and cook for 5 minutes.

5. Add the bell peppers, and then the eggplant. Cook for another 5 minutes, and stir well.

6. Pour in the vinegar, add salt, and stir again.

7. Enjoy right away, or keep in a sealed container in the fridge for 3 to 4 months.

8. Delicious on its own, as an accompaniment, or in sandwiches or burgers.

NOTES AND VARIATIONS

The pink peppercorns look like peppercorn but are actually dried berries. Fruity and slightly peppery, they add colour and flavour. You can replace them with juniper berries or omit them altogether.

Garlicky roasted
Asian eggplant

茄子

By Anita Feng

Asian eggplant is one of Anita's favourite vegetables because there are hundreds of ways to prepare it. Anita discovered this dish, very popular all across China, several years ago in a grill restaurant in Guangzhou, the capital of Guangdong. In this easy recipe, the eggplant literally melts in your mouth, and it goes perfectly with the sauce and fresh herbs. Traditionally, only the flesh is eaten, but the skin is still excellent to eat.

Preparation 10 min · Cooking 40 min · 4 to 6 servings ·

INGREDIENTS

5 medium Asian eggplants

¾ to 1 cup (180 mL to 250 mL) canola oil

2 tbsp (30 mL) toasted sesame seeds

3 green onions, green parts only, sliced

Fresh cilantro leaves (optional)

For the sauce

5 cloves of garlic, finely minced

2 Thai (bird's-eye) chilis, thinly sliced

1 tbsp (15 mL) soy sauce or tamari

2 tbsp (30 mL) tiánmiàn jiàng (sweet sauce
    or sweet soybean paste), or miso paste

2 tbsp (30 mL) sesame oil

¼ tsp (1 mL) five spice powder

½ tsp (2 mL) ground cumin

½ tsp (2 mL) granulated sugar

3 tbsp (45 mL) water

METHOD

1. Place the oven racks in the centre and upper positions. Preheat the oven to 410°F (210°C).

2. Cut the eggplants lengthways in two. Using a sharp knife, make incisions diagonally in the flesh, through half the thickness, taking care not to cut too deeply so that you don't cut through the skin.

3. Place the eggplant on a baking sheet, flesh side up, and slather the flesh with half of the canola oil. Place on the centre rack and roast for 15 minutes.

4. Meanwhile, mix the sauce ingredients in a bowl. Set aside.

5. Slather the eggplants a second time with the rest of the canola oil. Roast for 10 to 15 extra minutes, or until they are tender.

6. Spread the sauce uniformly across the roasted eggplants. Place on the top rack and grill for 5 to 10 minutes, or until the flesh is tender and pierces easily with a fork.

7. Sprinkle with sesame seeds and green onions. Garnish with cilantro leaves, if desired.

8. Serve with rice.

NOTES AND VARIATIONS

Asian eggplant can be replaced with napa cabbage.

Arctic char, miso eggplant, saké kasu

By Jérémie Bastien

茄子

Although this fish dish is inspired by Japanese cuisine, the majority of its ingredients can be found in Canada. In Jérémie's case, the char is fished in the Gaspé, the vegetables and ginger are grown at Le Rizen or on other organic farms in Quebec, and the misos and saké kasu come from Vancouver. You might have leftovers of some of the components of this recipe, so you can make it again or use them in other dishes.

Preparation and cooking 45 min • 4 servings

INGREDIENTS

11 oz (320 g) char fillet, cut into 4 portions
1 bunch of common ice plant (4 stems)

Miso eggplant
3 Asian eggplants
3 tbsp (45 mL) moromi miso

Green zucchini purée
2 green zucchini, grated
1 tsp (5 mL) finely chopped French shallot
1 clove of garlic
1 tbsp (15 mL) olive oil
Salt, to taste

Yellow zucchini purée
2 yellow zucchini, grated
1 tbsp (15 mL) grated fresh ginger
1 tbsp (15 mL) olive oil
Salt, to taste

Miso glaze
¼ cup (60 mL) white miso paste (shiro miso)
¼ cup (60 mL) saké kasu
1½ tbsp (22 mL) saké
1 tsp (5 mL) white soy sauce (or regular)
2 tbsp (30 mL) pure maple syrup
1 tbsp (15 mL) melted butter

Pickled mushrooms
5 oz (150 g) shimeji mushrooms (separated from their base into individual mushrooms)
¼ cup (60 mL) vegetable oil
2 tbsp (30 mL) granulated sugar
¼ cup (60 mL) apple cider vinegar

METHOD

For the miso eggplant
1. Grill the whole eggplant on a charcoal (or gas) barbecue.
2. Place in a sealable container (as it cools, the skin will loosen).
3. Peel the eggplant.
4. Using a knife, roughly chop the flesh. Transfer to a bowl and mix together with the moromi miso. Set aside.

For the green zucchini purée
5. In a pan, cook the garlic and shallot in the olive oil over gentle heat.
6. Add the grated zucchini and a pinch of salt, and then cook, covered, for 2 to 3 minutes to bring the water out of the vegetables.
7. Increase the heat, remove the lid, and cook for 3 to 4 minutes, stirring regularly, to dry out the zucchini.
8. Using a blender, purée until smooth. Add salt to taste, and chill on ice (to keep the bright colours).

For the yellow zucchini purée
9. In a pan, sweat the ginger in the olive oil.
10. Add the grated zucchini and a pinch of salt, and then cook, covered, for 2 to 3 minutes to bring the water out of the vegetables.
11. Increase the heat, remove the lid, and cook for 3 to 4 minutes, stirring regularly, to dry out the zucchini.
12. Using a blender, purée until smooth. Add salt to taste, and chill on ice.

For the miso glaze
13. Place all of the miso glaze ingredients except the butter in a blender or food processor. Blend until smooth, and then, with the machine running, gradually add the butter and purée until emulsified.

For the pickled mushrooms
14. In a pan over medium heat, fry the mushrooms in the oil.
15. Stir in the sugar, and then deglaze with the vinegar.
16. Reduce the heat to low and simmer for 5 minutes.
17. Remove from the heat and set aside, covered, for 15 minutes.

For the char
18. Cook the char for 3 to 5 minutes in the salamander broiler (or broil; see note next page). The flesh should just start to be cooked around the central bone, so adapt the cooking time to the size of the fish.
19. Peel off the skin and dry the flesh with a paper or kitchen towel. Slather 1 tbsp (15 mL) of the miso glaze on each portion of fish, and finish cooking with a blowtorch (or broil; see note next page).

To assemble
20. On each plate, assemble:
1 portion of char fillet
1 tsp (5 mL) yellow zucchini purée, spread with an angled spatula
1 tsp (5 mL) green zucchini purée, spread with an angled spatula
A quenelle (1 tbsp/15 mL) of miso eggplant
3 pickled mushrooms
1 stem of common ice plant →

NOTES AND VARIATIONS

• Canadian char is available between September and December. It can be replaced with rainbow trout or salmon.

• Saké kasu is the residue found in the fermentation process to make saké. You can replace the saké kasu with 2 tbsp (30 mL) tahini.

• Moromi miso is a condiment obtained from fermenting the ingredients used to make soy sauce, but in a reduced quantity of brine. Unlike the miso we add to soups, moromi miso is not smooth (it contains chunks of soybeans), and it is eaten alone or used as a garnish to flavour fish and tofu. It can be replaced with a smaller quantity of miso.

• Shimeji mushrooms are prized for their flavour in Japanese cooking. They are found in Asian grocery stores. They can be replaced with chanterelles or fresh or rehydrated shiitake mushrooms.

• Common ice plant is a leafy vegetable originally from South Africa whose juicy and slightly sour leaves are covered with frost or dew. Since it doesn't keep for long after being harvested, and can be found only at certain specialized farms, it is a great candidate for growing at home. It can be replaced with purslane, a sour succulent plant found in Mediterranean grocery stores.

• The salamander broiler is a cooking appliance for gratinating and caramelizing. You can also use a blowtorch or broil on the top rack in your oven.

Opposite page, miso eggplant.

Steamed pork-stuffed Asian eggplant

By Danielle Laou

茄
子

Our aunt Dany gave us this recipe for a typical Chinese dish that her mother used to make. She likes pork-stuffed eggplant because it is delicious, easy to make, and not too oily since it is steamed rather than deep-fried, the way our own mother used to make it (to our great delight!). Our aunt tells us that when she was a child, the cooking method was determined by the mood that day.

Preparation 40 min · Cooking 30 min · 4 servings ·

INGREDIENTS

2 Asian eggplants

1 to 2 tbsp (15 to 30 mL) fresh ginger, cut into fine sticks (a piece ½ to 1 inch/1 to 2 cm thick)

2 red Thai (bird's-eye) chilis, sliced

2 green onions, sliced

2 tbsp (30 mL) olive oil

2 cloves of garlic, minced

For soaking

1 tbsp (15 mL) vinegar (to prevent the eggplant from turning black)

1 tsp (5 mL) salt (to reduce bitterness)

Stuffing

8.5 oz (250 g) lean ground pork

¾ tsp (3 mL) salt

½ tsp (2 mL) baking powder

⅛ tsp (0.5 mL) baking soda

¼ cup (60 mL) water

1 tbsp (15 mL) cornstarch

1 tbsp (15 mL) olive oil

Sauce

1 tbsp (15 mL) soy sauce or tamari

1 tbsp (15 mL) oyster sauce

½ tbsp (7 mL) cornstarch

1 tsp (5 mL) sesame oil

½ tsp (2 mL) granulated sugar

Ground black pepper, to taste

METHOD

For the stuffing

1. Put the pork in a bowl, and then add the remaining stuffing ingredients. Mix by hand, always in the same direction, until you obtain a homogenous, sticky texture.

2. Throw the mixture against the bottom of the bowl five or six times to make it more elastic and smooth. Cover and set aside in the fridge.

For the eggplants

3. Rinse the eggplants, and then remove the ends. Cut into diagonal slices ¾ inch (2 cm) thick. Score each slice, cut-side up, at the centre, two-thirds of the way through so you can garnish each slice like a sandwich.

4. Add the vinegar and salt to a bowl of water. Soak the eggplants for 10 to 15 minutes. Drain, then pat dry with a paper or a kitchen towel to absorb surplus liquid.

5. Fill the eggplant slices with the stuffing. Put in a heat-proof container, and then sprinkle with ginger. Set aside.

6. In a cooking pot, rest a metal support, then fill with water so that the water does not go higher than the support. Bring the water to a boil. Put the eggplant container on the support. Drape a tea towel under the lid of the cooking pot to avoid condensation falling on the eggplants. Steam-cook for 20 minutes. Transfer the eggplants to a serving dish.

7. Pour the cooking juice from the eggplant container into a measuring cup and add water until you have 1 cup (250 mL). Set aside.

8. Sprinkle the chilis and green onions over the eggplants.

For the sauce

9. In a bowl, whisk together the ingredients for the sauce.

10. In a small saucepan over medium heat, pour 2 tbsp (30 mL) of the olive oil. Stir-fry the garlic, and then add the sauce. Cook, stirring continuously with a wooden spoon, until the sauce thickens slightly. Pour over the eggplants.

Bon appétit! *Maann maann sik!*

NOTES AND VARIATIONS

· The eggplant can be replaced with green bell peppers chopped into 2-inch (5 cm) pieces, which you can top with the stuffing before steam-cooking.

· The Thai (bird's-eye) chilis can also be replaced by red bell pepper.

· You can add roughly chopped fresh shrimp to the stuffing.

· Instead of the sauce, you can simply drizzle the eggplants with soy sauce and sesame oil.

Danielle Laou, unstoppable cook

Danielle Laou is our mother's older sister; they are the youngest two children of eight siblings. Danielle was the only one of our aunts and uncles to have settled in Montreal, so we would often go there to eat at her house with her husband, Bernard, and their children, Michaël and Sandra. What amazing gastronomic memories we have! Christmas dinners were notable for the astronomical quantity of delicious food, the many faces gathered around that we didn't see very often, and the fun group games. Dany, as she is called in French, or Yi Ma, as we call her, is an experienced, unflagging, and unbelievably generous cook. She is also very sociable and maintains a close connection with the entire extended family by phone and online.

Danielle remembers her father and uncles running a general store where she grew up in Nosy Be. It was originally a small shop, but they worked hard over the years, and it became the biggest one on their small island. It stocked, among other things, vegetables, flours, canned and jarred food, alcohol, and meat, along with clothes, material, toys, cosmetics, office furniture, hardware tools, musical instruments, radios, and much more. During the difficult years of the Second World War, her parents started making sweets to sell. Later on, when the shop grew, her father installed a machine for making lemonade with homemade syrup, and then started making popsicles. This was a time when people had to manage everything for themselves: Danielle's mother and aunt made cakes, waffles, fresh noodles, wontons, yogurt, and all kinds of ready-made snacks for the family as well as for customers. Danielle and her brothers and sisters have many fond memories of all those wonderful things to eat.

When they were at home, Danielle and our mother helped out a lot in the kitchen, especially preparing the food for the special day of January 1, New Year. The saat3 kei4 maa5, a dessert that resembles the puffed rice squares we all know, was one of the treats served on this occasion. For the green papaya syrup needed to make it, Danielle's mother would have her boiling the mixture for a good 3 hours. And she made enormous quantities of saat3 kei4 maa5: 6 lb (3 kg) of sugar to produce 6 lb (3 kg) of dough. Later on, once Danielle herself was the mother of a family and living in Quebec, she made it again, adding a little glucose instead of boiling the syrup for such a long time, and scaling it down to end up with just 7 oz (200 g) of dough. The syrup was ready in 10 minutes. The general store era was over! Our aunt remains convinced, after all this time, that her mother's saat3 kei4 maa5 is better than her own.

Today, Danielle still loves cooking and her cuisine is constantly evolving. She has taken Chinese dessert cooking classes in Hong Kong. Over the years, her cooking mostly stayed Chinese, but she adapts her recipes and explores new ones to match the tastes of her grandchildren and nieces. This requires a lot of research, and to do this she is constantly accumulating information by calling family members, spending hours on online searches, and archiving her wonderful finds, which she then loves sharing by email. She doesn't mind at all staying up late to finish a recipe or online research.

Danielle is seventy-five and still cooks with as much devotion as she did when she was younger, continuing to spread happiness all around her.

ASIAN CUCUMBER

黃
瓜

ASIAN CUCUMBER

Also known as: oriental cucumber
黃瓜 wong4 gwaa1/huángguā (yellow | squash)
In Cantonese also called: 青瓜 ceng1 gwaa1 (green | squash)

FAMILY: Cucurbitaceae

SPECIES: *Cucumis sativus*

HISTORY Originally from tropical Asia and likely India, the cucumber has been grown there for at least 3,000 years. It spread to the Far East and Mediterranean during antiquity. The Suyo Long and Tokiwa cultivars, both originally Chinese, are particularly good.

Asian cucumbers are more flavourful than English cucumbers or field cucumbers. They have the sought-after traits of Lebanese cucumbers — crunchy and refreshing, with few seeds and a thin skin — but the flesh stands out with its hint of lemon and creamy texture. They are an ideal choice for crudités, salads, spring rolls, sushi, and marinades. The Suyo Long cultivar has been available for a few years in markets and organic vegetable boxes. In the garden, Asian cucumber grows like any other cucumber variety.

Green, long, and slender, the most common Asian cucumbers have beautiful curves and bumpy skin with small spines and shallow ridges — not to be confused with luffa. This vegetable is mild to the taste and can measure up to 35 inches (90 cm) long.

In the garden

· It's vital to keep the young transplants under a floating row cover in the spring to protect them from the first wave of striped cucumber beetles. The cover can be removed once the first flowers appear; by this point the plants will be robust enough to withstand the next — less ferocious — waves of beetles.

· The cucumber will be more attractive and straighter if the plant has a support to climb.

· Constant watering guarantees sweet, juicy cucumbers.

· Most seed companies offer the Suyo Long cultivar, which is open-pollinated. At Le Rizen, this has been our preferred variety for several years, and we have obtained abundant harvests from growing it in the field without any staking, pruning, or manual pollination.

· To grow it in a container, plant in a pot that is at least 1 gallon (4 L). Ideally, use a large 5-gallon (20 L) pot and be sure to leave 10 inches (25 cm) between each plant. The challenge is to water regularly enough, since the soil dries out more quickly in pots than it does in the garden.

· The more mature the cucumber, the more seeds and juice. It's best to harvest by cutting the pedicel with secateurs once it has reached a diameter of 1½ to 2 inches (4 to 5 cm).

STORING
Keeps for up to one week, covered with a paper or kitchen towel and placed inside a sealable plastic bag or container in the fridge, or for up to 10 to 14 days after harvest in optimal conditions.

PREPARING
Prepare and use like any other cucumber: rinse, then slice, cut into sticks, or dice. It is not necessary to peel it or remove the seeds. You can rub off the small prickles on the skin with a dry cloth or with your hands under running water.

NUTRITION

Cucumber is 96% water. It is a source of vitamin K, which is particularly concentrated in the skin. This vitamin plays a role in blood coagulation and bone health. Several vegetables introduced in this book are excellent sources of vitamin K, including amaranth, mustard greens, and tatsoi. However, people taking certain anti-coagulants should take care not to change the amount of food sources of vitamin K consumed daily so as not to interfere with the medication.

IN THE KITCHEN

Edible parts	Ways to eat	Ways to cook
◦ Young leaves	◦ Raw	◦ Boil
◦ Young stems	◦ Cooked	◦ Sauté/stir-fry
◦ Flesh	◦ Pickled/ lacto-fermented	◦ Roast/grill
◦ Skin	◦ Dried	◦ Deep-fry
◦ Seeds		
◦ Flowers		

Asian cucumber is best eaten raw. In China, it is also eaten cooked or pickled. It goes well with garlic, tomato, onion, fresh cilantro, and dill, as well as with ginger, green onion, shiso, sesame seeds, and soy sauce.

RAW

· It is delicious as a crudité or in salads, sliced or diced.

· It is a good replacement for other cucumbers in pickles and lacto-fermentations. Cut into sticks, it can be quick pickled with black rice vinegar, sesame oil, garlic, and Sichuan peppercorn, refrigerated overnight, and then enjoyed cold.

· You can also make cucumber chips (see "Extending the life of vegetables" on page 314).

· Its shoots, young leaves and stems, and flowers can be used to garnish salads.

COOKED
Asian cucumber loses its crunch and becomes bitter when cooked. Either cook it very quickly or opt for cooking when it is very ripe or soft.

Our favourite ways to prepare it:
· Stir-fry lightly; for example, cut lengthways into two, and then in thin diagonal slices, and then toss with wood ear mushrooms and soy bean curd sticks or finely sliced pork, dressed with a sauce made from Shaoxing rice cooking wine, soy sauce, and oyster sauce.

· In Chinese cooking, very ripe cucumbers are peeled, diced, and added to soups at the end of cooking; for example, into a bone broth with peeled ginger.

· As with zucchini, the cucumber flower can be battered and then fried.

Cold noodles
(*Liáng miàn*)

By Maxime Robert-Lachaîne

黄瓜

Maxime loves noodle dishes so much he could eat them every day. According to him, when travelling in China, whatever the region, you just need to be able to remember the sinogram *miàn* 面 or 麵, which means "noodles," to be assured of a good meal. Whether the noodles are made of rice, wheat, egg, or mung beans, China is overflowing with regional variations on noodle dishes, stemming from centuries of traditions and culinary fusions across the country. Maxime's noodle recipe comes from Sichuan and is a firm favourite with everyone who tastes it. He often cooks this dish in summer since it is eaten cold — *liáng* meaning "cold."

Preparation 25 min • Cooking 35 min • 2 servings • 🌶🌶🌶

INGREDIENTS

10 oz (300 g) fresh wheat noodles or 7 oz (200 g) dried noodles

Oil of your choice

1 small carrot, julienned

⅓ to ½ Asian cucumber, julienned

1 handful of bean sprouts (optional)

1 clove of garlic, crushed in a mortar and mixed with 1 tsp (5 mL) cold water

2 green onions, green parts only, thinly sliced

1 tsp (5 mL) toasted sesame seeds

Sichuan peppercorn, roasted and ground, to taste

Aromatic soy sauce

¾ cup (180 mL) cold water

½ cup (125 mL) soy sauce or tamari

1 star anise

½ cinnamon stick

½ tsp (2 mL) fennel seeds

½ tsp (2 mL) Sichuan peppercorn

1 slice of fresh ginger (about ½ inch/1 cm thick)

3 tbsp (45 mL) pure maple syrup (or brown sugar)

Sauce

2 tbsp (30 mL) aromatic soy sauce (see recipe)

4 tsp (20 mL) Chinkiang black rice vinegar

2 to 3 tbsp (30 to 45 mL) chili oil, to taste

2 tsp (10 mL) sesame oil

1 tsp (5 mL) pure maple syrup

METHOD

For the aromatic soy sauce

1. In a small saucepan, combine the water and soy sauce, and bring to a boil. Add the spices and ginger. Reduce the heat and simmer gently for 20 minutes, or until you are left with about ½ cup (125 mL) of liquid.

2. Stir in the maple syrup. Pour through a fine sieve into a sealable container. Set aside.

To prepare

3. Bring a saucepan of water to a boil, and then cook the noodles until they are tender but still al dente. Drain and rinse in cold water. Transfer them to a large plate, tossing with a little oil to prevent them from sticking, and set aside to dry for a few moments.

4. Meanwhile, prepare the vegetables.

5. In a bowl, whisk together all of the sauce ingredients.

To assemble

6. Divide the noodles between two bowls, and then pour half the sauce into each bowl. Garnish with carrot, cucumber, and bean sprouts, and top with a little garlic purée. Sprinkle with the green onions and sesame seeds, and then finish with the Sichuan pepper. Mix well before eating.

NOTES AND VARIATIONS

· Asian cucumber can be replaced by Lebanese or English cucumber.

· For a nice addition (for 2 bowls), add ½ cup (125 mL) edamame or shredded cold chicken. Add a little more sauce to each bowl.

· Cinnamon sticks that are commonly sold in North America are originally from South China and are technically false cinnamon, called cassia. They are less expensive than true cinnamon from Sri Lanka, as well as being thicker and spicier.

· Aromatic soy sauce, or red sauce, as the chef who showed Maxime how to make it called it, is also used in tián shuǐ miàn (cold noodles that resemble udon) or in hóng yóu chāo shǒu (Sichuan dumplings with chili oil). Once made, it keeps well in the fridge.

Maxime Robert-Lachaîne
Checkmonwok

Maxime shares his passion for Asian food through his Checkmonwok project, which publishes recipes from China, Vietnam, Laos, and Thailand, as well as information to help people better understand and cook these recipes. Since it is difficult to obtain organic Asian vegetables in Quebec, Le Rizen is a real gold mine for him.

Asian cucumber and shiso cocktail

By Chloé Ostiguy

黄
瓜

This summer cocktail, simple and delicious, stars the freshness of Asian cucumber juice, the singular notes of your regional alcohol, and the unique flavour of shiso. This drink is perfect for special occasions, such as cocktails in the garden or summer brunches, or for a refreshing pause when the cucumber harvests are abundant and you don't know what to do with all the bounty.

Preparation 15 min (or 5 min if using sparkling water)
Makes 1 cup (250 mL)

INGREDIENTS

3 green shiso leaves
½ oz (15 mL) white vermouth
5 oz (150 mL) white wine
2 oz (60 mL) Asian cucumber juice (or sparkling water)
Ice cubes

For the cucumber juice
1 Asian cucumber, cut into batons

METHOD

1. Using a juicer, extract the juice from the Asian cucumber. Set aside.

2. Crush the shiso leaves in a mortar. Add the vermouth and crush again. Set aside.

3. Fill a large glass with ice cubes, and then pour in the mixture of shiso and vermouth. Add the wine and the cucumber juice. Mix with a long spoon, and enjoy.

NOTES AND VARIATIONS

· The Asian cucumber can be replaced with any variety of cucumber.

· The shiso can be replaced with fresh cilantro or basil.

· Add a few crushed blackberries or blueberries for colour.

· Some Quebec vineyards offer white vermouth and white wine — give them a try!

Chloé Ostiguy
L'Archipel

Chloé is the visionary chef-owner at the bar of L'Archipel in Cowansville, Quebec. Her mission, which she began a few years ago, was to supply her kitchen entirely with local goods. To do this, she works with farms of the region, including Le Rizen, to transform their fresh seasonal vegetables into delicious dishes year-round. Her vegetarian culinary creations have no limits, and here she enthusiastically offers her very own take on using Asian vegetables.

LUFFA

絲
瓜

LUFFA

Also known as: luffa gourd/angled luffa, Chinese okra/
smooth luffa, sponge gourd, dishcloth gourd
絲瓜 / 丝瓜 si1 gwaa1/sīguā (silk/thread | squash)
In Cantonese also called: 勝瓜 / 胜瓜 sing3 gwaa1 (win |
squash). Because 絲 in 絲瓜 has a similar pronunciation to
輸 (lose) in Cantonese, in that language they say 勝 (win)
instead of 絲, which gives the name 勝瓜.

Family: Cucurbitaceae

Series: *Luffa acutangula* (angled luffa), *Luffa aegyptiaca*
(smooth luffa)

HISTORY Luffa grows in tropical and
subtropical regions. It was originally from
South Asia and is eaten in Asia and Africa,
especially when it is young. It is also very
popular in China. Once mature, luffa is dried
and its fibrous flesh used as an exfoliating
sponge or scrubbing pad, and even to make
products such as carpets and shoes.

**Luffa is mainly known for
the sponge it forms once
dried. Its delicious taste is
a well-guarded secret: its
light, spongy texture feels
like biting into a cloud.
Hard to find outside Asian
grocery stores, it is certainly
worth the effort to grow it.**

In the same family as cucumber and zucchini, luffa is a climbing plant that can
reach 15 feet (4.5 m) in height and has the aroma of peanuts. The luffa fruit is somewhat like zucchini, with airier flesh and a sweeter flavour. It is eaten when young
because when it is mature it becomes fibrous, the skin hardens and turns bitter, and
the seeds swell and become bitter. There are two types of luffa: angled luffa, which
is slender and ridged and can measure up to 24 inches (60 cm) long, and smooth
luffa, which is often striped and shaped like a baseball bat. Although both types are
edible, the first is more commonly eaten because it is sweeter to the taste, while the
second is mainly used for making sponges because its fibre is easier to extract, and
its larger circumference when mature makes a decent-sized sponge.

NUTRITION

Smooth luffa is a source of vitamin C. It acts as an antioxidant while protecting
cells against oxidation. In addition, this vegetable encourages absorption of iron,
which is particularly important for vegans.

In the garden

• Choose the type of luffa to grow according to the desired use, either for eating or for making sponges. However, note that smooth luffa produces more fruits and is easier to grow.

• Whichever type you choose, make sure to choose a quick-growing cultivar.

• Luffa can be grown in a 5-gallon (20 L) container; put a layer of rocks or other good drainage material at the bottom, then cover with compost and earth, or a rich potting soil.

• Like cucumbers, luffa plants need stakes or a trellis to climb so that the fruit grows straight.

• To maximize fruit production, pull off the first flowers at the bud stage. You can also keep only the flowers that appear at least 3 feet (1 m) above the ground, which will allow the fruit to grow straight and receive more nutrients. Another tip is to pinch off the top of the main stem when it measures 5 feet (1.5 m) tall to encourage the growth of lateral shoots. If deformed fruits appear, remove them.

• The young fruits of both types of luffa are edible when well shaped and ¾ to 2 inches (2 to 5 cm) in diameter. The fruit's length varies with the cultivar and your preferences. At Le Rizen, our record is an angled luffa that was 3.6 feet (1.1 m) long. At this size, the fruit needs to be peeled, but the flesh is just as delicious.

• Note that harvesting luffa at a very mature stage will reduce the overall number of fruits per plant. In addition, an over-mature fruit will have coarse seeds that have to be removed before cooking. It is therefore better to harvest before passing the immature seed stage.

STORING
Keeps for a few days wrapped in a kitchen towel and then put in a basket in the pantry or placed in a plastic container or bag in the fridge. Keeps for 7 to 21 days after harvest in optimal conditions.

Note: Luffa is very fragile. Handle very gently to avoid damaging its skin or breaking it, which will reduce the amount of time it will keep.

PREPARING
Rinse the luffa. For angled luffa, peel the ridges with a peeler or knife. It is not necessary to peel young luffa if its skin is tender. Then slice the luffa to produce star shapes, or dice, cut into big chunks, or grate.

IN THE KITCHEN

Edible parts	Ways to eat	Ways to cook
• Young leaves	• Raw	• Steam
• Flesh	• Cooked	• Boil
• Young skin	• Pickled/	• Sauté/stir-fry
• Young seeds	lacto-fermented	• Roast/grill
• Buds and	• Dried	• Deep-fry
flowers		

Luffa is eaten like zucchini. It can be enjoyed raw or cooked, but it is better cooked with a sauce; like a sponge, it will absorb the liquids it's cooked in and take on the flavours. It goes well with seafood, chicken, and pork.

RAW
• Eat raw as a crudité.

• It can also be served like a cucumber salad, sliced or diced.

• The young leaves, shoots, flowers, and buds brighten up salads.

COOKED
It's important to choose ingredients that will not overpower its delicate flavour and to avoid overcooking since it is already tender.

Our favourite ways to prepare it:
• Steam-cooked or oven-roasted, and then drizzled with sesame oil and fish or soy sauce.

• Filled with a mixture of ground meat and vegetables, and then steamed or baked.

• Stir-fried with ginger and soy sauce, or with ginger, garlic, wood ear mushrooms, shrimp, and a sauce made from Shaoxing rice cooking wine and sesame oil.

• Simmered until tender, and then served with butter and lemon juice, or simmered briefly in a clear soup.

• Grated and then browned gently in a frying pan and added to an omelette.

• Battered and fried as tempura.

In China and Japan, young luffa is sliced and then dried and stored in a sealed container for use during the winter (you can dry it in the oven or, for other methods, see "Extending the life of vegetables" on page 314). In China, dried luffa cooked in stock is widely appreciated.

The young leaves, shoots, and buds can be stir-fried, fried, or simmered until tender and served with butter and curry powder.

When luffa reaches at least 2 inches (5 cm) in diameter, the young seeds can be oven-roasted like pumpkin seeds, either dry or with oil and salt.

Right: *Harvesting smooth luffa and angled luffa.*

Luffa spread

By Chloé Ostiguy

Chloé loves the fact that the texture and flavour of luffa are halfway between cucumber and zucchini. Luffa's silky texture means that it is perfect for making spreads. This one can be used in a sandwich, as a dip with crudités, or smothered over grilled tofu or vegetables.

Preparation 5 min · Cooking 10 min · Makes 1½ cups (375 mL) ·

INGREDIENTS

1 small to medium luffa (1.3 lb/625 g)
2 tbsp (30 mL) sunflower oil
½ tbsp (7 mL) tamari or soy sauce
½ cup (125 mL) fresh cilantro leaves
2 tbsp (30 mL) grainy mustard
1 tbsp (15 mL) white miso paste
1 tsp (5 mL) ground fennel seeds
1 tsp (5 mL) red pepper flakes

METHOD

1. Cut the luffa in half lengthways and then into ¾-inch (2 cm) thick slices.

2. In a large frying pan over high heat, heat 1 tbsp (15 mL) oil. Add the luffa and cook for 5 to 10 minutes, stirring occasionally, until it browns. Add the tamari, stir, and then remove from the heat.

3. In a food processor, blend the luffa, 1 tbsp (15 mL) oil, and the remaining ingredients until smooth. If needed, add a little cold water.

4. Cool before serving.

5. The dip will keep in a sealable container in the fridge for several days.

NOTES AND VARIATIONS

The luffa can be replaced by 2 or 3 zucchini.

Luffa and chicken stir-fry

By Danielle Laou

絲
瓜

Aunt Dany has always loved eating luffa. She makes sure to buy it the right size—that is, not too thick—so that it is still tender on the inside. She enjoys its soft texture and sweet taste, and uses it in stir-fries or makes into soup. Here she introduces a Cantonese stir-fry recipe that she likes to brighten up by using colourful vegetables.

Preparation 30 min • Cooking 30 min • Rest 10 min • 3 servings

INGREDIENTS

Chicken

2 deboned skinless chicken thighs (10 oz/300 g)
    or 1 to 2 skinless boneless chicken breasts
⅛ tsp (0.5 mL) salt
1 tsp (5 mL) soy sauce or tamari
1 tsp (5 mL) oyster sauce
1 tsp (5 mL) cooking liquor (or light cooking rice wine)
¼ tsp (1 mL) ground black pepper
½ tsp (2 mL) sesame oil
1 tbsp (15 mL) cornstarch
1 tbsp (15 mL) water
2 tbsp (30 mL) olive oil for cooking
2 cloves of garlic, thinly sliced
2 slices of fresh ginger (¹⁄₁₆ inch/2 mm thick),
    cut into fine batons

Dried mushrooms

0.3 oz (10 g) dried cloud ear or wood ear mushrooms
1 tsp (5 mL) granulated sugar
1 tsp (5 mL) all-purpose flour

Other vegetables

1 luffa (12 oz/350 g)
1 red bell pepper
8 oz (230 g) button mushrooms
1 onion, thinly sliced
2 cloves of garlic, minced
3 slices of fresh ginger (¹⁄₁₆ inch/2 mm thick)
2 tbsp (30 mL) olive oil for cooking
1 tsp (5 mL) salt
Ground black pepper, to taste

Sauce

½ tbsp (7 mL) oyster sauce
½ tsp (2 mL) soy sauce or tamari
½ tsp (2 mL) granulated sugar
2 tbsp (30 mL) cornstarch
1 tsp (5 mL) sesame oil
½ tsp (2 mL) ground black pepper
¼ cup (60 mL) water

METHOD

For the chicken

1. Rinse the chicken, and then cut it into pieces roughly ¾ inch (2 cm) wide and 1½ inches (4 cm) long. Put it in a bowl, add the salt, soy sauce, oyster sauce, cooking liquor, pepper, sesame oil, cornstarch, and water. Mix until the chicken is well coated. Cover and refrigerate for 10 minutes to marinate.

For the dried mushrooms

2. Rinse the dried mushrooms and place in a sealable container. Add the sugar, flour, and just enough water to cover. Seal the container, and then shake for 5 minutes (or soak in warm water for 15 to 60 minutes), or until the mushrooms are softened. Remove the hard part of the mushrooms, and then rinse with water. If the pieces are large, cut them smaller.

3. Bring water to boil in a saucepan, and then cook the mushrooms for 5 to 10 minutes, covered. Drain, and then set aside.

For the other vegetables

4. Peel the luffa skin if it is hard. Cut and discard the ends. Cut the luffa in half lengthways and then diagonally in ¾-inch (2 cm) thick slices.

5. Cut the bell pepper into chunks about ¾ inch (2 cm) wide and 1½ inches (4 cm) long.

6. Plunge the button mushrooms quickly into cold water to clean them, and then cut off the dirty part of the stem. Peel the skin (optional). If the mushrooms are large, cut them in half.

For the sauce

7. In a bowl, combine the sauce ingredients.

To cook

8. Heat a wok over medium heat, and then add the oil, garlic, and ginger for the chicken. When the oil is hot, add the marinated chicken. Brown each side for 45 seconds, then stir-fry for 15 seconds, or until the chicken is cooked through. Set aside.

9. Wash the wok if there is cooking residue in it. Heat the wok over medium heat, and then add the oil and garlic for the other vegetables. When the oil is hot, stir-fry the ginger for about 30 seconds. Add the onion, luffa, bell pepper, button mushrooms, dried mushrooms, and salt. Increase the heat to high, and then stir-fry for 40 seconds. Add the cooked chicken, and then stir-fry for another 20 seconds. Gradually add the sauce and stir well for 15 seconds.

10. Transfer to a serving plate and season with black pepper overtop.

11. Serve with rice.

NOTES AND VARIATIONS

• The luffa can be replaced with zucchini or cucumber. The dried mushrooms can be replaced with carrot.

• The chicken can be replaced with firm tofu, fish fillet, pork, beef, seafood, or scrambled eggs. You can macerate the chicken with a simple mixture of salt, soy sauce, cornstarch, and oil.

• The oyster sauce can be replaced with chicken stock or omitted.

Our grandfather Gaston, in his garden in Ambatondrazaka.

Culinary shocks

Over the course of their migratory journey, our family members have had to modify how they cook, since the Asian vegetables needed to make traditional dishes were not always available where they were at the time.

In Madagascar, access to Chinese vegetables changed depending on the region. Our mother's family lived in Nosy Be, an island far from the capital and other big towns, which had no Chinese restaurant. So they had to change their diet, since Asian vegetables were not available year-round. As for our father's family, they had settled in Ambatondrazaka, closer to the big cities and a large concentration of Cantonese families. This is probably why they had access to more Chinese vegetables. But certain Chinese products, such as tofu, bean sprouts, and preserved foods, quite simply never reached the Madagascar shores. It was therefore common for the Chinese community to make their own versions.

After going through this culinary shock in Madagascar, our grandparents, aunts, and uncles had to acquire other culinary norms when they arrived in Canada. Our uncle Jean started growing Asian vegetables that were difficult to find or expensive in Quebec, such as mustard greens, chayote, and bitter melon. On the other hand, he no longer germinated mung beans: "You can buy them for a few dollars at the grocery store!"

Uncle Bernard, Dany's husband, also started growing food when he arrived in Canada, and his garden is pretty impressive. He manages to grow unusual vegetables right in the heart of the city, including goji berries, luffa, and Brede mafane (a leafy green). Bernard saves most of his seeds, since it was difficult to get hold of Asian vegetable seeds when he started gardening.

As far as we are concerned, we were very lucky to have had access to Chinese vegetables, products, and restaurants during our Montreal childhood. Today, we are the ones who live far from Montreal, in varying degrees, and who have to contend with new culinary shocks. Outside the city, it can be more difficult to get hold of certain Asian vegetables and ingredients. Sometimes it's like being in Nosy Be!

We are grateful to the generations that came before us for having cultivated this attachment to Chinese cooking and its ingredients. Their resilience and creativity have allowed the flavours of our country of origin to be passed down to us. And in our turn, we wish to continue cooking—in our way—our culture of origin.

LEMONGRASS

香
茅

LEMONGRASS

香茅 hoeng1 maau4/xiāngmáo (fragrant | reeds/rushes)

FAMILY: Poaceae

SPECIES: *Cymbopogon citratus, Cymbopogon flexuosus*

HISTORY Originally from the tropical and subtropical regions of Asia, lemongrass is used as an aromatic in the countries of Southeast Asia, particularly in Thailand and Malaysia.

An aromatic herb with a citrusy flavour, lemongrass is a key element in recipes from Southeast Asia. Stalks of lemongrass are often found in Asian grocery stores or supermarkets: whole stems with the chilled vegetables, and its dried leaves with the spices or teas. You can also find it whole, or frozen in jars, in Asian grocery stores. The lemongrass grown locally has a great deal of potential, both in the garden and in the kitchen, when you learn to use all parts of it. In the garden, it is low maintenance as long as it gets as much heat as possible.

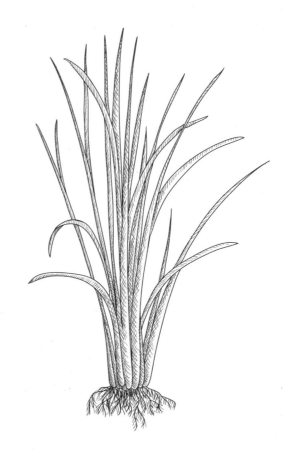

A large and beautiful herb, lemongrass produces pretty tufts of long, narrow leaves. Its yellowish green stems have a bulbous base prized for its tender edible flesh. Its citrusy flavour is delicate, and its aroma is akin to perfume. The outside part of the stems, and the leaves, are too tough for eating, but they lend a wonderful scent to a wide range of dishes. There are more than fifty different species of lemongrass, including the two most common. *Cymbopogon citratus* is the most widely spread species across the world, thanks to its large stem; it is also the one most commonly found in grocery stores. *Cymbopogon flexuosus* tolerates cooler temperatures and has an aromatic ginger note.

In the garden

- Lemongrass is a pleasant crop because it is unique in its genus* and, overall, relatively easy to grow. It simply needs enough fertilizer, moisture, and heat to produce a thick stem. Although here at Le Rizen we adore the species *Cymbopogon flexuosus*, we are planning to try other varieties in the future.

- Plan on sowing up to four times as many seeds as necessary, because this plant's germination rate is often poor. Another option is to buy a lemongrass stem with roots intact at the grocery store, soak it in water until the roots develop, and then plant it in a pot.

- Lemongrass can be harvested from mid-August. If frost is expected, the entire crop must be harvested because lemongrass cannot tolerate frost. It's best to harvest it wearing gloves — its leaves are very sharp. To harvest, pull the whole stalk with a bit of root, either by hand or with a knife. A faster harvesting technique is to break the stalk with your hands as close as possible above the root.

- If you don't want to start new seeds every spring, it is possible to bring lemongrass indoors over the winter and then replant outside in the spring. To do this, remove each plant from the soil and replant individually in 5-gallon (20 L) pots, leaving just 6 inches (15 cm) of the stem above the surface. Put the potted plants in a sunny place with good air circulation, somewhere well sheltered and away from frost. During their dormant period, water just enough to dampen the soil, about once a week. In the spring, water more regularly. When ready to move them back outside, divide each plant into several tufts that you can then either repot or plant straight into the garden.

STORING

The whole stalks with their fresh leaves will keep covered with a dry or damp kitchen towel and placed inside a sealable plastic bag or container in the fridge for a few days, or for 10 to 14 days after harvest in optimal conditions.

PREPARING

Rinse the stems and leaves, if desired. To separate the leaves from the stems, cut with pruning shears, especially if you have a lot to prepare, or with a knife, at the junction of leaf and stem. Then cut the stems into 4-inch (10 cm) sections. If desired, retrieve the tender flesh from the inside of the lower, thicker, stem sections and use immediately or freeze. Freeze the stem sections and outer layers in a sealed bag.

The leaves can be gathered to form a small bouquet, maximum 1 inch (2.5 cm) in diameter, and hung in the air. Once dried, they can be cut into 1-inch (2.5 cm) or smaller pieces using pruning shears, and then stored in a glass jar.

IN THE KITCHEN

Edible parts	Ways to eat	Ways to cook
• Flesh	• Raw (flesh)	• Steam
	• Cooked	• Boil
	• Pickled/ lacto-fermented	• Sauté/stir-fry
	• Dried	• Roast/grill

Lemongrass flesh can be eaten raw or cooked, while the leaves and stems need to be used in infusions. The flesh can be used whole, minced, or crushed. Lemongrass goes well with ginger, coconut, garlic, and chili.

RAW

The raw flesh can perfume vinegars, marinades, and curry pastes. For example, it can be crushed with red chilis, kaffir lime leaves, spices, and oil to make a Thai red curry paste.

COOKED

- The flesh can be cooked in all kinds of meals: stews, stir-fries, seafood, fish, chicken, pork, beef, rice, vegetables, and so on. We particularly love chicken and curries flavoured with lemongrass.

- Chunks of fresh or frozen stem can be added to long-cooking dishes like broths, soups, sauces, and stews, as well as to syrups for making desserts. Before adding, twist the chunks with your fingers to encourage the aroma to come out during cooking. Discard the stems after cooking.

- The leaves, fresh or dried, are used the same way as the stems, although they are less aromatic. They can be finely cut using scissors or pruning shears and placed in boiling water to make a tea. We love lemongrass tea: simple, flavourful, and comforting. Simply put about 1 tsp (5 mL) of lemongrass leaves in a tea filter (basket, ball, or teabag) and steep in 1 cup (250 mL) of water heated to 195°F (90°C) for 5 to 10 minutes.

NUTRITION

Lemongrass is a source of manganese. This mineral contributes to bone formation and protects cells from oxidation.

Tom kha gai soup

By Maxime Chanhda-Tremblay

According to Maxime, if you ask for soup in Thailand, you will be served tom kha gai. This is a creamy soup with a coconut milk base, and chicken, fish sauce, and typical Thai aromatics such as lemongrass and galangal, a cousin of ginger. The name tom kha gai literally means "soup | galangal | chicken." Since this traditional recipe is not well known in Quebec, Maxime loves being able to introduce it to his customers at his Asian grocery store.

Preparation 15 min • Cooking 15 min • 6 meal-size soups •

INGREDIENTS

1 lb (454 g) ground chicken

10 oz (300 g) mung bean vermicelli (or cellophane noodles)

3 to 4 Italian tomatoes (or several cherry tomatoes), diced

Cilantro leaves, to taste

Salt and pepper, to taste

Broth

3 to 4 sticks of lemongrass stem (6 inches/15 cm long; double the quantity for local lemongrass, which is thinner)

1 medium piece of galanga (about 1¾ oz/50 g), thinly sliced

6 to 8 kaffir lime leaves

1 Thai (bird's-eye) chili (optional), halved lengthways

1 can (400 mL) additive-free coconut milk

¼ to ½ cup (60 to 125 mL) granulated sugar

¼ to ½ cup (60 to 125 mL) fish sauce (nước mắm)

METHOD

1. Add 12 cups (3 L) cold water to a pot. Add the lemongrass, galangal, kaffir lime leaves, and Thai chili, and bring to a boil.

2. In a bowl, mix the ground chicken with a good pinch of salt. Shape into small balls.

3. Add the balls to the pot and stir gently to keep them separate. Add the coconut milk, sugar, and fish sauce. Season with salt, to taste.

4. Reduce the heat to medium-low and simmer until the chicken balls are completely cooked through (if you have a thermometer, it should reach 165°F/74°C).

5. Meanwhile, in a saucepan, boil water for the noodles. Turn off the heat, and then soak the noodles for 5 to 10 minutes. Drain well, and divide between the serving bowls.

6. Before serving, add the tomatoes and cilantro leaves to the soup. Adjust seasoning, if necessary. Ladle into the serving bowls.

NOTES AND VARIATIONS

· The mung bean vermicelli can be replaced with rice vermicelli.

Galangal and kaffir lime leaves are two aromatics used in Southeast Asian cooking.

· Galanga comes from the same family as ginger and is used the same way. It is slightly more citrusy and less peppery. Although it can be replaced with ginger in this soup, the end result won't be the same because of its unique eucalyptus note.

· Kaffir lime leaves come from a tree that originates in Southeast Asia: the kaffir lime tree, which is different from the trees that produce lime fruits as we know them. The leaves have a citrusy flavour, somewhere between lemon and lime, but are not acidic or bitter.

香茅

Grilled chicken with lemongrass and Siling labuyo chili (*Gà nướng sả ớt*)

By Alexandre Vovan

The first time Alexandre met Amélie, she ordered lemongrass chicken with disconcerting confidence. This dish would turn out to be one of their first topics of intimate conversation. Alexandre taught Amélie that traditionally, this dish was served with skin and bones, and that it was much more tender and flavourful this way. He promised her that one day, he would introduce her to his version so she could taste the difference. That day turned out to be the very next day, and after tasting Alexandre's version, Amélie never let go of him again! The couple's special recipe is printed here, and they hope it will make you fall in love with Vietnam and with locally grown lemongrass.

Preparation 30 min • Cooking 30 to 45 min • Resting 1 hour
4 servings • ⌇

INGREDIENTS

8 skin-on, bone-in chicken thighs
5 whole lemongrass stems (double quantity if using local lemongrass because it is thinner)
3 cloves of garlic
1 French shallot
6 Siling labuyo chilis (or 1 Thai)

Marinade

2 tbsp (30 mL) fish sauce (nước mắm)
1 tbsp (15 mL) light soy sauce or tamari
1 tbsp (15 mL) rice vinegar or fresh lime juice
2 tbsp (30 mL) liquid honey
¼ cup (60 mL) water
Ground black pepper, to taste

Glaze

2 tbsp (30 mL) liquid honey

METHOD

1. Cut and discard surplus fat on the thighs (leaving as little fat as possible). Wash the thighs well under cold water, drain, and put in a large bowl.

2. Cut and discard the thin green layers of the lemongrass stems, keeping the tender white flesh near the root (pull the fibrous layers off the lemongrass stems the same way you remove dry skin from an onion).

3. Crush the lemongrass flesh with the back of a chef's knife (or a meat tenderizer), and mince as finely as possible. Finely chop the garlic, shallot, and chilis.

4. Add the lemongrass flesh, garlic, shallot, chilis, and marinade ingredients to the large bowl with the chicken. Mix well, cover, and refrigerate for at least 1 hour (or overnight for maximum flavour).

5. Grill the chicken for 30 to 45 minutes over high heat until browned, and then over indirect heat, turning and brushing it with the marinade every 5 to 10 minutes. Toward the end of cooking, glaze with honey to lacquer the meat. Remove the chicken when it reaches an internal temperature of 165°F (74°C).

6. Serve with broken rice or noodles and a vegetable dish.

NOTES AND VARIATIONS

· We like to wash the chicken in cold water to remove residue like bits of feather.

· You can brush the marinade between the skin and the flesh by slicing an opening at one side of the chicken so that the skin stays attached to the flesh on the other sides.

· The Siling labuyo chili is a very spicy, small, triangular chili from the Philippines. In Vietnam it is called "forest chili" because it grows easily in nature. In Tagalog, the main language spoken in the Philippines, *Siling labuyo* means "wild chili." This chili grows very well here but is difficult to find, even in Asian grocery stores.

Alexandre Vovan

Les Vovans

Les Vovans are a Quebec woman who loves all things good and beautiful, from food to chopsticks, and managed to convince her partner to share their combined passion for Asian food with other people, and a man of Vietnamese origin who was born in Quebec. He is a true gourmet who inherited his knowledge and culinary secrets from his mother. Together, Amélie Lamothe and Alexandre Vovan have created a real Little Vietnam in Saint-Ours in Montérégie, Quebec, where they receive guests to share not just a meal but also a way of life, where cooking is a joyous activity and not just a chore. *"La vie à la viet"* (life Vietnamese-style) in Quebec is what Amélie and Alexandre offer at their cooking workshops and on their recipe blog, where Vietnam and Quebec mingle closely.

香茅

Lemongrass panna cotta

By Marie Wang

The inspiration for this recipe comes from the desserts served in dim sum restaurants: small cubes of milk-and-almond-based gelatin swimming in a bowl of canned fruit cocktail. Marie cooks this at home, and it has become the dessert she finds most comforting. She immediately thought of panna cotta when we asked her for a lemongrass dessert. She didn't know this aromatic when she was younger, but now she loves cooking and eating it!

Preparation 5 min • Infusion 30 min • Cooking 5 min
• Resting 3 hrs • 4 small ramekins

INGREDIENTS

1⅓ cups (325 mL) 10% cream

2 tbsp (30 mL) granulated sugar

3 lemongrass stems cut into 1¼-inch (3 cm) chunks

2 tsp (10 mL) powdered gelatin

2 tbsp (30 mL) water

METHOD

1. Pour cream and sugar into a saucepan. Crush the lemongrass slightly with your hands (to release the flavour) and then add to the pan. Boil for 1 minute, turn off the heat, and then let infuse at room temperature for 30 minutes.

2. Using a fork, discard the lemongrass chunks. Heat the cream over low heat for 5 minutes.

3. Meanwhile, in a small bowl, combine the gelatin and the water. Set aside for 5 minutes.

4. Away from the heat, add the gelatin mixture to the cream, and whisk for 1 to 2 minutes, until the gelatin is completely dissolved.

5. Pour the cream mixture into ramekins. Cover the surface with plastic wrap to prevent a crust from forming. Refrigerate for at least 3 hours, or until the cream is set.

6. Decorate with mint leaves, finely diced mango, ground cherries, or toasted coconut.

NOTES AND VARIATIONS

• To remove the panna cotta from the ramekin, carefully run warm water around the outside of the dish until the panna cotta comes loose, then put a plate over the ramekin and quickly invert. You can also eat the panna cotta straight from the ramekin.

• To make this vegan, use non-dairy cream (e.g., soy, cashew nut, coconut cream). The gelatin can be replaced with vegan gelatin or ½ tsp (2 mL) agar-agar. If using agar-agar, combine the cream and agar-agar in a saucepan and simmer for 1 to 2 minutes; pour the cream mixture into ramekins and refrigerate for 30 minutes.

• Panna cotta, which literally means "cooked cream," is a traditional dessert from northwest Italy. It can be flavoured with many different things, such as vanilla, coffee, lemon, or orange blossom, and it is traditionally garnished with caramel or sometimes covered with a fruit coulis. The best panna cotta Marie ever tasted is the one she had in southern Italy on a trip with her daughters, Amandine and Alizé.

香茅

FALL

秋天

THE FINAL SPRINT

After the oppressive summer heat, the arrival of cooler fall days is often positively welcomed. It's the time of final harvests, of closing down the garden, and of transforming its vegetables into products you can enjoy all winter long.

On the farm, the cold and damp settle in quickly once September arrives. The physical fatigue and the stress accumulated over the last few months make these fall days even more exhausting. Although our bodies are begging to rest indoors in the warmth, we have to stay motivated to harvest in rain and snow, with frozen hands, encumbered by heavy waterproof layers and boots that get bogged down with every step in the mud.

Despite everything, the last seedlings planted out at the end of August and the final harvests out in the field, which can stretch on until mid-November, are often accompanied by exhilarating joy, and feelings of pride and relief in reaching the last stage before the well-deserved winter rest. This is also the time to celebrate the season's accomplishments with the whole team, and then take stock of what can be improved for next season.

CLOSING UP THE GARDEN

Closing up the garden before winter is an important step, and not one to be neglected. The aim is to clear and cover the ground where things have been growing. The actions listed below will protect it not only from the winter but also from weeds and harmful insects looking for a place to shelter for the winter.

DEAL WITH THE BRASSICAS

All remainders of any bok choy, choy sum, gai lan, mustard greens, and Chinese cabbage plants — including roots, stems, and leaves — must be removed from the soil and then buried underground or placed at the bottom of the compost pile. If the roots show any signs of clubroot, a common fungal disease that deforms the roots and makes them rot, it's best to burn them or wrap them in a plastic bag and throw it into the garbage to avoid spreading the disease around the garden.

GOODBYE, WEEDS

Another good practice to adopt is to clear all growing surfaces and walkways of weeds and other debris, which are the preferred hibernation site of many harmful insects. At the end of the season, sowing green manure over the whole garden area is a beneficial practice to prepare for the cold season (see "Basic amendments" on page 94).

DRY, IN THE GARAGE, OR UNDER AN OUTDOOR SHELTER

All the seed equipment (multicell trays, pots), tools, insect netting, floating row covers, and occultation tarps should ideally be dried in the sun. Storing them without drying can lead to mould, which causes speedy deterioration of the material. You also need to tidy or cover all the containers, bins, wheelbarrows, and the vegetable-washing bath, because stagnant water encourages disease propagation and the presence of unwanted insects, especially mosquitoes. We also recommend dismantling the watering hose or irrigation system, or at least making sure that the water conduits are clear, because they can burst if any trapped water freezes. All soil amendments and potting soil must also be stored in a dry place. If you have leftover seeds, ensure that they are fully dry, then store in a sealed plastic or Styrofoam container, and keep in a cool place in the house, away from dampness and variations in light and temperature.

Essentially, closing up the garden is a big cleanup job. It's an ideal time to note what supplies are left so you can plan next spring's purchases, to repair netting and covers, to recycle or throw out any worn-out equipment, and to sell, donate, or exchange anything that has not been used for a long time.

Once the garden has been put to bed, you can watch the snow cover the ground with your mind at ease and the satisfaction of a job well done.

Rolling up the insect netting and floating row covers makes storage and handling easier.

Tidying away the bags of rocks and completely emptying the garden before winter allows you to work the soil early the following spring.

EXTENDING THE LIFE OF VEGETABLES: FREEZING, FERMENTING, AND SOME CHINESE METHODS

In Quebec, since we are in a North temperate region, nature dictates that vegetable growing is mostly seasonal: fresh food is abundant for the hottest six months of the year, but winter production of vegetables remains costly and marginal. Beyond the root vegetables, cabbages, and onions that the big farms manage to store and sell for much of the winter, how can we eat local year-round? Processing fresh food is by far the most economical and ecological method to extend the life of seasonal food and to eat local throughout the year.

For a market farm, adding a processing arm allows you to create value out of surplus, unsold, or downgraded vegetables that too often end up in the compost. Processing food contributes to the viability of market gardening as a job by distributing the workload across the year and ensuring financial stability while increasing the range of products offered.

The secret to getting started is quite simple: process small quantities of food throughout the season using different recipes and methods — freezing, dehydrating, lacto-fermenting, or canning. At the end, you will have a beautiful, colourful selection of products lining your shelves throughout the winter.

As inspiration, here we discuss the main ways to preserve our fifteen Asian vegetables.

See the "Preserving" table in the Appendix (page 345) for more detailed information on preserving techniques for each vegetable.

FREEZING

EQUIPMENT: chest or upright freezer, freezer bags, metal or plastic trays, plastic containers

This is the fastest method for preserving foods. For Stéphanie, a large chest freezer is an essential electric appliance in the home. Throughout the warmer seasons she fills hers with vegetables, pestos, meats, and local berries. In winter, it's a true pleasure to go shopping through her food stores. So you don't forget whatever is lurking at the bottom of the freezer and waste it, label and date everything you put in it, and keep an inventory of everything that goes in and out. Before storing vegetables in the freezer, try out some of the various techniques below. You can use freezer bags or a vacuum sealer for each of these methods.

FREEZING DIRECTLY

VEGETABLES: bok choy, choy sum, gai lan, celtuce, Malabar spinach, shiso, okra, Asian eggplant, luffa, lemongrass

When time is short, you just need to peel the vegetables (celtuce and luffa only), chop them, spread them out on a tray lined with parchment paper or a silicone baking mat (to avoid everything freezing in one large block), and place them in the freezer. Once the vegetables are frozen, transfer them to freezer bags. They will keep for up to 3 months at 0°F (−18°C) or lower.

BLANCHING

Blanching vegetables before freezing extends their storage capacity to up to 6 months. Cooking them briefly deactivates the enzymes that otherwise change the colour, texture, and flavour of vegetables over time. See "Preserving" on page 345 to find the recommended blanching time for each vegetable. Plunge the blanched vegetables into ice water, and then:

• For mustard greens, chrysanthemum, amaranth, and Malabar spinach: Using your hands, shape into small balls and squeeze out excess liquid before placing in freezer bags. They can then be used in green sauces for pasta, in cakes, or in savoury tarts such as quiches.

• For bok choy, choy sum, gai lan, Chinese cabbage, celtuce, okra, eggplant, and luffa: Arrange vegetables on a kitchen towel, which will absorb excess water, and then spread them out in a single layer on a tray. Freeze, and then transfer to freezer bags or containers and place in freezer.

ROASTING OR STIR-FRYING

All the vegetables in this book can be roasted or stir-fried in vegetable oil before freezing. Whether in the oven, barbecue, frying pan, or wok, with or without seasoning, the main thing is to let them cool down completely before dividing them into freezer bags. Vary the seasonings and the vegetables, which will help with meal ideas later on.

SOME SUGGESTIONS:

• Roasted eggplant slices with Italian spices for pizza topping.

• Stir-fried luffa slices for making luffa spread (see recipe on page 287).

• Boy choy, mustard greens, Chinese cabbage, or chrysanthemum leaves roughly chopped and roasted with oil, salt, and pepper, for using in fried rice, crêpes, or omelettes.

MAKING PESTOS OR JUICES

Leafy greens can also be made into pesto using a food processor or knife. Feel free to experiment with different combinations of greens, seasonings, and protein foods (seeds, nuts, tofu, etc.) to add variety to your stores. Once made, the pesto can be poured into freezer-safe containers and then frozen. Process cucumbers in a juice extractor, pour the juice into ice-cube moulds, and freeze. These ice cubes can later be used in smoothies, cold soups, or sauces.

TIP: If you want to avoid accumulating containers in your freezer, you can transfer the frozen contents to freezer bags once solid. Simply run the containers briefly under warm water to loosen the frozen pesto or juice before moving the blocks to a freezer bag and returning to the freezer.

DEHYDRATING

EQUIPMENT: dehydrator, dryer, or oven

Dehydration, which simply involves drying foods, has one great advantage: it turns large quantities of perishable food into a compact format that can be stored for a long time at room temperature. It's best to use a dehydrator or dryer to keep a constant heat between 100° and 125°F (40° and 50°C) during the entire drying process without risking cooking the vegetables. A conventional oven heated for a long time at the very lowest temperature, 150°F (65°C), can also work. The drying time depends on the size of the cut vegetable pieces and how much moisture the vegetable contains. The "Preserving" table on page 345 gives dehydration times for certain-size pieces of our fifteen vegetables.

It's best to dehydrate vegetables when they are very fresh, immediately after buying or harvesting. This technique needs patience because you have to cut the vegetables into identical-size pieces and lay them side by side to ensure uniform drying. Once they are drying, all you have to do is wait. When they have lost all moisture and are crisp (fruit vegetables and lemongrass) or crumbly (leafy greens), store in glass containers or sealed bags in a cool, dry place away from light.

A FEW IDEAS FOR PREPARING
AND USING DRIED VEGETABLES

• Powder: All dried greens can be powdered in a blender, and then used in smoothies or sprinkled over salad, pasta, or popcorn.

• Chips: The leaves of brassicas, amaranth, Malabar spinach, and shiso, as well as Asian eggplants and cucumbers in thin slices, can be seasoned and then dehydrated to make chips.

• Chunks: Okra sliced and cubed or sliced luffa or Asian eggplant dehydrate well, with or without spices, to be added as-is, or rehydrated before adding to, tomato sauces, lasagnes, pizzas, stews, and soups.

LACTO-FERMENTING

EQUIPMENT: funnel, fermentation containers (sealable glass jars, or ceramic, plastic, or stainless steel fermentation crocks)

Lacto-fermentation is a centuries-old process of fermenting that preserves without cooking. It is used for perishable foods such as vegetables, milk, meat, and cereals. Soy sauce, tamari, miso, and fish sauce are all lacto-fermented products.

Also called lactic acid fermentation, this technique consists of adding salt to the food, limiting contact with the air, and letting it macerate. In this salty, airless environment, the bacteria naturally present on the surface of the food develop and produce lactic acid, which will acidify the environment and preserve the product.

As well as increasing the life of food, lacto-fermentation improves its nutritional profile, producing certain beneficial compounds and reducing the levels of other elements that can impede nutrient absorption, for example. Lactic acid bacteria produced during lacto-fermentation may also have a probiotic potential: to limit the growth of pathogenic bacteria in the intestines.

To lacto-ferment vegetables, there are three main salting techniques:

• Brine is a salt-water solution in which you immerse the vegetables. In the Asian tradition, this technique is used to reduce the bitterness of leafy greens before transferring into fermentation jars.

• Dry-salting is used for vegetables that contain a lot of water, such as cabbages, and consists of putting salt on the vegetables, which will then release their juice. Afterward, you can rinse or not, spin or drain, and then ferment them with your choice of spices and aromatics.

• No-salt fermenting, or fermenting with very little salt, is possible, and foods prepared this way are ready to eat in just a few days. Salt's preserving capabilities can be partly replaced by mineral-rich ingredients like rehydrated seaweed, caraway seeds, dill seeds, or celery seeds or juice.

FOR THE LOVE OF KIMCHI
Korean in origin, kimchi is a lacto-fermented condiment that has been growing in popularity in recent years.

Traditional kimchi is made from Napa cabbage and Korean chili (gochugaru), and is recognizable by its bright red colour. It is a long-fermentation, long-term-storage kimchi, traditionally made with fall and winter vegetables submerged in brine. You will find a speedy version on page 325.

There is also a category of kimchi that is ready to eat instantly, or at least just a few days after being made. These kimchi are generally made from spring and summer harvests such as bok choy, mustard greens, amaranth, shiso, Asian eggplant, Asian cucumber, and even luffa.

CANNING

EQUIPMENT: a large cooking pot or autoclave, funnel, Mason jars, jar lifter

More recent than lacto-fermentation, canning is a well-known technique in the West. It has the major advantage of preserving foods for several years at room temperature, but it is more laborious to do at home.

First you cook the vegetables, and then transfer them to glass jars — such as Mason jars — that have been sterilized. To can acidic food such as marinades, ketchups, and salsas, you then simply bring a pot of water to a boil, carefully immerse the sealed jars upright in the pot on a rack, and boil for 10 to 30 minutes (depending on the recipe). Remove the jars from the pan and then allow them to cool completely. Once you hear the characteristic "pop" of the lid sealing, you know you are done. Less acidic food, such as soups, stocks, vegetables, and sauces, must be sterilized using an autoclave or pressure canner. This piece of equipment allows you to preserve under steam pressure, which is necessary to prevent propagation of harmful bacteria in non-acidic canned food (always follow the manufacturer's instructions).

PRESERVE YOUR VEGETABLES, FEED YOUR FRIENDSHIPS
Food preservation can often be seen as an additional task, one that takes a lot of energy, especially when you have already spent long hours in the garden growing your own vegetables. But all those sessions in the kitchen will be well worth it when winter rolls around.

Mix work and play by gathering family or friends to transform this chore into a joyful and unmissable annual meetup. Huge steaming pots, a large table for cutting Chinese cabbage and other veg from the garden, batch after batch ... Collective cooking means everyone can then go home with their own little meals. What a wonderful way to fill your pantry with local marvels from your very own garden.

A FEW CHINESE PRESERVES

When discussing practices as old as traditional Chinese cooking, it would be impossible to overlook food preservation techniques! According to chef Anita Feng, who has helped us greatly in understanding the differences between Chinese preserves, these products, in addition to adding a particular flavour, are also used to balance a dish by reducing the pronounced taste of another ingredient.

Our family members have highlighted four particular products that have been part of their lives. These often accompany pork dishes and are not usually eaten on their own, except for variations on the salted vegetables.

SALTED VEGETABLES
Cantonese: 鹹菜 haam4 coi3, pronounced "haam choy"

This lacto-fermented preserve can be made with different vegetables; our family mostly uses mustard greens. The vegetables are either mixed dry with a lot of salt or immersed in brine. The length of time the vegetables are lacto-fermented affects the taste, which is always fairly salty. Salted vegetables are mainly used in stir-fries to enhance the flavour of meat.

SPICY MUSTARD GREENS
Cantonese: 榨菜 zaa3 coi3, pronounced "tsaa choy"

A variation on the preceding method, spicy mustard greens are prepared by dry-salting its swollen stems, which are then mixed with ground chili. Tsatsai is the traditionally used mustard green variety. With a shorter fermentation time than for salted vegetables, spicy mustard greens are not overly vinegary but rather salty and spicy, although their flavour changes across regions and recipes. Sliced into strips, they add crunch and a marvellous lift to stir-fries and congee.

CHINESE SAUERKRAUT
Cantonese: 酸菜 syun1 coi3, pronounced "sünn choy"

Sauerkraut, which is usually associated with Alsace or Germany, is said to actually originally come from China. In the south and west of the country it is made with mustard greens, while in the north Chinese cabbage is used. Like the European version, Chinese sauerkraut is made with a brine. It is eaten in soups, stews, and broths, or with dumplings.

DRIED VEGETABLES
Cantonese: 菜乾 coi3 gon1, pronounced "choy gon"

The first dehydrator was, of course, the sun. In the Chinese countryside, it's still common to see rows of bok choy bundles hanging from ropes to dry after being blanched. Different varieties of mustard greens and cabbages can be dried this way, but in all cases the dried vegetables are served in soups or accompany steamed dishes. Once dried, they will keep for as long as they are kept dry. Anita Feng used to see her grandparents wrap them in newspaper and then put the whole bundle in a bag in a cupboard. Simple as that!

Note: Since these are traditional recipes, the Chinese names will vary between one region and another. In addition, the classifications of the different products are fluid, and some can belong to more than one of the categories given. The English names of the products are a liberal translation.

Our mother at a family gathering at the Madirokely beach.

Reconnecting with these preserved foods

We were not lucky enough to grow up with these four products, which are nonetheless typical of Chinese food. As mentioned earlier, our family in Madagascar had to make their own versions because they were difficult to obtain on the island. Beyond the culinary applications of the products themselves, having these skills was also very useful because it allowed for storing food for long periods.

We've been told that our paternal grandmother made salted and dried vegetables, especially when she managed the hotel restaurant. Our aunt Marie remembers the spicy mustard greens her mother used when making a steamed ground pork dish. And when they both lived in Sherbrooke in the 1970s, our grandmother made the most of each trip to Montreal and brought back boxes of salted vegetables and dried bok choy.

As for our mother's sisters, they remember that salted mustard greens were used when cooking ground meat, especially pork. Their father prepared Chinese sauerkraut with mustard greens, which was eaten during meals as a side vegetable, which they loved.

Today, in Chinese diasporas around the world, these preserved products are easily found in Chinese grocery stores. A growing number of small local businesses (including Le Rizen) are also preserving and fermenting locally grown harvests, and it's also becoming more popular for people to make these things at home. We encourage you to take inspiration from products already on the market and explore different techniques with Asian vegetables. Be creative!

CHINESE CABBAGE

紹菜

CHINESE CABBAGE

Also known as: Napa cabbage, Peking cabbage, pe-tsai
Cantonese: 紹菜 siu6 coi3 (? | vegetable)
黃芽白 wong4 ngaa4 baak6 (yellow | bud | white)
Mandarin: 大白菜 dàbáicài (large | white | vegetable),
often simply called 白菜 báicài

FAMILY: Brassicaceae

SPECIES: *Brassica rapa* subspecies *pekinensis*

Chinese cabbage, with Napa cabbage being the best-known variety, is the fall Asian vegetable par excellence. It features in numerous Asian recipes, such as Korean kimchi and Chinese hot pot. Sweet, crunchy, and tender, Chinese cabbage is adored by all. It keeps for several months in the fridge, especially if harvested with its roots. In Korea it is stored in the earth in the fall, and then dug up throughout the winter to eat or to make kimchi. If you like gardening challenges, Chinese cabbage is for you. It's also widely available in most supermarkets.

HISTORY Originally from China, where it has been grown for a long time, Chinese cabbage is a cross between the bok choy of the south and the turnip of the north. It was introduced to Japan around 1860 and into the United States in the late nineteenth century by the immigrant population and missionaries returning from China. Among the cabbages of Chinese origin, it is the species that has been the longest known in the West. The name Napa probably comes from Japanese.

NUTRITION

Chinese cabbage is an excellent source of vitamin K, a good source of folate, and a source of manganese, vitamin C, and vitamin B6. The latter contributes to the formation of red blood cells and the functioning of the nervous system.

Long and slender in shape, Chinese cabbage looks like romaine lettuce, although it can reach twice that size. Its ribbed leaves vary from dark green to greenish yellow, and are paler on the inside. It is particularly prized for its tenderness, its crunchy and juicy central ribbing, and its flavour, which is sweeter than that of regular cabbage. Napa cabbages are shorter, wider, and more compact. The Michihili is another common variety. Its long narrow leaves, detached from one another at the top of the vegetable, can measure up to 18 inches (45 cm) long.

In the garden

· Chinese cabbage is the most difficult of our selection of brassicas to grow because it takes longer to reach maturity (50 to 85 cool days) compared to the smaller, fast growing brassicas. In addition, given that it is sweet and tender, all sorts of caterpillars love to snack on its leaves and can cause major damage inside the cabbage that can't be detected from the outside.

· Author and market gardener Joy Larkcom understands its whims. In her book *Oriental Vegetables,* she describes Chinese cabbage as the demanding aristocrat of Asian vegetables that requires nothing but the very best right from the start.

· Spring sowing sometimes gives good results, which is why most organic market farmers give it a try. However, success depends on the temperature in May and June, because if it is too hot or too cold, or if there are too many temperature variations, the Chinese cabbages will be weaker and more vulnerable to insects. If you try the Chinese cabbage experiment in spring, sow indoors a little after the other greens, two weeks before the last frost date, then plant out thirty days later and cover with insect netting. Chinese cabbage is in large part water, so good watering is crucial.

· The best results often come from fall sowings. At this time of year you will need to be vigilant for aphids because they tend to multiply under the insect netting. At Le Rizen, we have been experimenting with strips of green lacewing eggs for a few years to try to prevent aphid infestations. We hook them from the hoops under the nets.

· At Le Rizen we grow the Bilko cultivar, which offers the biggest Napa cabbage and a high level of disease resistance.

· It is possible to grow a good Chinese cabbage in a pot. Use a container at least 20 inches (50 cm) deep filled with well-enriched soil, and water regularly. If you have limited space, you can grow it in a smaller container and harvest leaf by leaf.

· When the top of the cabbage is dense and firm to the touch, it is ready to be harvested. Cut at the base with a sharp knife, remove the outer leaves, which are often yellow, and store directly in a sealable bag or container in the fridge. The big green outer leaves can be left on to protect the cabbage during transport and storage. Although more fibrous than the paler interior leaves, they are perfectly edible, preferably cooked.

· Little black spots might appear on the cabbage. They are harmless and can be caused by a variety of factors: fluctuations in the garden temperature, too much fertilizer, or harvesting when the cabbage is too mature.

STORING
Keeps for about two weeks in a sealed plastic bag or container in the fridge, or for two to three months after harvest in optimal conditions.

PREPARING
Pull off the leaves and rinse. If desired, remove the base of the leaves, and then thinly slice, or cut into squares or strips.

IN THE KITCHEN

Edible parts	Ways to eat	Ways to cook
• Leaves • Flowering stems	• Raw • Cooked • Pickled/ lacto-fermented • Dried	• Steam • Boil • Sauté/stir-fry • Roast/grill • Deep-fry

Highly adaptable, Chinese cabbage is used like other cabbages. In addition, the central fleshy rib of its leaves can stand in for celery. Just like bok choy, it goes well with ginger, soy sauce, sesame oil, and sesame seeds.

RAW

· Chinese cabbage is a flavourful replacement for cabbage or lettuce in salads, sandwiches, and burgers. It's also delicious with julienned carrots and a creamy Asian sesame dressing, a new twist on familiar coleslaw.

· It can also be thinly sliced and rolled in a rice sheet with other ingredients.

· In China, Japan, and Korea, Chinese cabbage is commonly pickled or lacto-fermented, and used to accompany or enhance both cold and hot dishes.

· Its shoots and sprouts can be added to salads.

COOKED

Just like other Asian brassicas, Chinese cabbage should be cooked only briefly to preserve its delicate flavour and crunch.

Our favourite ways to prepare it:

· In a broth, thinly sliced or cut into squares, with noodles and shrimp, or simply added to a hot pot.

· Served cut into squares or strips, stewed in a cast-iron pot with fried tofu — a comforting winter dish that we often ate at Cantonese restaurants.

· Thinly sliced or diced, then stir-fried alone or with other vegetables, rice, noodles, fish, or meat.

· Finely chopped and mixed with ground meat to make a filling for dumplings.

· Thinly sliced and cut into squares with pork and shiitake mushroom slices to make a filling for imperial rolls.

· Slathered with oil and grilled on the barbecue (the big leaves).

The leaves can be dried and then added to soups and other dishes.

Kimchi

By Jean-Philippe Villemure

紹菜

An everyday condiment, kimchi is a delicious lacto-fermentation that enhances a variety of dishes. In Korea it is served with every meal, even breakfast! Jean-Philippe is a huge fan; he could not live without his daily dose of kimchi. Here, he shares an easy homemade recipe that honours the sought-after umami flavour of a good Korean kimchi.

Preparation 45 min · Resting 1 to 2 hrs · 🌶🌶
Ferment 3 days at room temperature + 10 days in the fridge
Makes 5 cups (one 750 mL Mason jar + one 500 mL jar)

INGREDIENTS

1 medium Chinese cabbage (about 2.5 lb/1.2 kg)
2 tbsp (30 mL) non-iodized, additive-free salt
    (for sweating)
2 to 3 green onions (or the green part of a small leek)
    (optional), cut in half lengthways and then into
    2½-inch (6 cm) chunks

For the spicy paste
3 to 4 cloves of garlic
1 piece of fresh ginger 1½ to 2 inches (4 to 5 cm) long
2 tbsp (30 mL) tamari (or fish sauce)
1 tsp (5 mL) granulated sugar
1 to 5 tbsp (15 to 75 mL) ground Korean chili
    (or ground paprika), to taste

METHOD

1. Cut the cabbage lengthways into four pieces. Rinse well under cold running water, and then drain. Cut each cabbage quarter into 1-inch (2.5 cm) wide strips, and then cut into 1-inch (2.5 cm) squares. Discard the hard base of the cabbage.

2. Put the cabbage pieces in a large bowl, and add the salt. Using your hands, massage the cabbage well so that the salt penetrates it.

3. Let sit for 1 to 2 hours at room temperature, stopping to stir 2 or 3 times.

4. Meanwhile, prepare the spicy paste. Using a food processor or mortar and pestle, purée the garlic and ginger. Add the rest of the paste ingredients, and then stir well. Set aside.

5. Drain the cabbage well in a colander or, for drier kimchi, in a spinner. For less salty kimchi, rinse quickly before draining.

6. In a large bowl, combine the drained cabbage with the spicy paste and green onions (if using).

7. Pack into very clean Mason jars, pressing down well and leaving a headspace of ¾ to 2 inches (2 to 5 cm), as fermentation will increase the volume of the kimchi. Seal with the lid but do not screw on too tightly (carbon dioxide needs to be able to escape). Place on a plate or in a container in case juice overflows from the jar.

8. Put in a dark place, at room temperature, and leave for 3 days. Do not open the jar — contact with oxygen could generate mould. After 3 days, refrigerate for 10 days for optimal flavour.

NOTES AND VARIATIONS

· Chinese cabbage can be replaced with bok choy, tatsoi, or mustard greens.

· Non-iodized salt is preferred for the texture of the brine, but it is not necessary.

· Kimchi made from Chinese cabbage or other brassicas keeps for at least 6 months in the fridge if you follow the guidelines closely; that is, limit contact with air as much as possible, always use clean tools for serving, and after using, press down the kimchi with a spoon or spatula so that it is still submerged in the juice.

· From the day it is made until a year later, kimchi is living and evolving. Some people like it young, while others prefer it mature or aged. In Korea, each fermentation stage is linked to a particular culinary use.

STAGES OF FERMENTATION

	Stage	Characteristics	Use in Korea
Day 1	Young	· Fresh that day · Crunchy and barely fermented · Smells of sea salt · Not much juice	Raw, in salads, or served with cold dishes, including bossam, very popular in South Korea, in which day-old kimchi, slices of spicy pork, and other condiments are wrapped in Chinese cabbage, shiso, or lettuce leaves and then dipped in sauce
Day 2 or older	Mature	· More tender but still crunchy · The paste has soaked into the cabbage · Characteristic kimchi flavour: pronounced, acrid, and sour · A little juice	Served in banchan, a small side dish usually placed in the middle of the table
After 3 months	Aged	· Soft texture · Dark red in colour · More pronounced odour · A lot of juice · Fizzes in the mouth	· Cooked dishes · Savoury kimchi pancakes, called kimchijeon · Stew, such as the famous kimchi jjigae

Glazed baluchoux with teriyaki sauce

By Amandine Chen,
with the support of Nirina Raharison

This recipe is inspired by stuffed cabbage. In French this is called a *baluchon*, but we call them *baluchoux* to incorporate the French word for "cabbage." Amandine wanted to create something tasty, simple, and beautiful: a delicious vegan dish, original yet accessible, and good for both everyday eating and special occasions.

Preparation 30 min • Cooking 15 to 30 min • Makes 12 baluchoux

INGREDIENTS

12 Napa cabbage leaves
Toasted sesame seeds, to taste

Stuffing

2 tbsp (30 mL) vegetable oil
1 medium onion, chopped into small pieces
2 tbsp (30 mL) minced fresh ginger (the equivalent of a ¾-inch/2 cm thick slice)
1 tbsp (15 mL) vinegar (white, cider, or wine)
½ cup (125 mL) dried seaweed (whole or flakes)
1 block (16 oz/450 g) firm tofu
1 medium potato, grated
3 cloves of garlic, minced
Salt and pepper, to taste

Teriyaki sauce

½ cup (125 mL) soy sauce or tamari
2 tbsp (30 mL) minced fresh ginger (the equivalent of a ¾-inch/2 cm thick slice)
2 cloves of garlic, minced
3 tbsp (45 mL) granulated sugar
2 tbsp (30 mL) vinegar (white, cider, or wine)

METHOD

For the stuffing

1. Heat a frying pan over medium heat and pour in the oil. Add the onion and ginger, and then brown for 1 minute, or until the onions are translucent. Add the vinegar, reduce the heat to minimum, and cook until the onions turn brown.

2. Meanwhile, rehydrate the seaweed according to the package instructions. Drain, and then mince if not already in small pieces. Crumble the tofu by hand into a large bowl. Add the seaweed, potato, and garlic. Season with salt and pepper.

3. Add the tofu mixture to the frying pan. Increase the heat to medium, cover, and cook, stirring occasionally to prevent sticking (if it is sticking too much, reduce the heat). When the potatoes are tender, turn off the heat.

For the cabbage

4. Meanwhile, bring a saucepan of water to a boil. One by one, pull off 12 leaves from the base of the cabbage and rinse under cold water. Once the water is boiling, immerse the leaves. When the water returns to a boil, or when the thick part of the cabbage is tender, transfer the leaves to a colander and drain. If desired, plunge into ice water to preserve the leaves' beautiful vibrant colour.

For the teriyaki sauce

5. Put all of the sauce ingredients in a frying pan or saucepan. Cook over medium heat, stirring occasionally, until the sauce reduces and becomes syrupy. (Be careful not to burn it or let it overflow; reduce the heat if necessary.) Set aside.

Optional

6. To enjoy the baluchoux hot, preheat the oven to 400°F (200°C).

To assemble

7. Set a cabbage leaf on your work surface, stem toward you. Make sure it is very flat. Place ⅓ cup (75 mL) of the tofu mixture in the middle of it. Fold up the cabbage leaf to make a little bundle. First fold in each side of the leaf over the stuffing, and then fold up the stem and end by folding down the top large part of the leaf. Set on a serving plate or an oven dish seam-side down. Repeat with the remaining cabbage leaves.

8. If desired, bake in the preheated oven for 15 minutes.

9. Before serving, use a spoon or brush to glaze the baluchoux with the teriyaki sauce.

10. Sprinkle with sesame seeds, and serve with rice.

NOTES AND VARIATIONS

· Any seaweed can be used, but the flavour will be different depending on which kind you choose.

· The seaweed can be omitted and grated carrot added for colour, or shiitake mushrooms for texture. You can also add cilantro leaves or green onions to the cooked tofu mix.

· The tofu can be replaced with ground meat, while the potato can be replaced with sticky or sushi rice (1 cup/250 mL uncooked rice).

· To make folding easier, you can thin the thick part of the leaf with a knife prior to filling with the tofu mixture.

Amandine Chen and Nirina Raharison

Amandine and Nirina are our cousins. Amandine is the eldest daughter of our aunt Marie, and Nirina is Amandine's cousin. Lovers of food and passionate about cooking, they love creating dishes with whatever they have on hand. Nirina studied nutrition with Caroline, and Amandine has been collecting culinary experiences in Europe. Always ready to help (and taste!), they are an integral part of our gastronomic family reunions. Amandine and Nirina are delighted to bring their own personal touch to their three cousins' project.

紹菜

A cousin baluchoux-making session.

Chinese cabbage sauté with bacon and chili

By Stanislas Pettigrew

紹菜

When Stéphanie met Stanislas, he was growing gigantic Chinese cabbages on the family farm. This recipe is Stanislas's favourite way of cooking the vegetable, because it needs only a few ingredients and little preparation, and is always satisfying when you want a quick, comforting meal. For him, the beginning of fall means it's time for a good Chinese cabbage sauté with bacon and chili.

Preparation 10 min • Cooking 10 min • 4 to 6 servings • 🥄

INGREDIENTS

1 tbsp (15 mL) canola oil

3.5 oz (100 g) diced bacon (¼ to ½ inch/½ to 1 cm)

3 to 4 tbsp (45 to 60 mL) chili powder

1.3 lb (600 g) Chinese cabbage (half a medium or one small cabbage), cut into 1-inch (2.5 cm) pieces

2 to 3 tbsp (30 to 45 mL) soy sauce or tamari

1 tbsp (15 mL) white vinegar

2 cups (500 mL) water

METHOD

1. In a frying pan over medium heat, heat the oil. Cook the bacon for 2 minutes.

2. Add the remaining ingredients. Do not mix.

3. Cover and simmer until the cabbage is tender but still crunchy.

4. Serve hot with rice.

NOTES AND VARIATIONS

• Chinese cabbage can be replaced by any other kind of cabbage.

• The bacon can be replaced with 1 cup (250 mL) rinsed and drained canned chickpeas. You can also use a combination: 2 oz (60 g) diced bacon and ½ cup (125 mL) rinsed and drained canned chickpeas.

• Chili powder is a blend of chilis, spices, and aromatics, not to be confused with ground chili, which is spicier.

Stanislas Pettigrew

Ferme Pettigrew

Stanislas is the third generation of Pettigrews to farm the family land in Frelighsburg, Quebec. He specializes in organic maple syrup. For four years, Stanislas and his family have welcomed Le Rizen's crops and have contributed greatly to the farm's development. As well as being an excellent farmer, Stanislas loves cooking and honouring seasonal vegetables. He has a particular fondness for simple, nourishing, and tasty recipes with lots of sauce.

January 1st in Nosy Be

It's January 1st on the island of Nosy Be, and time for a celebration!

All the families in the Chinese community of Hell-Ville, the main town of Nosy Be, have made hors d'oeuvres and little bites to share. Every year, the same flavours hit the taste buds: saat3 kei4 maa5 (a square made of puffy fried dough and sweet syrup), chips of sweet potato and taro mixed with roasted peanuts, salty/savoury taro or turnip cakes, baos, steam-cooked rice sponge cakes, fried dough balls coated with sesame seeds. The latter open up during cooking and bring laughing mouths to mind. Perhaps this is one of the reasons why they are made for the new year festivities.

Celebrations begin early in the morning. Everyone meets at the first house at the end of the main road, on which all the Chinese families of Hell-Ville have settled. Indoors, the hosts welcome the guests. People eat and exchange new year greetings. The children are all very happy to receive a red envelope, a traditional way of giving money in Chinese culture. And then it's off to the next house, chatting, drinking, eating some more, red envelopes changing hands, and so it goes on until everyone has reached the final house.

In the evening, all these people and their friends and family from neighbouring villages get together in the house doing duty as the Chinese community centre on the island. They enjoy yet another grand feast and they dance.

Aunt Monique tells this story, laughing and joking that the day was torture: far too many things to eat!

FINAL WORDS

With every migration, with every generation that passes, the flavour of the vegetables and the ways of cooking them change, and cultural mixing continues. In our opinion, the one constant across all cultures is a great collective love for food, which is even more appreciated when the dishes are shared around a table in good company.

There are many more Asian vegetables than the ones we have described in this book. The good news is that it is no longer necessary to travel far and wide to get your hands on these vegetables or to order dishes cooked as if you had. We see more and more dedicated people and businesses offering a range of Asian products. Support this growing community by buying directly from specialized market farms, exploring the Asian grocery stores near you, and eating at restaurants that include flavours inspired by Asian traditions or that cook local Asian vegetables in their own way. One of our goals with this book is to inspire the farming and food worlds to become interested in the potential of Asian vegetables and to play a part in helping these vegetables become better known in the name of diversity and food sovereignty.

At the end of these pages, we hope we have given you a taste for growing, cooking, and eating Asian vegetables, while also learning about our family and cultural heritage.

We wish you many happy moments of discovery, in both the garden and the kitchen, and we invite you to draw inspiration from your own roots.

Thank you for coming on this journey with us! We hope to see you somewhere on our route.

ACKNOWLEDGEMENTS

We would like to thank

Virginie Gosselin, for your talent, sensitivity, and efficiency, for the library of accessories you so generously shared with us, and for the magnificent photos that immerse us in a unique universe every time.

Élisabeth Brisset des Nos, for having believed in our project while it was still at the embryonic stage, for helping us navigate the publishing world, and for providing the very first literary guidance on our manuscript.

Noémie C. Adrien, for having picked up the torch so efficiently, for providing later literary guidance, and for staying on course for the due dates!

Julie Massy, for the artistic direction and your energetic help during the photo sessions.

For your recipes, your answers to our many questions, and your presence during the photo shoots: Jérémie Bastien, Rébecca Brilvicas-Pinsonnault, Maxime Chanhda-Tremblay, Amandine Chen and Nirina Raharison, Mong Chi Chong, Dana Cooper, Anita Feng, Danielle Laou, Guillaume Lozeau, Iscra Nicolov, Chloé Ostiguy, Félix Antoine Parenteau, Stanislas Pettigrew, Maxime Robert-Lachaîne, Jean-Louis Thémis, Jean-Philippe Villemure, Alexandre Vovan, Marie Wang, Yvonne Yau, and Yamei Zhao. Your recipes allow us to travel and enjoy Asian vegetables! Thanks also to your loved ones who came to the photo shoots: Inès Daoust, Amélie Lamothe, and Olivier Parent.

Our aunts Dany, Marie, and Monique and our uncles Jean and Bernard, who patiently answered our thousand questions about family history and Chinese culture and languages. Thanks also to Dany and Marie for the dishes made with love.

Our dear father, thank you for always being available to us and enthusiastic about everything we do, and for willingly diving into your memories to tell us about them. Thank you and Chi Nguyen for your help during the photo shoots.

A special thank you to Anita Feng, Yamei Zhao, Yvonne Yau, and Mong Chi Chong for patiently sharing your knowledge of Chinese culinary culture.

For the scientific review: Anne-Sophie Tardif (organic vegetable grower at the Coop de Solidarité des Jardins du Pied de Céléri), Daniel Brisebois (organic seed grower at the Ferme Coopérative Tourne-Sol), and Sophie Guimont (agronomist specializing in organic farming).

For Chinese language and linguistics review: Yanqing Zhang, Rao Shu Hang, Ting Zhang, Philippe Brin-Delisle, Jessie Deng, and Yao Zhang.

Claude Émile Racette, for your contribution to our understanding of traditional Chinese medicine.

Elisabeth Cardin and Jean-Martin Fortier, for your prefaces, which demonstrate your engagement with the agricultural and culinary revolution that you greatly inspire with your words, acts, and vision.

Marylin Merineau, for lending us your unique pottery pieces, fabrics, and other objects that decorated several of our photos.

Thank you to the people who took the time to test the recipes in this book: Marianne Bérubé-Lefebvre, Maude Boiselle, Amandine Chen, Céline Comeau, Lydia Liu, Vyna Mackay Chao, Michaël Poisson, Malaka Rached-d'Astous, Camille Tremblay, and Yvonne Yau.

Gabrielle Renaud, for your birthday in 2018, where Stéphanie spoke to your friend Élisabeth about our book idea without the slightest idea where it would all lead!

Friends, thank you just for being there.

And finally you, the reader, for your curiosity and interest in Asian vegetables, cooking, gardening, and family stories.

Between sisters

Caro, for your rigorous research and your impeccable follow-up, thanks to which we learned an enormous amount about foods, vegetables, and Asian cooking techniques.

Steph, for choosing one of the hardest but most essential jobs, for having enriched this book with your knowledge, accumulated with patience and resilience, and for the community you have created around Asian vegetables.

Pat, for deepening our knowledge of Chinese languages, for the poetry in our book, and for having uncovered the precious stories of our family that might otherwise have remained unknown, and that thanks to you we will be able to pass on to the next generation.

From Caroline

Thank you, Joey, for your presence, your support, your ideas, and for having tasted so much chrysanthemum and edamame.

From Stéphanie

Thank to you all the customers at Le Rizen, including restaurants and grocery stores, for your contagious enthusiasm, your culinary curiosity, and your unwavering support.

Thank you to everyone who has worked, done an internship, got their hands dirty on the farm, or in any other way contributed to Le Rizen's development.

Thank you to Jean-Philippe Villemure and Céline Comeau for the culinary creations behind Le Rizen's processed products. It is an honour to discover and appreciate local Asian vegetables with you.

Thank you to Stanislas and the Pettigrew family for having been so welcoming to Le Rizen between 2018 and 2021, and your contribution to its growth.

Thank you to Amélia Jasper-Laurin and Laura Michaud for being my stand-ins when we were making edits to the French book right in the middle of the 2021 season.

Thank you, Dad, for your assiduous help at the markets and with deliveries, commissions, and marketing advice.

Thank you to Bernard Alonso for having believed in the potential of Asian vegetables grown here and for having welcomed Le Rizen at its very beginning in 2016 and 2017.

Mong Chi Chong and Phyllis Tsai, thank you for your friendship, your big hearts, and for sharing your Zen knowledge, which has been such a useful guide to me over the years.

Lydie Vachon, thank you for your commitment to inspiring and accompanying people (including me) to draw on traditional Chinese knowledge for facing life's challenges as well as for enjoying every day.

David, thank you for your pen, which has embellished some of the sentences in this book, and for your gentle presence that lights up my life.

Sophie Maffolini, thank you for your light and the magical writing retreat in October 2020, which brought me so fluently and serenely here, writing these lines a year later.

Thank you to the wonderful community of Brome-Missisquoi, in particular to the supportive network of small businesses and organic market farmers, as well as Beat & Betterave for the precious Wednesday evening farmers' gatherings.

Thank you to La Via Campesina and to all the farmers I was lucky enough to meet on my way. You will always inspire me.

From Patricia

Thank you to Donna Chan, my Cantonese teacher, for your generous help outside class hours, and for making my dream of being able to speak Cantonese with my family ever more possible.

Thank you to everyone else who helped me by answering the thorny questions surrounding Chinese cooking and languages, and pointed me in the direction of the right resources.

Tom, thank you for discussions that always made me reflect just a little bit more.

Finally, an enormous thank you to the members of my family, who trusted me as I recounted their pasts and their presents. It was a joy to listen to you and to have the privilege of retelling, in my turn, a little bit about you.

FOLLOW US

Share your harvests, recipes, discoveries, and stories of Asian vegetables using **#AsianVegetablesBook**

Follow our different projects and get in touch!

STÉPHANIE
lerizen.ca   🛅 Le Rizen   📷 le.rizen

CAROLINE
carolinewangnutrition.com   🛅 Caroline Wang, diététiste/dietitian

PATRICIA
hoyi.ca   🛅 Patricia Ho-Yi Wang — Artiste   📷 patricia.hoyi.wang   🎵 Patricia Ho-Yi Wang

Garden Glossary

ACCLIMATIZATION
The necessary period of transition from the greenhouse or indoor seed trays to the garden. Helps young plants gradually adapt to the sun, wind, and cold.

BOTANICAL FAMILY
The first order of plant classification, a botanical family connects several genuses coming from the same parents. The names of botanical families end in -aceae in English.

BROADFORK
A U-shaped hand tool that allows you to hold its handle while digging its 12-inch (30 cm) teeth down into the ground to loosen the soil without turning it over. Used before planting a crop that has a long root system.

COTYLEDONS
The first two leaves that grow from a seed are not true leaves; they are cotyledons. These do not resemble the plant's real leaves and fall off naturally as the plant grows.

CROSS-POLLINATION
Cross-pollination happens when insects pollinate the flowers of vegetables in the same species. If you plant the seeds of a cross-pollinated vegetable, you will end up with a vegetable that is different from the parent.

CULTIVAR
A cultivated variety that is the result of hybridization, selection, or mutation, generally reproduced for its characteristics (colour, shape, resistance to certain diseases, etc.).

FLOATING ROW COVER
Thin fabric placed over plants to protect them from wind and mild frost while still letting light through.

FLORAL BUD
With leafy greens, all the stems will form a flowering bud; this is the stage of flowering that precedes blooming.

FLOWERING STEM
The flowering stem is the most common term in market gardening to describe an edible part of the plant made up of a stem with a flower bud.

GENUS
A genus includes all the species of a plant. The first word of the scientific name (nomenclature) of every plant is its genus in Latin.

HOE
A long-handled weeding tool that allows you to stand up while pulling out weeds between rows or plants before they develop roots. Hoeing also breaks up the crust that can form on the surface of the ground, allowing water and air to penetrate the soil.

INTEGRATED CROP MANAGEMENT
An approach to managing harmful insects that has five steps: knowledge, prevention, monitoring, intervention, and evaluation.

MULTICELL TRAY
Plastic tray, 10 x 20 inches (25 x 50 cm), made up of identical cavities, which can be larger or smaller depending on your needs and choices, to be filled with potting soil for sowing seeds.

OCCULTATION TARPS
Thick black plastic that is laid over a growing area to destroy the remains of a crop or to choke out weeds.

POTTING UP
The action of transferring a plant from one pot into a bigger one to encourage growth. *Potting* is the action of putting a plant in a pot.

PRESSURE SPRAYER
A container that you can carry over your shoulder or wear as a backpack that has a manual pump for spraying diluted treatments over crops.

REPLANTING
Although this is usually synonymous with transplanting, in market gardening it refers more specifically to the action of replanting young seedlings (when they have two true leaves) into trays with larger cells or into separate pots.

ROW
In a growing area it is typical to sow seeds or plant out seedlings in rows aligned lengthways, which makes weeding easier. The rows can have varying distances between them depending on the size of the vegetable being grown. This will also determine the spacing between plants in a row.

SPECIES
A species is a group of plants that can reproduce among themselves by their seeds. Usually plants of the same species share certain traits. In the nomenclature system, the second word of the scientific name of a plant is its species in Latin.

TRANSPLANTING/PLANTING OUT
In market gardening, the action of taking plants out of their multicell trays or pots and planting them in the ground.

TREATED SEED
Treating seeds includes several processes, such as covering them with fertilizer, fungicide, or pesticide, or coating them to improve their handling.

TWO-WHEELED MINITRACTOR
This tractor is about twice the size of a lawnmower. Different tools can be attached to it so it can carry out the majority of the ground work needed for market gardening in a small area.

VARIETY
An individual plant within a species that has distinctive traits. These traits can be reproduced by growing from seed, and transmitted from generation to generation. The varieties of a single species can cross-pollinate among themselves.

INDEX

RECIPES

SALADS

Japanese sesame salad (*Goma-ae*) **157**

Celtuce leaf and dried cranberry salad **183**

Laotian meat salad (*Laap*) **235**

Cold noodles (*Liáng miàn*) **277**

SOUPS

Nabe with miso and butter **159**

Amaranth soup **213**

Tom kha gai soup **297**

APPETIZERS

Chrysanthemum-stuffed crêpes (*Bings*) **167**

Dungeness crab with celtuce, mint, goat yogurt, oxalis **179**

Spring rolls with shiso and duck **237**

Crispy roasted okra (*Kurkuri bhindi*) **249**

Luffa spread **287**

CONDIMENTS

Quick-pickled celtuce **183**

Tomato rougail **217**

Lacto-fermented okra **251**

Asian eggplant achar **259**

Kimchi **325**

SIDE DISHES

Roasted bok choy **117**

Speedy steamed choy sum **131**

Grilled gai lan **143**

Lightly braised gai lan with miso and pancetta **145**

Gai lan with sizzling oil (*Biang biang gai lan*) **147**

Maple-sautéed chrysanthemum **169**

Malabar spinach stir-fry with ginger and Sichuan pepper oil **225**

Okra with mushrooms **253**

Garlicky roasted Asian eggplant **261**

BEANS AND TOFU

Chrysanthemum pesto noodles with edamame **171**

Lentil and amaranth dhal (*Thotakura pappu*) **215**

Malabar spinach and black-eyed peas curry (*Valchebaji ani gule*) **227**

Glazed baluchoux with teriyaki sauce **327**

FISH AND SEAFOOD

Gaspé turbot, lobster, and tatsoi with XO sauce **119**

Arctic char, miso eggplant, saké kasu **263**

CHICKEN

Luffa and chicken stir-fry **289**

Grilled chicken with lemongrass and Siling labuyo chili (*Gà nướng sả ớt*) **299**

MEAT

Rustic sticky rice with bok choy **123**

Cantonese fried rice with choy sum **133**

Amaranth romazava-style **217**

Steamed pork-stuffed Asian eggplant **267**

Chinese cabbage sauté with bacon and chili **331**

DESSERTS

Shiso and lychee sorbet **239**

Lemongrass panna cotta **301**

BEVERAGES

Asian cucumber and shiso cocktail **279**

RECIPE CREATORS

JÉRÉMIE BASTIEN, Monarque restaurant
Gaspé turbot, lobster, and tatsoi with XO sauce 119
Dungeness crab with celtuce, mint, goat yogurt, oxalis 179
Arctic char, miso eggplant, saké kasu 263

RÉBECCA BRILVICAS-PINSONNAULT
Japanese sesame salad (*Goma-ae*) 157
Nabe with miso and butter 159

MAXIME CHANHDA-TREMBLAY, Épicerie Chanhda
Laotian meat salad (*Laap*) 235
Tom kha gai soup 297

AMANDINE CHEN AND NIRINA RAHARISON
Glazed baluchoux with teriyaki sauce 327

MONG CHI CHONG
Malabar spinach stir-fry with ginger and Sichuan pepper oil 225

DANA COOPER, Fraîche!
Lightly braised gai lan with miso and pancetta 145
Spring rolls with shiso and duck 237

ANITA FENG, J'ai Feng
Chrysanthemum-stuffed crêpes (*Bings*) 167
Quick-pickled celtuce 183
Garlicky roasted Asian eggplant 261

DANIELLE LAOU
Steamed pork-stuffed Asian eggplant 267
Luffa and chicken stir-fry 289

GUILLAUME LOZEAU, Le Super Qualité restaurant
Lentil and amaranth dhal (*Thotakura pappu*) 215
Malabar spinach and black-eyed peas curry
(*Valchebaji ani gule*) 227

ISCRA NICOLOV
Okra with mushrooms 253

CHLOÉ OSTIGUY, L'Archipel
Asian cucumber and shiso cocktail 279
Luffa spread 287

FÉLIX ANTOINE PARENTEAU, Sauce Prune
Gai lan with sizzling oil (*Biang biang gai lan*) 147

STANISLAS PETTIGREW, Ferme Pettigrew
Chinese cabbage sauté with bacon and chili 331

MAXIME ROBERT-LACHAÎNE, Checkmonwok
Cold noodles (*Liáng miàn*) 277

**JEAN-LOUIS THÉMIS, Cuisiniers sans frontières
and Parti culinaire du Québec**
Amaranth romazava-style 217
Asian eggplant achar 259

JEAN-PHILIPPE VILLEMURE
Lacto-fermented okra 251
Kimchi 325

ALEXANDRE VOVAN, Les Vovans
Grilled chicken with lemongrass and Siling labuyo chili
(*Gà nướng sả ớt*) 299

CAROLINE WANG
Roasted bok choy 117
Maple-sautéed chrysanthemum 169
Tomato rougail 217

CAROLINE AND PATRICIA WANG
Chrysanthemum pesto noodles with edamame 171

MARIE WANG
Cantonese fried rice with choy sum 133
Shiso and lychee sorbet 239
Lemongrass panna cotta 301

STÉPHANIE WANG, Le Rizen
Speedy steamed choy sum 131
Grilled gai lan 143
Celtuce leaf and dried cranberry salad 183
Crispy roasted okra (*Kurkuri bhindi*) 249

YVONNE YAU
Amaranth soup 213

YAMEI ZHAO, Rendez-vous Café
Rustic sticky rice with bok choy 123

FAMILY ANECDOTES

Chinese medicine and us 34
A playground 45
The fish and seafood of Madagascar 121
From Marie-Thé to Marie Wang 134
It's never too late (to learn to cook) 173
Soups and fruits 211
A chef's vision 241
Danielle Laou, unstoppable cook 268
Culinary shocks 291
Reconnecting with these preserved foods 319
January 1st in Nosy Be 333

SOURCES

MAIN SOURCES

Fortier, J.-M. (2015). *Le jardinier-maraîcher: Manuel d'agriculture biologique sur petite surface* (2nd ed). Écosociété.

This is an excellent work on the tried-and-tested practices of a pioneering bio-intensive market farm, including project planning and garden design.

Harrington, G. (2009). *Growing Chinese Vegetables in Your Own Backyard: A Complete Planting Guide for 40 Vegetables and Herbs, From Bok Choy and Chinese Parsley to Mung Beans and Water Chestnuts.* Storey Publishing.

Harrington provides a complete overview of a selection of Asian vegetables in both the garden and the kitchen.

Kiang-Spray, W. (2017). *The Chinese Kitchen Garden: Growing Techniques and Family Recipes from a Classic Cuisine.* Timber Press.

Wendy Kiang-Spray tells the story of her Chinese family immigrating to the United States, where she and her father grow big beds full of Asian vegetables. She discusses several of the vegetables we have written about here, and more. The book also includes her favourite recipes, numerous gardening tips, and anecdotes about Chinese culture.

Larkcom, J. (1991). *Oriental Vegetables: The Complete Guide for Garden and Kitchen.* Kodansha.

This is perhaps the most complete agronomic reference written (in English or French) exclusively about Asian vegetables to date. We strongly recommend it to anyone who wants more detailed information on all aspects of growing Asian vegetables.

Ministry of Agriculture, Food, and Rural Affairs. (2012). *Specialty Vegetables.* Government of Ontario. www.omafra.gov.on.ca/CropOp/en/spec_veg.

The Ontario government devotes a whole section of its website to information on growing "speciality and non-traditional" vegetables to encourage local producers to take a greater role in this fast-growing market.

COMPLEMENTARY SOURCES

Chun, L. (2012). *The Kimchi Cookbook.* Ten Speed Press.

The founder of the American company Mother-in-Law's Kimchi offers 60 recipes for kimchi and kimchi-based dishes. In this book you will find recipes for kimchi made from bok choy, shiso, eggplant, cucumber, and of course, Chinese cabbage.

Dawling, P. (2019). Optimizing Your Asian Greens Production [slides]. SlideShare. www.slideshare.net/SustainableMarketFarming/optimizing-your-asian-greens-production-dawling-2019.

Pam Dawling has managed the market production of the intentional community of Twin Oaks, Virginia, for twenty years. Slides of her detailed presentations on growing Asian vegetables are available online.

de Vienne, E., and de Vienne, P. (2007). *La cuisine et le goût des épices.* Trécarré.

Ethné and Philippe de Vienne, the spice hunters running the company Épices de Cru, have written a book offering a world tour that introduces spices in stories, flavours, recipes, and pictures. Here you will find recipes for spice blends to make at home and other practical information for finding the sweet spot of the tastes and flavours that make the perfect recipe. Their website is also full of information: https://epicesdecru.com.

Jodoin, M. (2011). *Entre fourchette et baguettes: Plaisir et sagesse au menu.* Éditions Li Shi Zhen.

A fairly complete work that introduces the concepts of traditional Chinese medicine, connecting it with food and offering recipes.

Savaria, M. (2020). *La saison des légumes.* Mariève Savaria.

Mariève Savaria's love of vegetables, talent, and creativity are all highlighted in this book, which contains a thousand and one tips for cooking vegetables in season, including foraged vegetables, and preserving them for later. A reference work for anyone who wants to increase their food and culinary autonomy.

Semences du Patrimoine Canada. (2013). *La conservation des semences* (6th ed).

This is a complete guide for beginners as well as experts wanting to learn more about seed saving.

Solomon, K. (2014). *Asian Pickles: Sweet, Sour, Salty, Cured, and Fermented Preserves from Korea, Japan, China, India, and Beyond*. Ten Speed Press.

This book explores 75 lacto-fermentation and marinade recipes from across Asia. Use it with the vegetables from this book or to make side dishes to accompany our recipes.

The Woks of Life. https://thewoksoflife.com.

A practical web resource for all things Chinese cooking: from ingredients to recipes, including their Chinese names. A small goldmine of information in the Chinese culinary universe.

Wittman, H., Desmarais, A.A., and Wiebe, N. (2011). *Food Sovereignty in Canada*. Fernwood Publishing.

This collection of texts written by people working in the fields of agricultural research and policy offers numerous perspectives on understanding the challenges and possibilities relating to food sovereignty in Canada.

ADDITIONAL SOURCES
General
European and Mediterranean Plant Protection Organization. (2021). EPPO Global Database. https://gd.eppo.int.

A bank of species names, common names, and taxonomy.

L'encyclopédie visuelle des aliments. (1996). Québec Amérique.

L'encyclopédie visuelle des aliments. (2017). Québec Amérique.

Farming
Espace pour la vie. (n.d.). *Carnet horticole et botanique*. https://espacepourlavie.ca/carnet-horticole-et-botanique.

Iannotti, M. (2014). *The Timber Press Guide to Vegetable Gardening in the Northeast*. Timber Press.

Institut de la statistique du Québec et ministère de l'Agriculture, des Pêcheries et de l'Alimentation du Québec. (2020). *Profil sectoriel de l'industrie bioalimentaire au Québec – Édition 2019*. https://statistique.quebec.ca/fr/fichier/profil-sectoriel-de-lindustrie-bioalimentaire-au-quebec-edition-2019.pdf.

IRIIS phytoprotection. www.iriisphytoprotection.qc.ca.

Johnny's Selected Seeds. www.johnnyseeds.com.

Kim, H. (2012). Première rencontre globale sur l'agroécologie et les semences paysannes, Thaïlande. https://sites.google.com/site/youthlvcna/agroecology/Agroecology-Schools.

La Via Campesina. (2003). *Souveraineté alimentaire*. https://viacampesina.org/fr.

Leach, K. (2021). [main presentation]. Ecological Farmers Association of Ontario's 8th annual conference, virtual conference. https://efao.ca.

National Farmers Union. (n.d.). *Agroécologie*. www.nfu.ca/fr/campaigns/agroecology.

Tang, L., Wu, D., Miao, W., Pu, H., Jiang, L., Wang, S., Zhong, W., and Chen, W. (2019). Sustainable Development of Food Security in Northeast China. *Strategic Study of Chinese Academy of Engineering, 21*(5), 19—27. www.engineering.org.cn/en/10.15302/J-SSCAE-2019.05.016.

Union paysanne. www.unionpaysanne.com.

West Coast Seeds. www.westcoastseeds.com.

Cooking and preserving
Canadian Produce Marketing Association (n.d.). *Home Freezing Guide for Fresh Veggies and Fruit*. Half Your Plate. https://halfyourplate.net/homefreezingguide.

Bouchard, V. (2020). *Cuisiner sans recettes : guide de résilience alimentaire*. Écosociété.

Katz, S.E. (2012). *The art of fermentation*. Chelsea Green Publishing.

Nutrition
Bélanger, M., LeBlanc, M.-J., and Dubost, M. (2015). *La nutrition* (4th ed). Chenelière Éducation.

Cortés-Rodriguez, V., Dorantes-Alvarez, L. Peredo-Lovillo, A., and Hernández-Sanchez, H. (2018). Lactic acid bacteria isolated from vegetable fermentations: Probiotic characteristics. *Reference Module in Food Science*. https://doi.org/10.1016/B978-0-08-100596-5.22601-2.

Institute of Medicine. (2006). *Les apports nutritionnels de reference : le guide essentiel des besoins en nutriments*. The National Academies Press. https://doi.org/10.17226/11758.

Septembre-Malaterre, A., Remize F., and Poucheret, P. (2018). Fruits and vegetables as a source of nutritional compounds and phytochemicals: Changes in bioactive compounds during lactic fermentation. *Food Research International, 104*, 86—99. https://doi.org/10.1016/j.foodres.2017.09.031.

Weaver, C.M., Heaney, R.P., Nickel, K.P., and Packard, P.I. (1997). Calcium bioavailability from high oxalate vegetables: Chinese vegetables, sweet potatoes and rhubarb. *Journal of Food Science, 62*(3), 524—525. https://doi.org/10.1111/j.1365-2621.1997.tb04421.x.

Weaver, C.M., Proulx, W.R., and Heaney, R. (1999). Choices for achieving adequate dietary calcium with a vegetarian diet. *The American Journal of Clinical Nutrition, 70*(3), 543—548. https://doi.org/10.1093/ajcn/70.3.543s.

Composition of food
Agricultural Research Service. (2019). *FoodData Central*. U.S. Department of Agriculture. https://fdc.nal.usda.gov.

China Food Nutrition Network. (n.d.). *Food Composition Database*. www.neasiafoods.org.

Ministry of Education, Culture, Sports, Science and Technology of Japan. (2015). *Standard Tables of Food Composition in Japan* (7th revised version). www.mext.go.jp/en.

Chinese medicine
Racette, C.É. (2010). *Manger le dragon: compendium de diétothérapie en médecine chinoise*. Centre collégial de développement de matériel didactique.

Languages
Garnaut, A. (2011). *Mandarin*. Lonely Planet.

McWhorter, J. (2019). *Language Families of the World: The Languages We Call Chinese* [video]. Kanopy. https://www.kanopy.com/en/product/languages-we-call-chinese.

Wong, C. (2014). *Le Cantonais*. Assimil.

This is the only work we found that teaches Cantonese to French speakers.

Culinary culture
Zhou, Y. (2012). *La baguette et la fourchette: Les tribulations d'un gastronome chinois en France*. Fayard.

APPENDICES

PRESERVING

	REFRIGERATING	FREEZING		DEHYDRATING		
	Optimal preserving temperature (°F/°C)	Preparation	Blanching time	Preparation	Duration (hours) at 125°F (52 °C)	Texture obtained
AMARANTH	32 to 36/0 to 2	1 inch (2.5 cm)	Leaves: 1 minute Stems: 2 minutes	Remove tough stems and spread leaves out side by side.	3 to 7	Crumbly
ASIAN CUCUMBER	35 to 55/7 to 13	Slice thinly.	Freeze directly without blanching.	Cut into ¼ inch (0.5 cm) thick rounds.	4 to 8	Crisp
ASIAN EGGPLANT	46 to 54/8 to 12	Slices ¼ inch (0.5 cm) thick. Add ½ cup (125 mL) fresh lemon juice to 4 cups (1 L) water.	4 minutes	Cut into rounds or slices between ¼ to ½ inch (0.5 to 1 cm) thick.	4 to 8	Crisp
BOK CHOY	32/0	1 inch (2.5 cm)	Leaves: 1 minute Stems: 2 minutes	Cut in two lengthways (stems and leaves), lay the halves flat on a chopping board, then cut lengthways into ½-inch (1 cm) slices.	4 to 7	Crumbly
CELTUCE	32/0	1 inch (2.5 cm)	3 minutes	Cut into rounds or sticks ¼ inch (0.5 cm) thick.	5 to 6	Crisp
CHINESE CABBAGE	32/0	1 inch (2.5 cm)	1.5 minutes	Cut widthways into layers ¼ to ½ inch (0.5 to 1 cm) thick, and lay flat in dehydrator.	4 to 8	Crumbly
CHOY SUM	32/0	Whole	2 minutes	Cut both stems and leaves lengthways so that stems are ¼ to ½ inch (0.5 to 1 cm) thick.	3 to 7	Crumbly
EDIBLE CHRYSANTHEMUM	32/0	1 inch (2.5 cm)	Leaves: 1 minute Stems: 2 minutes	Lay leaves out side by side or cut in two lengthways (young stems and leaves).	3 to 7	Crumbly
GAI LAN	32/0	Whole	2 minutes	Cut leaves and stems lengthways so that the stems are ¼ inch (0.5 cm) thick. Leave florets whole.	4 to 8	Crumbly
LEMONGRASS	36 to 43/2 to 6	Stems: cut into 4-inch (10 cm) strips.	Freeze directly without blanching.	Cut leaves with secateurs into chunks of ½ to 1 inch (1 to 2.5 cm).	2 to 4	Crisp
LUFFA	50 to 54/10 to 12	Slices of ½ inch (1 cm)	2 minutes	Cut into ½ inch (1 cm) thick rounds.	4 to 8	Crisp
MALABAR SPINACH	32/0	1 inch (2.5 cm)	Leaves: 2 minutes Stems: 3 minutes	Remove tough stems and lay leaves side by side.	3 to 7	Crumbly
MUSTARD GREENS	32/0	1 inch (2.5 cm)	Leaves: 1 minute Stems: 2 minutes	Remove tough stems and lay leaves side by side.	2 to 7	Crumbly
OKRA	46 to 50/8 to 10	Whole. Remove pedicel.	3 minutes	Cut into ¼ inch (0.5 cm) thick rounds.	4 to 8	Crisp
SHISO	50/10	Freeze the leaves whole, spread out on a tray, and then bag. Or chop and freeze with water, oil, or stock in an ice cube tray.	Freeze directly without blanching.	Remove tough stems and lay leaves side by side.	4 to 8 at 110°F (43 °C)	Crumbly

INDOOR SOWING

	Plants per sowing to feed one person	Growing time in days	Days in the garden	Date of first indoor sowing (spring)	Date of last indoor sowing (fall, unless otherwise specified)	Dates of indoor sowing at Le Rizen (successive sowings)	Ideal germination temperature	Tips for germination
AMARANTH	1 to 2 plants	40 to 50	55 to 65	3 weeks before last frost	13 to 14 weeks before first frost	11 May 8 June 26 June	Min. 50°F (10°C) Ideal 70° to 75°F (21° to 24°C)	Barely cover seeds with soil.
ASIAN CUCUMBER	1 vine, or 2 plants kept short	70	110	3 to 4 weeks before last frost	2 weeks before last spring frost	5 May	Ideal 75° to 80°F (24° to 27°C) Min. 60°F (16°C) at night and 70°F (21°C) during the day	Soak seeds overnight or pre-germinate. Sow two seeds per hole, with the seed standing on end rather than lying down.
ASIAN EGGPLANT	2 to 3 plants	95	130	6 to 7 weeks before last frost	Not applicable (1 single sowing)	10 April	80° to 90°F (27° to 32°C)	Soak seeds overnight.
BOK CHOY	4 to 10 plants	45 to 50	45 to 50	7 weeks before last frost	6 weeks before first frost	7 sowings 21 days apart, starting on 10 April	64° to 75°F (18° to 24°C)	
CELTUCE	2 to 5 plants	66	45	7 weeks before last frost	11 weeks before first frost	10 April 24 April	59°F (15°C) ideal Below 75°F (24°C)	
CHINESE CABBAGE	3 to 5 plants	70 to 80	45	5 weeks before last frost	10 to 11 weeks before first frost	22 April 13 July	Min. 75°F (24°C)	
CHOY SUM	3 to 5 plants	40 to 50	50 to 60	7 weeks before last frost	11 weeks before first frost	10 April 5 May 13 July	64° to 75°F (18° to 24°C)	
EDIBLE CHRYSANTHEMUM	2 to 7 plants	50 to 55	50 to 60	7 weeks before last frost	6 weeks before first frost	10 April 5 May 20 July 17 August	70°F (21°C)	
GAI LAN	3 to 5 plants	40 to 50	60 to 100	7 weeks before last frost	10 weeks before first frost	10 April 5 May 8 June 20 July	75° to 80°F (24° to 27°C)	
LEMONGRASS	1 plant	150 to 155	150	10 to 11 weeks before last frost	Not applicable (1 single sowing)	18 March	70°F (21°C)	Barely cover seeds and germinate in the dark. Water lightly.
LUFFA	1 to 2 vines	95	125	4 weeks before last frost	Not applicable (1 single sowing)	20 April	Ideal 75° to 80°F (24° to 27°C) Min. 60°F (16°C) at night and 70°F (21°C) during the day	Soak seeds for 24 hours. Sow 1 to 3 seeds per hole, with the seed standing on end rather than lying down.
MALABAR SPINACH	1 vine, or 2 plants kept short	75 to 85	140	4 weeks before last frost	2 weeks before last spring frost	28 April 12 May	64° to 70°F (18° to 21°C)	Soak seeds for 24 hours or nick them.
MUSTARD GREENS	2 to 5 plants	50	45 to 50	7 weeks before last frost	9 weeks before first frost	10 April 5 May 5 June 3 July 31 July	64° to 75°F (18° to 24°C)	
OKRA	6 plants	70 to 80	125	5 weeks before last frost	Not applicable (1 single sowing)	27 April	81 to 90°F (27° to 32°C)	Soak seeds overnight or nick them.
SHISO	1 plant	75 to 80	85	6 weeks before last frost	15 weeks before first frost	20 April 21 May 18 June	68°F (20°C). Takes 7 to 21 days to germinate.	Just barely cover seeds. They need light to germinate.

Growing time corresponds to the number of days between sowing in trays and the first harvest.

Days in the garden is the number of total days spent in the ground, from planting out to the final harvest.

Dates of first and last indoor sowings take into consideration the vegetable's growing time as well as the expected dates of the last spring frost and the first fall frost. In Brome-Missisquoi, the risk of frost is practically zero after 31 May, and the fall frosts generally occur around 15 to 30 September. We are optimistic, so we think of 30 September as the date of the first fall frost, especially for crops that have a floating row cover to protect them. You can adjust the dates to your own region; for example, adding 15 days to the date of first sowing if your final spring frost is 15 June.

Nicking seeds means roughing the seed coating with sandpaper or notching it with a knife to speed up germination.

PLANTING OUT

	Date of first planting out at Le Rizen	Number of rows per 30-inch (75 cm) bed	Spacing between plants in the row (in)	(cm)	Date of expected first harvest
AMARANTH	28 May	3	8	20	30 June
ASIAN CUCUMBER	15 May	1	20	50	12 July
ASIAN EGGPLANT	28 May	2	12	30	16 July
BOK CHOY	1 May	4	6	15	4 June
CELTUCE	7 May	2	12	30	23 June
CHINESE CABBAGE	8 May	2	24	60	5 July
CHOY SUM	1 May	4	8	20	29 May
EDIBLE CHRYSANTHEMUM	1 May	4	6	15	4 June
GAI LAN	1 May	4	8	20	31 May
LEMONGRASS	28 May	2	24	60	17 August
LUFFA	28 May	1	24	60	26 July
MALABAR SPINACH	28 May	2	12	30	7 July
MUSTARD GREENS	1 May	3	8	20	4 June
OKRA	28 May	2	24	60	26 July
SHISO	28 May	2	8	20	7 July

This table contains information about planting out in the ground with the intention of harvesting when the vegetables are semi-mature to mature. For a harvest of mesclun or younger plants, the plants can be spaced closer together.

The date of first planting out is determined by the date on which all risk of frost has passed in the spring, which is late May in Quebec.

The expected harvesting date is the date of indoor sowing + average growing time at Le Rizen, slightly adjusted to take into account the recorded dates of the first harvests of prior years.

Copyright © Les éditions Parfum d'encre 2022
English translation copyright © 2023 J. C. Sutcliffe

Original edition published in French under the title *Légumes asiatiques : jardiner, cuisiner, raconter*, by Parfum d'encre, an imprint of Groupe d'édition la courte échelle inc. First published in English in 2023 by House of Anansi Press Inc.
houseofanansi.com

House of Anansi Press is committed to protecting our natural environment. This book is made of material from well-managed FSC®-certified forests, recycled materials, and other controlled sources.

House of Anansi Press is a Global Certified Accessible™ (GCA by Benetech) publisher. The ebook version of this book meets stringent accessibility standards and is available to readers with print disabilities.

27 26 25 24 23   1 2 3 4 5

Library and Archives Canada Cataloguing in Publication

Title: Asian vegetables : gardening, cooking, storytelling /
the Wang sisters: Stéphanie, Caroline, and Patricia ; translated by J.C. Sutcliffe.

Other titles: Légumes asiatiques. English

Names: Wang, Stéphanie, author. | Wang, Caroline (Caroline Ho-Yane), author. | Wang, Patricia (Patricia Ho-Yi), author. | Sutcliffe, J. C., translator.

Description: Translation of: Légumes asiatiques. |
Includes bibliographical references and index.

Identifiers: Canadiana (print) 2023044900X | Canadiana (ebook) 20230449018 |
ISBN 9781487012052 (hardcover) | ISBN 9781487012069 (EPUB)

Subjects: LCSH: Cooking (Vegetables) | LCSH: Cooking, Asian. |
LCSH: Vegetable gardening. | LCGFT: Cookbooks.

Classification: LCC TX801 .W3613 2023 | DDC 641.6/5—dc23

Book design: Julie Massy
Photography: Virginie Gosselin
Typesetting: Catherine Charbonneau

The content of this book is informative in nature. For personalized advice regarding your health, we invite you to consult your health care providers.

House of Anansi Press is grateful for the privilege to work on and create from the Traditional Territory of many Nations, including the Anishinabeg, the Wendat, and the Haudenosaunee, as well as the Treaty Lands of the Mississaugas of the Credit.

Canada Council   Conseil des Arts   ONTARIO ARTS COUNCIL
for the Arts   du Canada   CONSEIL DES ARTS DE L'ONTARIO
                                          an Ontario government agency
                                          un organisme du gouvernement de l'Ontario

With the participation of the Government of Canada | Canadä
Avec la participation du gouvernement du Canada

We acknowledge the financial support of the Government of Canada through the National Translation Program for Book Publishing, an initiative of the Action Plan for Official Languages — 2018–2023: Investing in Our Future, for our translation activities.

Printed and bound in Canada

MIX
Paper from
responsible sources
FSC® C016245
www.fsc.org